COMING UP
FROM THE STREETS

This book is dedicated to:
Paddy and Diana
Mr P and Kit

COMING UP
FROM THE STREETS

THE STORY OF

TESSA SWITHINBANK

EARTHSCAN

Earthscan Publications Ltd
London • Sterling, VA

First published in the UK and USA in 2001
by Earthscan Publications Ltd

ISBN: 1 85383 544 7

Typesetting by PCS Mapping & DTP, Newcastle upon Tyne
Printed and bound in the UK by Creative Print and Design Wales, Ebbw Vale
Cover design by Danny Gillespie
Cver photograph by Chris Anderson

For a full list of publications please contact:

Earthscan Publications Ltd
120 Pentonville Road, London, N1 9JN, UK
Tel: +44 (0)20 7278 0433
Fax: +44 (0)20 7278 1142
Email: earthinfo@earthscan.co.uk
http://www.earthscan.co.uk

22883 Quicksilver Drive, Sterling, VA 20166–2012, USA

Earthscan is an editorially independent subsidiary of Kogan Page Ltd and
publishes in association with WWF-UK and the International Institute for
Environment and Development

A catalogue record for this book is available from the British Library

Library of Congress Cataloging-in-Publication Data

Swithinbank, Tessa.
    Coming up from the streets : the story of The big issue / Tessa
    Swithinbank.
        p.cm.
    Includes bibliographical references and index.
    ISBN 1-85383-544-7 (pbk.)
    1. Big issue. 2. Homelessness–Great Britain–Periodicals–History.
3. Homeless persons–Services for–Great Britain. 4. Homeless
persons–Employment–Great Britain. 5. Periodical vendors–Great Britain.
6. Street vendors–Great Britain. I. Title.

HV4545.A4 S94 2001
052–dc21

                                                                        2001004050

CONTENTS

FOREWORD

Anita Roddick

LIKE THOUSANDS OF other people across the UK, I've got to know a fair number of *The Big Issue* vendors in the paper's ten-year existence. You strike up a conversation and before you know it you're sharing stories. It's the most primal form of human communication and, as far as I'm concerned, it's been one of *The Big Issue*'s most meaningful achievements, because it's turned homelessness from a distant 'something' into an intimate group of 'someones'.

In doing that, *The Big Issue* has armed us with a sense of how a society can fail its citizens by denying them shelter, a fundamental human right. So, its story is a surprisingly comprehensive portrait of not-so-great Britain in the 1990s, a decade that seesawed through extremes of disillusionment and optimism to end up back where it began. Well, maybe not quite, but one lesson that was inescapably confirmed in the 1990s was that there is very little faith left in politics, politicians or their agents. When the time comes to exercise our democratic right and choose our leaders, it would seem that the most reliable choice open to us at the beginning of the new century is self-help.

That is, of course, another right that homelessness takes away – the freedom to choose. In trying to restore it, *The Big Issue* has evolved as textbook social entrepreneurialism. I recognize many of the triumphs and trials that make this story such a riveting and valuable one, from its activist origins to the latter-day challenges that success poses to the founder's ideals. Oh yes, a word about that founder – John Bird is the incarnation of my conviction that passion is the most persuasive force known to humankind. His passion is practically a force of nature. Stand in its way and you are crushed if you aren't carried along.

Fortunately, there are hundreds – maybe even thousands – of people who would say that John's passion has carried them to places they never thought they'd see, with *The Big Issue* as their means of transport. He's done it in the healthiest possible way – in a partnership with the people he wants to help. I've never been a believer in cheque-book charity; a hand-up is better than a hand-out. There's ample proof of that in the success stories of *The Big Issue* vendors who've managed to get back on level ground, whose work has renewed their sense of dignity and security.

The idea of partnering is something I've been used to at The Body Shop. It is the foundation of our commitment to trading with economically marginalized communities around the world. But *The Big Issue*'s success awes me because homelessness isn't only about economic deprivation. People of all ages and backgrounds end up on the streets because of domestic violence and sexual abuse, for example. To create successful partnerships with such a range of people in need has called for a rare kind of compassionate pragmatism, without forgetting that, at the same time, *The Big Issue* has been evolving as a quality paper that hundreds of thousands of people want to read every week.

I'm a sucker for a good story, and there are plenty in *Coming Up From The Streets*. In some, I identify with John Bird, the editor-in-chief, who maybe doesn't do things the way everyone wishes he would. In others, I recognize the cynics waiting to leap at the first shortfall or perceived compromise. Or I can detect the perennial worry that commercial success will somehow damp the fire. As I mentioned earlier, the substance of these stories is familiar from my own experiences. There's never been a road map for the social entrepreneur to follow, so it's useful to find out exactly what other people must deal with. But, perhaps, this is the road map taking shape. When I'm asked about my hope for the future, I usually answer that I would like to see the spirit of enterprise make a seamless shift from servant of private greed to vehicle for public good. *The Big Issue*'s story proves just how possible – and essential – that is.

PREFACE

A John Bird

WHEN GORDON RODDICK asked me to start a street paper in March 1991, I had no idea that ten years on it would have such a worldwide presence. Gordon was obsessed with the concept. He had asked me earlier to get involved and I wriggled out of it. I didn't want to get involved with a charity, since it was alien to my sentiments. Later, though, he insisted it would be a business not a charity. Eventually, I agreed and thus began the great adventure.

This book, I believe, shows what an adventure it was. It does not paint *The Big Issue* as a completely formed object in its early stages. It shows the problems we encountered. It shows the mistakes we made. And it shows that both myself and my team learnt on the job.

Learning by doing is certainly one way of achieving your ends. But it can also be wasteful, repetitive and woolly-headed. But without a blueprint to follow, we had little choice. We had to get on with it.

Now, ten years on, *The Big Issue* has become one of the most successful social interventions in living memory. It has kept the tragedy of homelessness to the fore; it has given homeless people the chance of moving out of homelessness; and it has opened up a huge debate around how homeless people need to be involved in their own transformations.

The Big Issue remains dynamic and forceful. But like all innovations it has to change, develop and improve in order to continue. More than anything, I believe that this book captures the contradictions of *The Big Issue*. How it bit off more than it could chew. And how it has had to cope with its failures as well as its enormous success.

In a nutshell, *Coming Up From The Streets* is an honest attempt at showing those contradictions. And how 'helping the homeless to help themselves' is its most noteworthy credo.

In reading this book, I hope you will remember the energies and dedication of the thousands of homeless people who have rallied to such a worthwhile effort. Without such dedication, *The Big Issue* would have been dead in the water.

ACKNOWLEDGEMENTS

MANY, MANY THANKS to all those people who helped me enormously by reading and commenting on the manuscript in its various stages: Vicki Barker, John Bird, Maria Clancy, Rory Gillert, Lynn O'Donoghue, Peter Raynard, Gordon Roddick, Lucie Russell and Lyndall Stein; to Sue McLeod for accessing her invaluable research facilities; to all *The Big Issue* vendors and staff, and others outside the organization who took time to be interviewed; to Jonathan Sinclair Wilson, Pascale Mettam and Frances MacDermott at Earthscan who spotted and supported a good story; to editor Kathleen Tansey; and to all my friends and family – and cats – who kept my spirits up during the difficult times. I would finally like to express my gratitude to *The Big Issue* for giving me the opportunity to write its first history, and to all *The Big Issue* vendors for their encouragement and support.

The Big Issue *Is Born – John Bird, Anita Roddick and Sheila McKechnie (front row, top) and Gordon Roddick (far right, bottom) celebrate the magazine's launch in 1991 with some of the first* Big Issue *vendors*

INTRODUCTION

THE BIG ISSUE is a contradiction and a conundrum. The magazine, sold by homeless people on the streets of cities throughout Britain, has helped thousands of people earn a living since its launch in 1991. It has had a profound and sustained impact on the public's perception of homelessness, combined with an unsentimental and hands-on approach to tackling social exclusion.

It set out to propel people back from the edge into mainstream society. But not simply a job creation scheme, it was about self-esteem, people winning control over their lives, self-help, breaking dependencies and sustainability.

It was one of the most dynamic and exciting publishing phenomenons of the 1990s. *The Big Issue* topped the 1997–98 circulation figures of weekly current affairs magazines in the UK with national sales of 280,000. It has won a whole array of journalistic awards. It is international, with editions in Cape Town, Los Angeles and Melbourne and has led the way for a worldwide street paper movement. From Madrid to Miami and St Petersburg to Serrekunda, street papers are helping thousands of homeless and socially excluded people to help themselves. How this happened is described in this book.

The Big Issue was set up as an alternative to the traditional methods of helping homeless people. Its originality was in being a street paper which is sold by people who have an opportunity of moving on and making decisions about their own lives. Spawned by an international company, from an idea that originated in New York, the magazine was put together by a businessman and a printer, neither of whom had a charity background.

Now, the magazine and its vendors feature in TV sitcoms, in Ruth Rendell and Russell Hoban novels, on billboards, in cartoons, corporate advertisements and in school projects. It is supported by big business, the police and government. It has a vibrancy and energy remarked upon by many who come into contact with it. And it is an organization which, while campaigning against homelessness, is also a publishing business, a film maker and a book producer.

In its initial stages, the company staggered along from month to month encountering disasters, financial problems and set-backs, many of which will be described here – often in the words of those involved. The tale of *The Big Issue* is one of meteoric growth combined with amateurish organization, and it still suffers from being thrown together in a hurry. Despite now turning over £4m per annum, the inherent contradictions within the company stoke up an enduring battle to keep its radical edge and yet to ensure the business continues to expand to provide an income for those who need it. *The Big Issue* has been described as having a multiple personality disorder and a split soul.

As described in Chapter 1, conditions for *The Big Issue*'s launch in 1991 were ripe, with homelessness at its peak. The public was dissatisfied with the government's response, and single-issue, direct action politics were beginning to replace the more prevalent left-wing politics.

When *The Big Issue* arrived on the scene in September, it entered in methodological opposition to the traditional charity work of handouts and dependency. It brought a businesslike approach to homelessness, encouraging homeless people to think of themselves as consumers. And whilst there are no definitive answers to the social problems the welfare state and voluntary organizations both try to address, there are arguments which may point towards getting rid of the dependency culture, and implementing a more business-like approach to social problems.

This book is predominantly about *The Big Issue* in London because it was the first one, although the four other Big Issues are portrayed in a comparative way. No doubt the founders of the others will write their own stories in time.

The Big Issue

1–5 Wandsworth Road, London, SW8 2LN
Tel: +44 (0)20 7526 3200   Fax: +44 (0)20 7526 3201
Email: press@bigissue.com   Web: www.bigissue.com

1

HOMELESSNESS

HOMELESSNESS IN BRITAIN is not new. It has been with us for centuries.

> 'Time and time again through the centuries the number of homeless people has increased as a direct result of factors such as economic downturn, the cessation of war and climatic catastrophe. The response of those in authority is to clamp down even harder on the increased numbers 'of no fixed abode', regardless of how valid their reasons may be for having found themselves in their predicament'.[1]

The patterns of causes have changed over time, but poverty has persisted as a key factor.[2] It is the period between 1979 and the launch of *The Big Issue* in 1991 that concerns this book. This particular phase manifested itself not only in a relentless rise of homelessness in general, but also in an unremitting rise in street homelessness, particularly amongst young people.

Many believe that the fallout from the Tory government's monetarist economic policies created the unemployment (which rose above 3 million) and poverty which caused this particular surge in UK homelessness in the 1980s. The social fracture of Thatcher's Britain reflected itself in frightening statistics. In the ten years to 1989, for example, whilst the annual income of the average UK household increased (and the average income of the richest 20 per cent increased even more), at the lower end of the sprectrum average real income dropped.[3] Since then the gap between rich and poor has widened.[4]

Talking of 'The Homeless' became commonplace as they became an established part of our society. All along the Strand, in the heart of the capital, south to Charing Cross and northwards to Lincoln's Inn Fields, hundreds of people were sleeping outdoors: by night in tents, on theatre steps, in cardboards boxes and doorways; by day, begging on the streets.

Not only were people sleeping rough, but hostels and bed and breakfasts were bulging, and thousands of empty buildings were being squatted. Shelter estimated that over half a million people were homeless in England alone in 1991.[5] The government had its own definition of those who were statutorily[6] homeless.[7] In 1991, 170,500 households were accepted as homeless by local authorities.[8] Between 2000 and 3000 were sleeping on the streets of the capital in 1990 and up to 8000 on any one night in England.[9]

There are many reasons why people become homeless. Often homeless people carry the baggage of abuse, poor education and lack of motivation. Those who make up the majority of homeless people, and who are the most vulnerable, are teenagers coming out of care, people who have left the armed forces, ex-prisoners, people with mental health problems, those from broken marriages and relationships, physically abused women or abused young people leaving home and lone parents with their children on low income or on benefits.

Single men are numerically at the top of the list, but they are at the bottom when it comes to priority for housing. They make up the majority of street sleepers. And once on the streets their problems are compounded. Many start drinking or taking drugs, or are already addicted, and their ability to remain motivated gradually disappears. Invisible and marginalized, they are more likely to suffer illness, they are not able to eat properly or economically. They are cut off from their families.

The average life expectancy of a male street sleeper is 42.[10] It is hell out on the streets. Former street sleeper Jim Lawrie says:

'It's dog eat dog. There's a lot of horrible people amongst those who sleep out as well. I've had things stolen off me, people clout me and all sorts. Why are people like that? It's because they are a product of a society that has failed them. It is not them that has failed. It's society that's failed the homeless. Why have we got so many people with mental health problems living out on the streets?'

Women tend to work out different ways of staying off the streets, although their number is steadily increasing. They sleep on friends' floors or are trapped in poor accommodation because of low income or violent relationships. Because many are with their children, they have more support in terms of provision of hostel beds and access to bed and breakfast accommodation, but the problems tends to be more 'hidden', or they are not even considered homeless in the public or media's perception.

D (28), a writer who sold *The Big Issue* for three years, was homeless for a couple of years in her mid twenties. Originally from Suffolk, she came to London three years ago, having graduated in social sciences. She is still in contact with her family. She has never had to sleep on the streets and is sometimes challenged about her 'alleged' homelessness. D is typical of the 'hidden,' young, single people who are unable to buy their way into the private market, afford the high rents of the private sector or obtain decent council housing.

She was interviewed by two newspapers. Three other vendors were also interviewed and told their stories, which were quite classic ones. She says:

> *'I'm sorry to say that I think they were secretly hoping that my step dad was sexually abusing me and I had to leave home at the age of 13 onto the streets. When I wasn't that, half way through telling my story they stopped me and asked "so have you ever actually been homeless?" and I was cross. I was sleeping on my friend Annie's floor, actually. But I'm lucky, I have always had my mates.'*

Before that, she was squatting. It was not until the good squats ran out, the ones where there used to be a good family-type community, that she actually considered herself to be homeless. She then went to live on various friends' floors. 'It was not having my own space, when I started thinking I might qualify as homeless,' she says. Perhaps it was a lifestyle decision for her?

> *'At any point I could have got on the lists as a vulnerable young single female and got stuck into a 'hard to let' flat. I can't think of anything worse. Hell. Stuck in a flat not knowing anyone...'*

She stayed in one squat with no running water, no kitchen, no bathroom, nothing. The rest of the house was disgusting. She adds, 'You could choose the lifestyle to a certain extent but generally you don't choose to live like that. It's not a positive choice.'

D thinks it is important that it is acknowledged that people do not have to be on the streets to have all their confidence stripped away, to feel so completely vulnerable all the time, that they never belong anywhere. That horrible feeling takes a long time to get over.

D's story shows how homelessness is not simply a situation in which someone lacks a roof over their head. People are excluded from being part of a community or a neighbourhood because they lack a stable home. FEANTSA[11] identifies homelessness as 'the most extreme manifestation of social exclusion'.

Besides unemployment and poverty, the bricks and mortar issue is a major contributor to homelessness. Historically, the British housing problem has consisted of the fact that there are far more households than dwellings.[12] Social house building never caught up with housing needs after the Second World War when the shortage of dwellings was estimated at something over 2 million. From the 1960s to around 1990, the numbers of people accepted annually as homeless, that is in temporary accommodation, by local authorities in Britain, multiplied between ten- and twentyfold, depending on the area.[13] Housing aspirations changed too, as young people starting families did not wish to remain in their parents' home. They wanted a home of their own. And by the 1990s, many people decided to live alone. These factors created further pressure on the housing stock.

Britain's deep social inequality is reflected in the tenure of housing. During the last Conservative government, there was a decline in local authority new building to its lowest peace time level since 1920. This decline was complimented by the Thatcher government's policy of encouraging home ownership. Since 1980, there has been such a rapid increase in home ownership that nearly 70 per cent of households in Britain own (or are buying) their homes. The remainder rent from local authorities, housing associations[14] or private landlords. The deregulation of rents in the private sector brought soaring rents and a severe shortage of affordable accommodation became the norm.

The problem for social housing was compounded by the Housing Act of 1980 which gave council tenants the right to buy their homes at a discount on market rates. Under the 'Right to Buy' legislation social housing stock plummeted from 6.5 million units in 1981 to under 4.5 million by 1997.

It turned out that the best houses were sold, leaving the least desirable to degenerate, creating what are labelled 'sink estates' or 'hard to let accommodation' into which the poorest people or homeless people are placed by the local authorities.[15] As Anne Power explains:

> 'Council estates have become increasingly unpopular and stigmatized as they became tied to slum rehousing, then became housing of the last resort for people who might otherwise become homeless. By the eighties, a vast stock of about 10,000 council estates – nearly 4 million homes – was seen as a fail-safe to house the poor in an increasingly unequal society.'[16]

Then, at the end of the 1980s soaring interest rates affected mortgages (from under 10 per cent in May 1988 to 14.5 per cent by October 1989), resulting for many people in mortgage arrears, repossessions and negative equity. Having been encouraged by the Thatcher government to buy their homes, thousands then lost them when the interest rates were hiked up so sharply, causing increased homelessness.

The public perception of homelessness was focused on its most manifest symptom. It was the visibility of street sleeping, particularly amongst young people, that aroused the public, voluntary sector and some members of the government's concern and therefore brought the whole issue of homelessness into public discussion. Hundreds of people began begging on the streets of London.

Within the voluntary sector and statutory authorities providing services to the homeless, there were also changes. David Warner, former CEO of Homeless Network,[17] was there and says:

> 'A number of different things came together during the early eighties that led to the massive explosion of people on the streets in the late eighties. Firstly, the closure programme of old DHSS spikes [hostels for single people], which probably started about 1981/82.'

The voluntary sector had lobbied for these inhumane places to be replaced. The government subsequently developed a programme of replacing them, so that meant that one aspect of the circuit had disappeared. The hostels were to be replaced with a more diverse range of accommodation mainly through housing associations.

At the same time, there were very large working men's hostels, privately owned, which increasingly had become dumping grounds for people who were 'social misfits'. Refurbishment work on these to make them decent places to live meant reducing the bed spaces. These measures impacted across London particularly, but also elsewhere.

The 1980s saw a reconfiguration of the way that accommodation services for vulnerable people were provided. A net reduction in places led to an increase in visibility of those people on the streets. Homeless people did not like these big hostels, nor do many like going into present day ones. No one asked them what they wanted. 'I've been in hostels,' says Jim Lawrie, currently vending *The Big Issue*:

> *'I've been in Salvation Army hostels. Their attitude in the past has been "it's really your fault, but God loves you." They used to go and recruit the sinner. I was in one 20 years ago in Middlesex Street. It was dormitory accommodation and you used to have to sleep with your boots under the end of the bed, or someone would nick them in the middle of the night.'*

It was a very Victorian attitude. He adds:

> *'They've moved on since then, got more modern hostels. Some of the attitude is the same. But I'm not kicking them really hard, because they are needed. They are part of the front line. Loads of people have told me that they hate these hostels. I make a point of not going into their hostels, or not going into hostels at all.'*

Then, a crucial policy change in the mid 1980s triggered an immediate crisis for vulnerable young people, leading to the rise of young people's homelessness. Modifications to the social security structure in 1985 and again in 1988 further eroded benefits to the homeless and in particular to young people.[18] Sixteen and seventeen year olds lost entitlement to income support from September 1988.[19]

The benefit changes combined with the crisis of unemployment in the North led in the late 1980s to the migration to London of people who were suffering increasing poverty, particularly young people who left home as a consequence of benefit changes. The numbers of young people with no income rose from 70,000 in 1988 to 97,000 in 1993.[20] And there was this perennial and increasing shortage of affordable rented housing.[21]

Mark McGreevy, Director of the DePaul Trust,[22] worked in hostels and day centres in the early 1980s with people who were sleeping rough but who were all 'traditional old lads'. Then suddenly, after the change in legislation, within three to six months he witnessed a massive rise, which was most marked in young people. 'That had never been seen before. Rarely did you see a young person out on the street before 1988.' In 1988, The Passage Day Centre saw about 350 people a day, and almost half the people that came in within this 12 month period dropped to the under 25 age range. 'No one would convince me that the pace that it happened between 1987 and 1989, that that was some kind of cultural phenomena. It had to be led by a policy.'

Nick Hardwick, then Director of Centrepoint which works with young homeless people, emphasizes that at this time, in the 1980s, kids weren't called 'homeless', they were 'runaways'. This implied that they could be counselled and sent back home. This attitude was still prevalent when he wrote the lead article for the first edition of *The Big Issue* in 1991, 'Why don't the homeless just go home?':

> *'Why didn't they go home? The idea that people didn't have homes was not an argument that had been completely won. It was seen as a social condition, something about the way you behave, rather than you haven't got anywhere to live.'*

He remembered that before 1985 kids were never seen begging and sleeping on the streets. Centrepoint carried out the first survey, in 1987, that proved that there was a youth homeless problem as opposed to a runaways problem. He adds:

> *'We did this big survey of the experiences of people using our centre and we didn't ask a question about begging because nobody begged. And yet by 1988 that had completely changed and there was a lot of people begging on the streets and as far as*

young people were concerned, that was a direct result of the 1988 Act.'

From the government's point of view, Sir George Young, Housing Minister 1990–94, did not agree that there had been a sharp rise in the overall numbers of homeless people under the Tory government.[23] Unlike those working directly with homeless people, Sir George relied on statistics. However, he did concede the point on young homeless people. He explains:

'How people measure [homelessness] is that they look at the number of people accepted as homeless by local authorities and that is the thermometer. By definition, hardly any of those were ever actually "homeless", they were all threatened with homelessness. They presented themselves to the local authorities, and they were accepted.'

He maintains that 50 per cent went straight into permanent accommodation. Nearly all the rest went straight from where they were, from the private landlord who was evicting them or the building society who was repossessing them, into good quality, but temporary accommodation. He says, 'So when you produce the figure that 250,000 people were accepted as homeless, people assume that those people were actually homeless. They weren't.'

The figures went up, but in the early 1990s they peaked and started going down. The reason for this, he explained, was that in some parts of the capital, the homeless route was seen as the only route into social housing.

'If you looked at the total number of people moving into social housing, you probably find that that was static, or even possibly going up a bit, but that route was becoming more popular. It's understandable, the ways the figures were presented, that people presumed that more and more people were actually becoming literally homeless, but they weren't. Very few of those people were actually ever homeless.'

Sir George did agree on the drastic increase in young people's homelessness:

'These were people who were not covered by the legislation. The people we have just been talking about [above] are covered by the Homeless Persons legislation – they are the ones who appear on the statistics. With young people, who are not covered by the legislation, indeed there was an increase and that is one of the reasons that we introduced the Rough Sleepers Initiative, because a lot of them were young people.'

One of the keys to the subsequent policy changes is acknowledged by Victor Adebowale, CEO of Centrepoint until recently. Some of the Tory ministers were very concerned about what was going on. He says:

'People, like former MP Charles Hendry, very concerned, very supportive of what we were trying to do, still is. Because he understood, bothered to read up and talk to people. The majority of the Tory Party, that was the problem. That's why we had that poster – "Politicians put young people in boxes." Why? Because they don't actually bother to find out. It's just about not caring. It's about not knowing the consequences and thinking, "well, if it works for the majority, hell, we can live with a few homeless people".'

THE ROUGH SLEEPERS INITIATIVE

Charles Hendry was Conservative MP for High Peak 1992–97.[24] He was joint Chair of the All Party Group on Homelessness and Housing which he joined in the autumn of 1992. Homelessness and the issues surrounding youth at risk were the areas in which he took a particular interest. He felt there were not enough people within the Tory Party who were taking an interest in social issues.

'I think we came to be seen to be a party which was particularly interested in economics. Even the human aspects of economics got slightly overlooked. I think that one of the reasons why people turned against us, in the way they did, was that we were seen to be too one-sided.'

He also explains how difficult it was to stir up a great deal of interest in housing or homelessness amongst MPs, 'even though for many of our constituents, their houses and homes and heating are the most important issues'. Every time there was a debate on the issue, he says, the chamber of the House of Commons just emptied. That was when the crisis was at its worst.

With the All Party Group, Charles consulted with the voluntary sector representatives. Charles believes that Nick Hardwick, as the Director of Centrepoint, was one of the most important people in getting homelessness put on the agenda because he was someone highly regarded in the sector. At this point, the voluntary sector realized that Sir George Young was prepared to listen. Nick Hardwick was seconded with a group from the voluntary sector to the Department of the Environment to advise the government on the Rough Sleepers Initiative (RSI).

In 1990, he took Michael Howard (Housing Minister before Sir George Young) and Chris Patten, Secretary of State for the Environment, out onto the streets to see homeless people for themselves. Nick and his staff had already taken a number of Tory politicians out, but it was always a bit risky because they never quite knew who they were going to find.

> *'I got this frantic call the night before saying, "what should they wear?". I said "wear what you wear at the weekend". So Michael Howard appeared in his gardening clothes, with ordinary shoes, black socks, jeans that stopped just above the ankle.'*

They walked down the Strand where there was a group of kids whom Nick knew. 'We all got down on our haunches and there was Michael Howard and Chris Patten talking to these kids in a shop doorway.' As they walked off down the Strand:

> *'a group of what you would describe as toffs, who clearly were going out for a night at the theatre, speaking in this very upper class accent just as they passed, said "It's an absolute bloody scandal. Why doesn't the government do something? I haven't supported them for generations to see this".'*

They then walked down into the Bullring in Waterloo, which at that point was at its worst, where between 200 and 300 people lived.

'The place was full and people were lighting fires, so you had this low pall of smoke. When we were down there, a guy was having an epileptic fit and rolling around. Then there was this guy who didn't have any legs, on a trolley, who came up towards us, pushing himself with his hands, and he looked grim. He spat on his hand, put his hand out and said "pleased to meet you". They shook him by the hand.'

Nick worried about the security of the ministers, particularly when Chris Patten went wandering off.

'He just stood there in the middle of this and said "This can't go on, can it? This simply isn't acceptable". Soon after, Michael Howard pushed the first RSI through the Treasury.'

Shelter did similar 'seeing and believing tours'. 'They were amazing', recalls Sheila McKechnie, then Director of Shelter.

'We did a few jointly with the Prince's Trust who were the other players in this at the time. At the time when government ministers were being taken round, so were lots of businessmen, and they were equally shocked. The Bullring was fearsome. There were a lot of things going on on the streets and a hell of a lot of bullying of young people... There was always much more violence towards young people on the streets. People used to asked me, "why don't you get young black beggars?", and I would say because the public would kill them. You cannot safely beg as a black person on the street.'

The result of all this was that the government put £99.2m from 1990 to 1993 and £86m from 1993 to 1996 to sweep people off the streets. The initiative offered block grant payments to agencies to offer street sleepers accommodation in shelters and to work towards their resettlement in temporary or, preferably, permanent housing. By September 1991, according to Nick Hardwick, writing in the first *Big Issue*, 1500 had been housed who otherwise would have been on the streets. Some additional funds were given in grants to organizations and projects providing advice and assistance to single homeless people.

Sir George Young replaced Michael Howard as the Minister of Housing. He talks about the RSI and its place in Conservative housing policy.

'The RSI wasn't the main thrust, it couldn't be, because the number of rough sleepers as defined by the Department was about 3000. (I know Shelter came up with a much bigger figure.) The RSI was part of housing policy. It was by no means the only thing or the most important thing.'

There were, he says, a lot of people with housing problems – people living in the private sector, people in council houses that were badly maintained and falling down, the difficult to let estates.

'In terms of visual impact and impact on the media, the RSI was quite successful because you could do a count each quarter and monitor the progress. It was much more difficult to do that with the difficult to let estates where you were looking at a five year programme to turn that round. The RSI was successful, not so much as for what I did, but what the voluntary sector did with the resources that they were given by the Department and the heroic work of a lot of individuals who are still at it.'

The RSI worked, concludes Nick Hardwick.

'At that point, there were 3000 people on the streets and the numbers were just going sky high. And you were talking about a lot of people who just didn't want to be there another minute. It was very desperate. We did shift a lot of people and we did get the situation under control and then we won the battle later on.'

Nick believes that the lasting value of this experience was the setting up of relationships between the voluntary sector and the government.

'At that time the relationship was a bit more spiky because the consensus wasn't there about what we were doing. So at Centrepoint we had a whole lot of people who were deeply sceptical whom we had to keep satisfying. There was much more of a tradition of argument with the Tory government. We still had a very strong feeling that we could work together [with government] but that didn't limit our right to be critical.'

When Nick joined Centrepoint in 1985, both the definition and arguments surrounding homelessness differed from today's. The political argument he had to fight was that tackling homelessness should be solely the goverment's responsibility. Some people argued that Centrepoint should close down because its operation let the government off the hook. And the local authorities were the only ones who should be running direct access accommodation.

David Warner explains:

> 'The voluntary sector, from the formation of Shelter in the sixties, had been very good at campaigning and arguing for change without necessarily being prepared to then engage with policy makers on the delivery of that process of change. So you would have organizations like Shelter and CHAR, as they then were, standing up and being critical and campaigning, but not then being prepared to sit round the table and actually work out solutions.'

He adds:

> 'What happened in London is that we successfully borrowed the techniques of lobbying and campaigning to get public support for something and then we made the next fundamental step (and I don't know whether consciously or unconsciously) of actually sitting round the table with government and helping them work out how they could solve the problem.'

Sheila McKechnie believes that during this period Shelter's campaigning profile was second to none on the issue. However, all was not rosy between some Tory MPs and charities. One particular incident illustrates the sometimes spiky nature of the relationship. Charles Hendry believed that there was a confusion in people's minds between rough sleeping and homelessness in general, and that it 'suited some people's arguments to confuse the two'. Some of the people who caused this confusion came from the voluntary sector, he maintains.

He referred Shelter to the Charity Commission because:

> 'they produced a leaflet saying there were 2 million homeless people. Next to that there was a photograph of a person in a

sleeping bag on the street. They said anyone who is in unsuitable accommodation is homeless, anyone who is staying on a friend's floor is homeless, anyone is in a slightly overcrowded home with their parents is homeless. It wasn't a definition that most people would recognize.'

The reality, he believes, was somewhere between those sleeping rough on the streets and the Shelter definition. He thinks that Shelter subsequently modified the figures.

Sheila explains that this incident was specifically over educational material on homelessness for schools and there was one phrase that had caused him concern.

'But instead of discussing it with us, he went to Conservative Party Central Office. We got a letter. I took that head on... We had fairly extended correspondence with the Charity Commission and in the end they accepted our position and not Charles Hendry's.'

Thus in the late 1980s the voluntary sector came to be seen as the people directly picking up the pieces, particularly in the context of homelessness in London. The state retreated from the direct provision of welfare services, partly because of a general climate of fiscal restraint, by channelling money through the voluntary sector. They in turn provided the relevant services to homeless people.

Whilst acknowledging the absolute necessity for short-term emergency work, *The Big Issue* believed charity wasn't going far enough to promote social change. Criticisms also come from other quarters towards the charity sector and are harsh.

Definitions of homelessness are revealing of vested interests. Some critics argue, for example, that public and policy and voluntary sector activities are designed not so much to help homeless persons as to maintain existing institutional arrangements and to forestall radical change. 'Compassion... is little more than the passion for control.'[25]

'There is a difference of opinion about the extent to which the voluntary sector assists or hinders the development of self-help initiatives on the part of homeless people. Disenchantment exists amongst some homeless people after repeated exposure to

caregivers conducting "needs assessments" without knowing much about the capabilities of people being evaluated. A paternalistic approach breeds resentment.'

Some people complain that the voluntary agencies engage in band-aid solutions or cosmetic exercises, whilst avoiding challenges to underlying problems.[26]

There has also been deep dissatisfaction amongst homeless people themselves at the way they are not listened to, or have to abide by the rules of 'those who say they know best'. At the National Speakout,[27] nine years on from the launch of *The Big Issue*, homeless people were still saying that no one was listening, Sam Hart wrote in *The Big Issue*:[28]

'Homelessness is big business. Hundreds of millions of pounds have been thrown at the problem – yet it refuses to go away... Agencies agree that there is unlikely to be a reduction in this figure [400,000 homeless people in the UK] in the near future, despite a huge network of charities, church groups and government teams dedicated to alleviating it.'

Sam continued:

'An obvious solution would be to consult those with experience of the problem – homeless people. Yet their input has been limited – until now. "Homeless people have a unique insight, yet are usually ignored," says Jerry Ham of Groundswell, a network which develops self-help initiatives for homeless people. "The attitude of larger charities tends to be: 'We know what's best for you. Listen to us...' " "When I was staying in shelters they were full of rules and regulations, but nobody asked me what would help me best," says Groundswell volunteer and former rough sleeper Steve Scott. "It's simple. If you've got a problem you ask an expert. We're experts, why don't they ask us?".'

At the Speakout, homeless people talked about the shortage of hostel spaces for both gay and straight couples. Very few hostels admitted dogs, forcing many people to sleep rough rather than abandon their pets. They would like choice like everyone else, wrote Sam:[29]

'Lack of services for those most damaged by society was a common theme. Drug-users and drinkers pointed out that they are effectively excluded from the system because hostels do not allow drugs or alcohol on the premises.'

As Ruth Turner, founder of *The Big Issue in the North*, has said:

'We have always encouraged homeless people to think of themselves as consumers. We say, you don't have to accept that advice, or help, if you don't want to. If you don't like that approach, go for another one. The policy of making homeless people only have one offer of accommodation, and then if they don't accept it reject them, is wrong. They should have choice like anyone else. It's about having the same aspirations as you would for your friends or your family.'

Charities are not businesses and cannot generate jobs for people, although the rules are becoming more flexible.[30] Jobs, along with decent, permanent accommodation, are what most homeless people want. The non-profit (voluntary sector/charities) attitude is very different from a business mentality.

'Non-profit organizations are oriented toward getting people to give them money. Businesses are oriented towards making money. What's needed is to put the two together so social service agencies can learn to be more businesslike... and businesses can learn to be more socially beneficial.'[31]

Charities, though, were beginning to change. In July 1995, Geoff Mulgan, then director of the think-tank Demos, summed up the nature of this change.[32] Whilst recognizing that charity is one of the things that the British seem to be very good at, he acknowledged that those who contribute to charities, or depend on them, have no say in how they are run. In the past this has caused few problems, but now people are demanding more.

'All these anxieties boil down to a similar concern: that the charity world is out of step with the nineties, and that the very idea of charity is no longer as self-evident and beyond reproach as it might once have seemed.'

He continues:

> 'But if the old idea of charity is unsatisfactory for those giving,
> the same is true for those on the receiving end. Few feel comfort-
> able being dependent on someone else's charity... As Raymond
> Williams put it: "It is not surprising that the word which was
> once the most general expression of love and care for others has
> become so compromised that modern governments have to
> advertise welfare benefits as 'not a charity but a right'".'

This is surely, states Mulgan, why many of today's most successful initiatives place so much emphasis on the responsibility and
self-respect of those in need – with enterprises like *The Big Issue*
magazine turning the homeless from supplicants into sellers.

Despite the changing nature of charity, Mulgan believes it was
wrong to conclude that it was therefore irrelevant. 'The original
ideas of charity – care and help – remain no less valid today than
they ever were'. John Bird takes the argument a step further. He
believes that modernizing charity as an efficient social engine to
break poverty, provide emergency relief and aid recovery into
society is what is needed.

Similarly, there has been much discussion around the changing role of the welfare state. Sir William Beveridge's 1942 report
on social security, which the government subsequently imple-
mented in post-war Britain, outlined the creation of a safety net
for male breadwinners of families who found themselves
temporarily without work or housing. The new welfare state was
not supposed to provide a lifetime service, and the success of the
system depended on high employment levels. However, high
employment and levels of social need since the 1980s have eroded
Beveridge's original plan and put extreme financial and social
burdens on the welfare state, initiating a gradual chipping away
in social spending over the years.

William Beveridge believed it was important that the new
system did not destroy people's motivation and drive so that they
would become dependent on the state. A few years into the
system, however, Beveridge claimed that this was beginning to
happen. The discussion re-emerged when unemployment soared
and the social security bill did likewise during the 1980s. Aspects
of the welfare state were attacked from the Right and encouraged
new thinking from the Left. The Commission on Social Justice, for

example, launched in 1992 by the then Labour leader John Smith, reported that: 'in place of a benefits system, which helps to keep poor people poor, we need a revolution in welfare to enable people to earn their way out of poverty'.[33]

Sheila McKechnie talks about the constant debate around the disabling nature of the welfare system. 'This was usually from the Tory right, and that has tended to obscure the very genuine criticism from the more centre left position. There is a welfare dependency syndrome.'

Charles Leadbeater, economist and research associate at Demos, has linked the rise of social entrepreneurship to the failing welfare state. The inadequacies of the welfare state have prompted radical and innovative alternative ways of tackling social exclusion. He describes social entrepreneurs as those who are 'bridging the gap between the private and public sectors, the state and the market to develop effective solutions to social problems',[34] involving such things as innovative drug treatment programmes or the provision of high quality housing schemes.

> 'The welfare state is, first and last, about helping people. It is also about survival. To survive it needs to behave like any other industry: devise new approaches to welfare and promote self-reliance rather than long-term dependency on the state.'

Business also has a part to play, and the 1990s saw a re-configuration of the private, public and government partnership in addressing today's major social issues. There is now a recognition that business can be part of this process and that it cannot be left to government or the voluntary sector alone. There is an increasing willingness on the part of some businesses to recognize and meet the challenge of tacking both social and environmental dislocation. They have taken up the challenge, issued by consumers, employees and pressure groups, of social responsibility towards their wider community and environment.

As Anita Roddick states, with over two decades of experience in the world of business:

> 'I don't think anyone would argue that business now dominates the world's centre stage. It is faster, more creative, adaptable, efficient and wealthier than many governments... so in terms of power and influence, you can forget the Church and forget

politics, too. There is no more powerful institution in society than business.'

She stresses the importance for business to assume a moral leadership in society. She continues:

'Many governments' economic agendas seem to take no account of caring for the weak and the frail and the marginalized. If governments are not interested, then I believe that business – rich, powerful and creative – has to take responsibility. If not us, who?'[35]

It is not surprising, therefore, that today's political activity on the streets has eschewed anti-government demonstrations and centred on confronting the attitudes of global business.

There are no absolute answers. A multi-faceted approach to social exclusion is what is needed. But there are many arguments which point towards getting rid of the dependency culture and implementing a more business-like approach to social problems. This is not an argument for getting rid of charities or the welfare state, but to harnessing a more inclusive approach to social issues. This could be by concentrating more on the prevention of social problems; an expansion of the self-help ethos; the welfare state re-inventing itself to prepare people for employment; or encouraging the business world to become more responsive to social issues.

CHAPTER 2

THE *BIG ISSUE* IS BORN

'BIG ISSUE, BIG ISSUE. *Buy this week's* Big Issue...'

Chris, 36, used to sell *The Big Issue* at Finchley Central tube station in North London. A train driver from Glasgow, he had suffered a nervous breakdown in 1992 and had a serious gambling habit and huge financial problems.

In October 1994 he packed his job in, boarded the train for London and for the first week slept in Euston station before he was moved on by the police. The police told him he was listed as a missing person. He told them that he wanted to sort himself out. He had no contact with his family for three weeks and they believed the worst.

> *There was a body fished out of the River Clyde and my family thought it was me. It was all over Glasgow that I was dead. I contacted the police first and said I was a missing person but I was not missing any more. Then I contacted my parents.'*

Chris met a guy who introduced him to *The Big Issue*. He knew *The Big Issue* in Scotland and used to buy it, but never dreamt he would end up selling it down in London. At *The Big Issue*'s Farringdon offices, he was given a badge and offered a pitch at Finchley Central. The housing staff helped him find a flat. He was also asked if he needed counselling, but he was already attending

Gamblers Anonymous. Chris vended for nine months, moving on to a full-time job in *The Big Issue*. Now he works for a big London employer.

Chris is one of the success stories of *The Big Issue*, but the story didn't start in London. An earlier chance encounter between the head of an international company and a homeless man inspired an initiative that has revolutionized the methods of tackling social exclusion. During a business trip to New York in 1990, the Chairman of Body Shop International, Gordon Roddick, passed Grand Central station. He remembers:

> *'This huge black guy holding a pile of papers came over to me. He was very friendly. I bought a copy of* Street News, *and chatted to him for a bit.'*

Street News was the first homeless street paper. It was launched in November 1989, the brainchild of Hutchinson Persons. Initially it had a huge circulation (circa 150,000 a month). Its success was partly due to its novelty and partly because of the huge numbers of homeless people at that time on the streets of New York.

The *Street News* vendor told Gordon that the greatest thing for him when selling the paper was the chance to talk to people. He had come out of a penitentiary and moved away from his former neighbourhood.

> *'He said, "Normally when I am standing on the street with my hand out, nobody wants to talk to me. They chuck me a coin and walk on. But with the paper people look me in the eye. They are curious about me and what I am doing, and why I am doing it." He told me it wasn't so much the cash, which was great. It was the human contact. It was the enablement he felt that he was a part of the throbbing race of life and not a bit of garbage sitting on a corner asking for someone's indulgence.'*

Author Lee Stringer, formerly homeless and a crack addict in the 1980s, became involved with *Street News*[1] first as a vendor and then a journalist. He describes his first meeting with the paper at its office in West Forty-Sixth Street in the winter of 1989:

> *'The first time I laid eyes on this place, a pair of old street geezers were perched on upturned milk crates just outside the door,*

oblivious to the winter chill, garbed in black caps, T-shirts, and money aprons that said Street News. *Each had a wad of bills pinched between his fingers and they were comparing the thicknesses of their respective accumulated earnings…Trailing out the door and snaking half way down the block was a line of eager people waiting to get in, all summoned there by nothing more than word of mouth.'*

The scene, he said, 'had an exhilarating, up from the streets kind of momentum'.

Buying the papers for a quarter each, they sold them for 75 cents. 'The papers flew out of our hands, for all over the city the streets were filled with homelessness and compassion.' People could make $60 a day. However, the situation wasn't to last. The sales started to decline and it began to be published irregularly. Since then the paper has been owned and edited by a number of people. By 1994 Lee describes it thus: 'For three years its circulation had been dwindling, a situation I attributed to its languishing content – 24 pages of lackluster filler…' He hoped that as a writer he could help it emerge from the doldrums. But there were a number of forces working against *Street News*'s success.

Street News's decline owed much to its concentration on pure street sales. It did little to aid people other than give them a livelihood. Added to this, was its weak editorial content, as Lee Stringer states, and a sense of pride in the product was never developed. When Persons left and the ownership kept changing hands, there was no consistency. Also, Mayor Giuliani had begun his campaign to sweep homeless people off the streets of Manhatten. The attitude towards homeless people changed. When *Street News* first came out, Lee could sell a hundred papers on the No 6 train. 'That was back when Wall Street was really pumping and the train would be full of stockbrokers. Those guys really got off seeing a guy hustle.' A few years later, 'although Wall Street is pumping again, the mood is different. Standing up and reeling off a speech is not the attention-getter it once was.' The ultimate insult is from a guy who calls him over: 'He gives me a dollar but refuses a paper.' *Street News* is still going but has never regained its former position.

However, Gordon was inspired by the encounter with *Street News*. He decided to try and replicate the idea in the UK, where homelessness was an ever increasing problem. Here was an interesting concept. A socially marginalized person was being given the opportunity to do two things: one was to earn a badly needed legitimate income by selling a newspaper; the other was to build up his or her self-confidence so that they could think about getting back into mainstream work. One motive fuelled the other. With the income they could eat, so they did not have to rely on handouts. And by selling the paper they could talk to people who in turn would begin to understand their predicament.

The street paper concept was given to the communications department of The Body Shop. For a year, staff talked to lawyers, publishers and organizations working with homeless people. The issue was how to sell the paper and generate the profit to address the homeless question.

The reports from the communications department were disappointing. The conclusion was that the newspaper would have to be sold through newsagents. It was felt that English people would not like being approached in the street by vendors. Vendors would need a hawker's licence and the police would be a problem. The social security issue would be too difficult to monitor. The paper would make enemies by interfering with the pitches of London's daily newspaper, the *Evening Standard*.

But Gordon was adamant that the only way was for the paper to be sold on the streets by the homeless so that they could earn their own income. His initial thoughts were that the remaining profit would be channelled into a homeless organization. He says:

> 'The purpose was also that the homeless themselves should sell the newspaper in order to have the human contact. And if you have newsagents you have no contact at all.'

GORDON RODDICK AND JOHN BIRD – SOCIAL ENTREPRENEURS

The idea was put on the back burner until Gordon talked the project over with an old acquaintance, John Bird. John and Gordon had first met in Scotland in 1967. 'I was on the run from the police. Just before Christmas 1967,' recounts John:

> 'This large Scotsman came into a pub in Edinburgh with a load of his rugby mates where I was drinking. It was a kind of evil little pub and we all knew each other. I went over to him and we started talking, strangely enough about poetry. We found out we were both poets.'

They met on and off for a couple of years but then lost touch. John and Gordon's backgrounds were very different. Gordon was educated at a public school called Merchiston Castle in Edinburgh (where later John was employed as a gardener) and hated it. After school he studied agriculture, but did not finish his studies. He then became a poet and travelled the world. Gordon met Anita in the late 1960s. They had two girls, got married and Anita opened her first Body Shop in March 1976. Two months after the opening of the shop, Gordon decided to take off to South America for two years. He wanted to ride a horse from Buenos Aires to New York. Having completed 2000 miles in one year, he returned after one of the horses was killed falling over a precipice. By this time, Anita had opened a second shop in Chichester, and with Gordon's involvement The Body Shop expanded rapidly.[2]

John was born in 1946 in the slums of Paddington, London, into an Anglo-Irish working class family. The community was strong and, despite the poverty, he always felt safe. This security disappeared when he arrived back from school one day at the age of five to find his family's belongings dumped onto the pavement. His parents hadn't paid the rent for months. As John's family were Catholic, the five boys were sent to a Catholic orphanage in Mill Hill, North London. John sank.

'My brothers became part of the system and I didn't. I started running away. The nuns were tough. They were my first experience of intense, injected charity, which put me off it for life.'

Three years later the family were rehoused in Fulham and the boys came home. Immediately, John started to get into trouble. Shoplifting, housebreaking and truancy meant he was periodically brought before the juvenile court. The magistrate was a well-known social reformer called Baroness Wootton who, when John was 14, with a number of convinctions to his name, sent him to a detention centre. John still remembers the words she used to announce the sentence: 'We're going to send you for a short, sharp shock because people like you have got to respect other people's property.'

The detention centre was a boot camp run by ex-army personnel and the inmates were punched and terrorized. This type of regime did not cure him of his stealing, so the next time round he was sent to an approved school at Peper Harow in Surrey, a beautiful 18th century country house with walled gardens and parks. This regime suited John and, he believes, many of the other boys, as it involved both education (he did some GCE classes although he never passed the exams) and job training. Gardening, writing and art were just some of the skills he acquired.

For the next 25 years, John's life encompassed a vast range of different experiences. Though still a petty criminal, he talked his way into Chelsea Art School. He got married and had a daughter. Although still getting into trouble, he was writing. When his marriage failed, he left for Paris to avoid the police once more. In the revolutionary fervour of the late 1960s, he became a Trotskyist, joining the Socialist Labour League. He became a printer, got married for a second time and had two more children. He wrote plays for fringe theatre, and settled down to earn his living as a printer and publisher. In the mid 1980s he saw Gordon on television, with Anita. 'I thought this guy's become incredibly rich, so I thought I should beat a path to his door,' which he did and they met occasionally over the next few years.

So it was that over a meal in a Sussex pub in early 1991 with John, Gordon resurrected the idea of starting a street paper. But what was the risk of asking someone like John to take on such an enormous project? Gordon says, 'The risk was on the integrity of the person. If you can appeal to John's passions, then there's nothing that he won't do to get there.' John claims that Gordon asked him because he had been a printer and produced a number of magazines. He had sold papers on the streets (the *International Herald Tribune* in Paris and the Trotskyist *Workers Press* in London). He had been homeless, having run away from home at the age of 15 and slept on park benches all over the capital. He was an ex-offender. And that probably was the profile of a number of the people he was expected to work with.

The history of *The Big Issue* is a reflection of the lives of two men from diverse backgrounds. The two entrepreneurs, Gordon and John, represented something quite unusual. *The Big Issue* was not about Gordon wanting to cash in on further business opportunities. In fact, he made it clear he wanted *The Big Issue* kept completely separate from The Body Shop in the public's perception. Nor was it about John building a traditional business from which he could make money to pass on to his children.

It was a new idea, a socially responsible business spawning a social business. It would be a business solution to the problem of homelessness, rather than a charitable solution. As Anita Roddick has stated about her attitude to business:

> 'Since 1984, the year The Body Shop went public, as far as I am concerned the business has existed for one reason only – to allow us to use our success to act as a force for social change, to continue the education and consciousness-raising of our staff, to assist development in the Third World and, above all, to help protect the environment.'[3]

Since The Body Shop had led the way in advancing the concept of social and environmental responsibility in business, it was no surprise that Gordon would help create *The Big Issue*.

THE FEASIBILITY STUDY

John set out to do his own study on the feasibility of running a street paper in London. His initial thoughts were that if he did a street paper, he would work with homeless people, the police and the business community. The problem with the street paper in New York, he felt, was that people would only buy it if they felt sorry for the homeless person, or if they were interested in the social problems of homelessness, so its appeal was limited. It was, in a way, an elitist publication, simply banging a drum about homelessness. The street paper in Britain had to be different.

Gordon and John agreed that the paper would be totally independent of sponsors and independent of the homeless sector. It would not raise the expectations of homeless people by promising them the earth. Gordon insisted that it operate as a business. It would give homeless people an opportunity of earning money, but would only do more when it was in a position to do so. The paper would not be given to homeless people, it would be sold to them and they would sell it on to the public with a mark-up. This flew in the face of the philosophy of many of the other organizations working with homeless people as it provided an income. The paper would re-energize the work ethic in people's lives: it would be a method of motivating them and help to create choice.

This was in the early days of Prime Minister John Major's Conservative administration, when homeless people were seen by many as aggressive beggars who were a social nuisance on the streets. As an alternative to begging, the paper would enable homeless people to relate to the public.

John needed to know three things. If he gave homeless people an alternative to begging and a way of earning a legitimate income, would they be happy with this? Would the police support them and would the people of London support the initiative? He needed to know the reactions of all the players in London's community as the project would have far-reaching effects on all of them.

John looked at the work done by The Body Shop communications department. Interestingly, Richard Preston, who had done much of the work, was very positive about a potential street paper. He offered John his time and advice. He was the expert and knew more about the homeless sector's responses to the idea. He was John's first adviser and they met constantly throughout the study.

TALKING TO HOMELESS PEOPLE AND HOMELESS ADVOCATES

John's first task was to talk to London's homeless. He talked with homeless people on the streets and with people sleeping rough in the Bullring and Lincoln's Inn, which were the two biggest and most well-established sites of rough sleepers in the centre of the capital.

Communities of homeless people had lived in Lincoln's Inn Fields on and off for decades. The offices around the square were occupied by the Royal College of Surgeons and members of the legal profession and at the time they were pushing hard for homeless people to be evicted. The Bullring was a round concrete underpass near Waterloo station which in the 1970s became a well-known homeless community. During the 1980s, over 200 people would sleep there each night. The numbers did not decline until the government initiatives of the early 1990s.[4]

The biggest difficulty was explaining the new idea to homeless people who had been involved with charity for much of their lives. Homeless people demanded to know why he wanted to sell something to them rather than give it away. John argued that people have been giving away things to homeless people for hundreds of years and nothing had changed.

> *'I didn't think it was good for people, not for moral purposes,
> but because if you can live as a scavenger, why would you ever
> want to get off the streets? It saps your morale, your sense of
> creativity and you become a glorified forager. That is not good
> for people who want to get out of homelessness.'*

Many homeless people were willing to talk to him, but others
were more dismissive. Some thought he was yet another do-
gooder, who would be giving out Bibles and sandwiches. Others
supposed he was a member of a left-wing political party, or that
he was setting up a business to make money out of homeless
people. A number told him to keep his nose out of their business.
He was threatened with being roughed up.

John also found that the idea of getting off the streets was
alien to some homeless people. They did not believe they could
or even wanted to. On the other hand, they were angry with all
the things that left them homeless, on the streets relying on the
kindness of strangers. They wanted to be empowered by earning
their own money and breaking from dependency. They talked
about the difficulties of finding work which was virtually impossible because they had no permanent address and often turned
up for a job looking dishevelled and dirty. Therefore, how could
they make money, other than by robbing or by begging?

So the response from the homeless community was mixed.
Many people told John that they would want to sell a product
that would not just be another form of begging. He told them that
it would be a professional paper, a paper that would be well
printed, well designed and a lot of people would want to buy it.
In retrospect he admits, 'I didn't even know what the hell I was
doing really, talking like this.'

John visited two organizations for their reaction to the idea of
a street paper. He went first to the London Connection, a day
centre and job creation organization for young people in the West
End. John believes they were sceptical of him because he was not
a typical advocate.

> *'I didn't have any deep, profound, psychological knowledge of
> the street or social dislocation. I had no charity expertise. I
> didn't have a CV in social improvement. I was a printer cum
> publisher. My only experience was that I had lived the crisis of
> many of the young homeless people.'*

But there he met Pete Husbands, a London Connection support worker. Although not impressed by John, Pete later proved one of his earliest supporters. John meanwhile went to the North Lambeth Day Centre which at the time ran a paper produced by homeless people. They were positive and very interested but did not have the time to get involved.

Until the paper was up and running, the concept was difficult to grasp. The initial suspicion that ran through the voluntary sector about a paper to be sold by homeless people was understandable. It was not the self-help element, which was already being espoused by some within the voluntary sector, but the commercial aspect that was a challenge to the philosophy these organizations embraced. A few people from the sector had also mentioned to John that they were worried that homeless people could not be relied upon or trusted to work in the commercial environment of selling a paper. John just did not believe this, but as someone who had never professionally been involved with working with homeless people, he had stepped into a world that had decades of experience.

Before *The Big Issue* started, Nick Hardwick, then Director of Centrepoint, had been approached about the possibility of setting up a street paper in London. Nick's opinion was that it would never work here, so the idea was shelved. He says:

> 'I then got asked to do the first article by John. I was reasonably bold and recovered some lost face. Other people at that point were saying don't touch it with a barge pole.'

The editor of *ROOF* magazine at Shelter had brought some copies of *Street News* back from New York. Then Sheila McKechnie at Shelter had received a visit from the man who had taken over from Hutchinson Persons. 'We were thinking of doing it [a street paper] in Shelter, so there was a little bit of tension at the beginning, discussing it with The Body Shop.' Shelter's basement was put forward as a possible headquarters. 'We thought it was a brilliant idea. No question', she says. However, Shelter decided not to go ahead with it and thought that it should be run as an independent project.

There were some good reasons for being cautious about the idea, believes Nick:

'On the one hand the homeless sector is bedevilled by people saying "I'm going to set up something to help you", getting a lot of important people to sign their names to it and then turning out to be extremely exploitative or criminal. People come along, you don't know who they are, and they could turn out to be dodgy.'

So it was not the commercial aspect of *The Big Issue* that made him cautious. Once the magazine was established, the issue arose about how to work with it. Nick explains:

'We came to the decision by the first issue that we would endorse it. But if other people were cautious I think that's to do with whether it seemed to be a genuine help. It was nothing to do with The Big Issue, but more to do with our experience of other people setting up things to help homeless people.'

For Mark McGreevy of the Depaul Trust, his experience of a street paper goes back to a visit to New York in 1989 when he talked to a few vendors selling *Street News*. His impression was that vending wasn't something they wanted to get involved in permanently. He also noticed the way the public treated them: for every person that showed an interest there must have been a hundred that just walked by. He says:

'I went down into one of the subway stations one night with one of the vendors and there were a mass of people sleeping out with newspapers beside them. I didn't see the point in it as they were sponsored by a corporate interest. I thought it may be just solving a corporate conscience.'

This coloured his view and made him deeply cynical when he went to the first meeting of Homeless Network to discuss *The Big Issue*. The ten people at the meeting were invited to be on the board. 'I said, thanks, good luck, but no.' Some people were more positive than others. Mark did not believe in the kind of jobs it would produce, the kind of level of income it would generate and the reasons behind it. Being corporate driven, even by an ethical company like The Body Shop, he doubted it would be successful. 'However, I eat my words,' he admits.

David Warner was working in the homeless sector when *The Big Issue* was launched but was not directly involved. Talking to people who were around at the time, he picked up two instinctive responses to John's idea:

> *'The first was, it's a load of crap, it will never work. The second one was, it's probably a load of crap, it will never work, but we can't be seen to be publicly too critical of it, because it might work. So the wiser people within the sector in London took the view that it was an interesting idea.'*

Next, the police were contacted. They were an important factor because of their daily contact with homeless people, especially in the West End. John met with Janet Newman and Mary Asprey who were working with street children in conjunction with the Suzy Lamplugh Trust. They had started looking for missing children in 1989 and Janet had set up a Missing Persons Helpline in her bedroom. They introduced him to officers from the Juvenile Protection Unit and the Homeless Unit at Charing Cross police station. The police appeared supportive and they put the word round about the possible launch of the paper.

On a visit to Scotland Yard, John was told that people did not have the right to sell a paper on the streets. Fortunately he was able to produce a copy of the 1871 Peddlars Act, having obtained it from Scotland Yard's PR department. The Act showed that selling a publication on the streets was legal.

No one could predict whether the public would buy a street paper. The New York experience proved nothing and the meteoric rise and fall of *Street News* did not look encouraging. The only conclusion that John could reach was that it was worth a try. 'So long as we didn't fall into the trap of producing an unreadable publication, we might stand a chance,' he reflected. 'If the paper was popularist in its coverage, social issues with arts and reviews, then the chance of success would increase.'

THE RESULT

John's six-week feasibility study was based on his instincts, rather than gathering lengthy statistics on who was for the paper or who was against it.

> *'I looked at it as a Londoner, as to what I wanted to happen in London rather than what homeless organizations wanted. And I*

*was always struck by the kind of anger of the people on the
streets, the people who scream out in the middle of the day. So I
was looking at it as a London phenomenon rather than simply a
homeless one.'*

His conclusion was a further refinement of his previous discussions with Gordon: the paper would be set up as a private
company, with two shares, a controlling 'A' share would be
owned by John, and a 'B' share held by The Body Shop. John
would be paid a wage. *The Big Issue* would soon define itself as a
social business, and not for profit of any individual. If there were
profits, they would be spent on social support for homeless
people. 'We would be as commercial as we could be and make a
profit,' John once graphically described it. 'Then we would mug
ourselves on the way to the bank and give the profits away for
the advantage of homeless people.'

The paper would be a self-help initiative, with people buying
the paper, initiating a businesslike approach by its vendors. John
did not think of providing a system of social support at that
point, since the voluntary sector was there for emergency social
support for homeless people. He wanted to avoid the problems
of duplication.

John also believed homeless people needed a feeling of
belonging which was a support mechanism in itself. He wanted
people working with them to be those who had straightforward
relationships with them – ex-homeless people, homeless people,
people who had been in trouble themselves. 'I was trying to
develop the idea of poachers turned gamekeepers. To get
homeless people who had been through it all themselves but who
had lifted themselves out.' At this point, John believed that if
people were given the means of making a legitimate income and
didn't have to resort to begging, then those who were relatively
able-bodied, or relatively stable, would move out of homelessness. Alternatively, they would be able to sustain themselves to
the extent that they were not seen as a blight on the social
landscape.

John also believed that the first positive outcome of selling a
paper would be that the police would have a healthier relationship with the homeless. They would not have to keep stopping
them begging, or questioning them about crime. In a sense,
homeless people would be decriminalized by their legitimate

activities of selling a paper. The media, the government, local government and businesses would then find it difficult to put homeless people down as no-hopers who were passing their social problems on to the general public.

Despite his mixed response from both homeless people and the voluntary sector, John pushed ahead. After completing the feasibility study with Richard Preston, he received the go-ahead to launch. The Body Shop provided the initial finance of £30,000 to carry the business through to the launch. He had four months, from May to September 1991, to build a team and produce the first edition. He says:

> 'As it developed, it became obvious that we were really flying by the seat of our pants. We didn't know where we were going. We didn't have a grand plan. As far as I was concerned, it was a social experiment which may or may not work.'

John's experience as a printer and small publisher stood him in good stead. But what he was not experienced in was people management. The launch team was recruited in the arbitrary fashion that became the hallmark of *The Big Issue*. John had met a writer/guitar player/song writer called Phil Ryan and over tea in his West Hampstead flat suggested he become his first employee.

> 'What I liked about Phil was his humour and confidence. Like me, he was up for anything. He was a good speaker and could wax lyrical about almost any subject. He was an encouraging guy to be with. And, like me, he could do with a challenge. He became my right hand man and did many of the things I couldn't do or wouldn't do.'

It was in Phil's flat that *The Big Issue* name was first dreamt up. John insists that he came to the meeting with the name in mind. Phil, though, says that John wanted to call it Issue, and Phil added Big. Whatever the reality, it was John and Phil who started the laborious task of turning the idea into a reality.

Alex Cooke, who was in the middle of a politics degree at Sussex University and had completed a study of *Street News* in New York, came next. She threw herself into the initiative and was their first volunteer. Later, John convinced her to take a year out from university and devote her time to the paper. The paper's first arts editor, VJ, an aspiring young actor, was recruited having met John in a café in Richmond, where she waitressed.

Pete Husband's friend, Andrew Giaquinto, of Haymarket Press, did all the production work on the magazine. It was Andrew who in a matter of minutes produced *The Big Issue*'s distinctive logo, working as a volunteer. He was paid in Italian dinners and gave endless hours to perfecting *The Big Issue*'s appearance. The Right Type, a company run by Nina Ozols, an old friend of John's, provided typesetting facilities. An office was rented in the basement of one of the Georgian houses on Richmond Green. It was big enough to accommodate four people, but within a matter of weeks it was overrun with staff and volunteers.

The four summer months of 1991 were spent planning editorial, put together by a host of volunteer freelancers. Advertisers such as VW, Shelter, Mates, the London Institute and British Gas, with Coca-Cola on the back cover, were lined up for the first issue. The money for the advertisements came out of these companies' community budgets.

John asked Nick Hardwick to do an article entitled 'But why don't the homeless just go home?' John saw it as a bold statement that would run well on the first cover. It talked about the causes of homelessness in London and the need to tackle them and recommended changes to the Social Security systems and better support for people leaving institutions. Nick wrote that:

> *'The cost of keeping people homeless is far greater than the cost of housing them and providing a chance to make the transition from reliance on benefits and handouts to working and contributing to society.'*

The feature neatly paralleled *The Big Issue*'s philosophy of breaking people from dependency, providing work as an alternative to begging and subsequently from the benefit system.

There was also a provocatively entitled article, 'The dangers of safe sex', an interview with Anita Roddick, articles on cultural activities in the capital and charity profiles, fulfilling the idea of a general interest magazine. A tabloid format was chosen because it would be cheaper to produce, and the paper was to be sold for 10p to the vendors who would sell it on to the public for 50p. The first print run was 50,000, based on the premise that the selling period would be four weeks.

John employed his youngest brother Pete to do the distribution with him storing the papers in his garage and distributing them from the back of a van in the West End. He was to tour homeless meeting places, sign people up and sell them papers.

The mainstream press reported the imminent launch of the paper in the middle of August 1991. An ad agency, Still Price: Lintas, donated their services for free by organizing posters in tube stations with photographs by David Tack, and a 60 second cinema ad. Phil recruited some homeless people to sell the paper, with fingers crossed that they would turn up on the day. About 20 turned up on the morning of the launch, some from the Bullring, others from Lincoln's Inn Fields. A number were recruited from outside St Martin-in-the-Fields that very morning. *Big Issue* bags, hats and T-shirts were given out to the prospective sales force.

Members of the press and representatives of organizations working with homeless people were invited. Sheila McKechnie, Director of Shelter, chaired the meeting, with Anita and John giving the launch speeches. Gordon brought supporters and Diana Lamplugh came, representing her Trust. Homeless people spoke. And on 11 September 1991 *The Big Issue* was launched in the Crypt of St Martin's, the very epicentre of London's homeless crisis.

3

GETTING GOING

THERE WAS FRANTIC activity after the launch. Around 50 homeless people, a few women but mostly single men who were sleeping rough, started vending on the streets of central London. Word spread along the street, bringing in more and more vendors.

A system for selling around the West End was drawn up with vendors allocated specific pitches. They were given advice on selling techniques and numbered badges with their photograph. But there were constant fights over pitches, especially in the most lucrative West End areas. This reflected the problems of the first vendors who were rough sleepers, many heavy drinkers. Staff were continuously having to rush out to stop the altercations. Two coordinators were nominated, themselves vendors. Their role was to oversee the pitches, help monitor the vendors out on the streets and report back on how the paper was selling. Coordinators have subsequently proved a very useful and practical way of keeping equilibrium on the streets.

Len was one of the original vendors (badge 59) and continued to sell until recently in a London suburb. Now in his late fifties, he first vended in Leicester Square and then Oxford Street. He recalls a fight over his pitch after another vendor had stolen it:

> *'I floored the other guy. I was arrested and spent a couple of hours in a cell. Then the policeman let me go, although he shouldn't have because technically it's an offence to fight in the street.'*

The vendors were given ten free papers as a starter but were responsible for buying the second round. There was an ongoing battle over this for the first six months. Vendors found it difficult to accept that they had to buy the papers, rather than be given them for nothing. They also had to look after their money so that they could buy more papers. The distribution team was accused of being exploiters of homeless people. The big challenge was that the homeless vendors needed educating out of the hand-out scenario, and into a self-help frame of mind. John believes that the flip side of post-war welfarism is that people, and not only homeless people, believe they have a right to donations, charity or welfare. This view was extended to the new street paper, and the battle continued until the principle of buying and selling was accepted.

Distributed by van in the West End, the paper was picked up by the vendors at certain stop-off points such as the Bullring, Charing Cross or Lincoln's Inn Fields. Notices were put up around the area. But the van did not always turn up on time and kept breaking down. A swarm of people would turn up only to hang around because the van was late. Frustration escalated into fights. Many would demand free papers and when they arrived, bundles would be stolen. 'It was terrible', remembers John Bird. 'It was almost like we were at war with homeless people.' The sooner a premises could be found, the better.

In an attempt to curb some of the more erratic behaviour that occurred on the pitches, especially drinking and fighting, the staff drew up a set of rules. Each vendor had to sign the Code of Conduct.[1] This stated that they could not drink or take drugs whilst selling and could not be abusive to the public. They had to be over 16 years of age, the UK's official school leaving age. They also had to agree not to be sexist or racist and were to sell without causing problems to the public, the police, or other vendors. The code provided a reference point from which staff could discuss with vendors the necessity of a good standard of conduct on the streets. John says he told a group of vendors:

> 'We don't want Mad Maxes selling the paper. Be polite. Be sober. We want to break down stigmas against the homeless. It doesn't look good if you're drinking or on drugs.'

Initially, the public was unsure about the purpose of *The Big Issue* despite a burst of media coverage on the paper. Apart from the *Evening Standard*, Londoners were only used to left-wing or religious papers being sold on the streets. Len remembers being approached by a man asking if *The Big Issue* was a communist paper. When he confirmed that it was not, Len was given a £20 tip. The public's reaction was reflected in an initial burst of sales, followed by a drop off at the end of September. Of the 50,000 printed, 30,000 were sold, and the first issue ran for seven weeks rather than for four. *Big Issue* staff felt so exhausted by the experience that a decision was made not to produce a paper in October. But, with the second issue published on 1 November, sales took off. The 50,000 print run ran out almost immediately and they had to order a reprint.

One hundred thousand copies of the third issue were printed at the beginning of December 1991 and immediately sold out. This quickly became the sales pattern. The public had responded in the most positive of ways. However, a monthly paper created problems for the vendors. They had good sales for the first two weeks of the month, and were left with a dribbling income for the last two as sales tapered off. As for how much the vendors were earning, this was difficult to say. It depended on a number of factors: how long each person stayed out selling; whether it rained or snowed; how good their selling techniques were; and whether it was a lucrative pitch. It is likely that monthly income was between £40 and £150, which meant they were selling anything up to 400 copies each.

The other earnings factor which raised its head immediately after the launch was that of signing on – or claiming benefit. The staff reminded vendors that, if they were signing on, they should inform their benefit office that they were selling *The Big Issue*. The rules were that no more than £5 could be earned daily over and above benefit without having it reduced.

This was a real dilemma for the vendors. They were trying to lift themselves out of dependency on the state, but could only do so if their income was sufficient. There was little financial incentive to being on benefit as people could barely live on the amount. It became apparent that there needed to be a discussion and a period of adjustment. This was also a first for the Department of Social Security (DSS). Negotiations began with local DSS offices in London and subsequently around the country as *The Big Issue* expanded. The matter blew up later in 1994 with a raid on *The Big Issue* offices by two investigators from the Employment Service's Fraud Unit (see more in Chapter 6), who were trying to obtain a list of vendors.

The day after *The Big Issue*'s launch in September 1991, Lucie Russell, now Chief Executive of *The Big Issue* Foundation, phoned the office in Richmond. She became a volunteer for three months. The way everything ran at the beginning was chaotic and stressed, Lucie remembers. The whole atmosphere was charged; it was exciting but also frightening because of the huge numbers of people the staff were responsible for. Weekly management meetings were held in the restaurant in Dickens & Jones in Richmond, but in reality there was little organizational structure and everything was unpredictable. Within a few weeks, the number of vendors had jumped to 150. There was a period when it looked perilously near to going under due to the large number of vendors and the small number of staff.

Lucie Russell believed in the importance of having some sort of support for the vendors, contradicting John's initial thoughts on only using the voluntary sector for support. A social worker by profession, she convinced John that when working with vulnerable people, simply expecting them to sell a paper and not offering them any support was not viable. Lucie began by providing a lot of personal support herself for those with drink, drug or other problems when they came to collect their papers, then referring them to outside agencies. This became a combination of both internal and external support with people subsequently employed to offer services such as housing and counselling when finance allowed.

THE VENDORS

Within six months the number of vendors had leapt to around 400 necessitating the expansion of the distribution team to deal with their day-to-day needs. The team began employing ex-vendors who, it was felt, would be able to relate directly to the issues that arose with the other vendors. But it was difficult having ex-homeless people working with the homeless, and the staff were about to learn a big lesson. To some extent, this reflected the opinion of a few people in the voluntary sector to whom John had spoken initially. Ex-homeless people could not necessarily take to a daily work environment.

The team's policy was to be very open in all their dealings with the vendors. John remembers that they were very green when it came to realizing the extent of 'the canniness of the dispossessed'. This manifested itself through the crossing of boundaries by some ex-vendors whose behaviour and survival tactics from the streets were brought into the working environment. Some found it difficult slotting into a 9 to 5 work day. In addition, in spite of being on the streets themselves, they did not necessarily know how to deal with vendors' problems. Many tried to rip off the company by stealing money, which happened at times in the first six months. The company's learning curve was sharp, based on the premise that homeless people were desocialized by the experience of being on the streets.

A further matter at this time was dealing with some vendors' anger and dislike of people who tried to help them. Vendors' anger was constantly vented on *Big Issue* staff. John remembers:

> 'On one occasion a guy came on our mobile phone, cursing and swearing, asking where the papers were. He said he was going to stab us if the papers didn't turn up.'

The staff confronted the anger and would not be physically intimidated. By employing people who would stand up to the abuse, some equilibrium was established.

An office was found in Marylebone at the West London Day Centre for a short period. Now vendors could come to the office and begin to see *The Big Issue* as a supporting organization. For a few months order seemed to be established. Then they were asked to leave because of trouble between vendors and the day centre's users.

A second distribution point was established in the Student Union of the London School of Economics (LSE), near Lincoln's Inn Fields. One of those sleeping in the Fields at the time was Ray Gray (66), who now works in *The Big Issue*'s administration department. Ray had been working as the post and telegraph officer in Brecon post office when his wife died in 1988 and he had a breakdown. Having kept up his mortgage payment for six months, it eventually became financially impossible. 'One Friday morning, the bailiffs were there and I was out on the street. The only thing they left me was my red Mini,' he says.

Ray drove up to London in March 1989 to look for work and a policeman at Euston station advised him to go to the St Pancras Hostel where he stayed for three nights. A resident told him about Lincoln's Inn Fields, so he went down to take a look. It seemed acceptable so he bought a one-man tent and settled in. Ray remembers that around 40 people, a few of whom were women, were sleeping there. Most were in their twenties and thirties, but one elderly man used to sleep on a bench. There was no trouble and the police left them alone. Ray obtained a part-time washing up job which brought him around £30 a week to survive.

> 'Nobody nicked my stuff, which was only blankets anyway. It was great because we used to look after each other. I went to Euston to get a bath and a shave, and I'd keep myself to myself, although I made a few friends.'

However, in 1991 a group came up from the Bullring and, Ray maintains, the Fields became more violent, eventually leading to a personal disaster. A man in the next tent to his had suggested to Ray that he sell *The Big Issue* which he had started to do early in 1992. This created jealousy between him and two of the new residents:

> 'There were two guys, one from Scotland and one Scouser, and they couldn't sell the paper because they were boozing all the time. I was doing alright because I was selling The Issue [as vendors call it] down at the Embankment. I used to give my money to the Father of the local church and he used to save it for me. I never carried a lot of money on me. I knew that if I took it back it would disappear.'

Ray kept away from the drinkers.

> 'But they found out I was making money, because they could tell by the number of papers I was buying. They used to say "you've done alright out of The Big Issue". And I used to say, "yea I've stuck at it and I don't drink".'

He arrived back one summer day to find the police, ambulance and fire brigade gathered around the burnt-out shell of his tent. He had a good idea who the perpetrators were. Another *Big Issue* seller had his tent ripped to shreds. Ray immediately moved out of the Fields and later camped out in a wood north of London until *The Big Issue*'s housing unit found him a flat in Brixton where he now lives.

The Big Issue continued to be distributed at the LSE until the Easter holidays of 1992 when problems emerged. A report in the university's magazine, *The Beaver*, stated that *The Big Issue* had unfortunately been asked to stop its activities at the LSE due to 'begging, inappropriate behaviour towards women by vendors and vendors walking around the building causing security problems'. By this time, however, a new distribution building in Victoria had been found.

VENDOR MEETINGS

What did the vendors think of *The Big Issue* and how it operated? Firstly, they came to sell it in their droves. Secondly, they came to tell the staff at monthly meetings about their progress, the response of the public and improvements that could be made in the organization.

The early meetings were chaotic and very loud. Only by shouting above the cacophony could John control the meetings, but they were full of a vitality and openness. The meetings were held in the crypt of St Martin-in-the-Fields with which *The Big Issue* had a good working relationship until, unfortunately, the vendors' meeting before Christmas 1991 when they arranged a Christmas party.

After the meeting, drink was brought in. This was a mistake, and *The Big Issue* paid for it. It took until the late hours of the night to clear the church of drunken vendors. The church wrote to John after Christmas and accused him of breaking their no-drinking code. John says:

> *'It never occurred to us that there was this code. I have to say at the time I was a bit belligerent at the letter, because most of the vendors greatly enjoyed the party. Most behaved impeccably, though a handful did go over the top.'*

Vendors tended to sound off at meetings about anything that was bothering them. This meant they would also sound off about *The Big Issue* saying that the magazine was making money out of homeless people. One meeting highlighted the volcanic nature of such events.

In early 1992, up to 600 vendors turned up to a meeting in Notre Dame Hall in central London's Leicester Square. They were again told that they could not pick up the new issue unless they came to the meeting. John remembers:

> 'We had this theatre full of screaming vendors. It was absolutely phenomenal. We were saying that there had to be less aggression, less drunkenness, more good social behaviour. It was a madhouse. I didn't have a microphone so I had to scream from the stage.'

Undercover police officers were present at the meeting, worried about the homeless people who might be unleashed in huge numbers onto the streets afterwards. More worrying, though, were the police wagons and police with riot gear outside the hall. John went out and recommended that they leave, insisting that there would be no trouble.

> 'I said to the police that the vendors would go nuts if they saw the police outside, because they would have felt betrayed that we would have led them into a trap.'

The police took the hint, quickly jumped into their wagons and went off. A crisis had been averted and there was no trouble. Vendor meetings then tapered off when the new distribution office was opened in March 1992 in Victoria and vendors could talk to staff about matters that were concerning them.

ADDRESSING PROBLEMS

John held regular monitoring meetings with the police which were very positive and the staff found them very supportive. John says:

> 'In a matter of months after the launch, I was talking to coppers on the beat who were saying that people who were incredibly badly behaved in public before were now beginning to behave themselves because they were being disciplined by the marketplace.'

Petty crime in the West End is said to have decreased as some homeless people now had the opportunity to earn a legitimate income. However, there were occasions when vendors would cause public disturbances. The police would phone *The Big Issue* office and a member of staff would rush down to one of the West End stations. A newspaper reported a judge suggesting to a man who was up before him on a charge of begging that it would be more useful for him to sell *The Big Issue*.

Nick Hardwick was impressed by what was a real sense of ownership by homeless people of the product. They did not, he believes, have a similar sense about any other organization:

> '*I don't think that homeless people felt at all that they owned Centrepoint. This was something that had been done for them. Whereas I think people did feel ownership of* The Big Issue *in a way that was very empowering for those individuals and that was brilliant.*'

Despite all the difficulties and the problems, talking to many of the vendors, this still appears to be the case.

Very quickly *The Big Issue* became famous in London, largely because of its unique method of distribution and because the public began conversing with homeless people. Vendors were coming back to the office telling the staff about the chats and exchanges of views they were having on the streets with their customers. Many made new friends and their confidence began to rise as they felt less isolated and alienated. Many members of the public began to see homeless people as people who were down on their luck, and not to be despised.

1992 – THE MOVE TO HAMMERSMITH AND VICTORIA

In March 1992, the Richmond office from which the paper had launched was at bursting point and the business needed more space. The editorial and production staff moved into an office block in Hammersmith, West London, which had just been vacated by Colourings, The Body Shop's cosmetic division. The Body Shop had the building on lease and *The Big Issue* was not charged rent.

The Empty Homes Agency (EHA) obtained a rambling old furniture warehouse in Victoria for the distribution and outreach work, given rate-free by Westminster Council. The property company who owned the building also gave it without rent. In spite of the dereliction, it was a godsend to the *The Big Issue's* development.

After the move to the Victoria office, a telephone line was installed for the public to phone in to report negative – or positive – incidents with vendors. This was anything from vendors not giving the right change (something pointed out as very important in the sales training) to drinking whilst selling. This was another way of monitoring people's response to *The Big Issue*. Despite the fact that most calls were to complain about vendors, it proved a useful way to disperse the wrath of the public and explain the nature of the paper.

Once the distribution team had moved in, Housing Minister Sir George Young paid a visit and was impressed. 'It was the element of self-help, the training that they gave to the vendors, and it was the ethos of the place,' Sir George remembers.[2] 'It was the concept of giving people independence by training them in skills of selling and moving them away from straightforward asking for charity.' Lucie Russell had approached the Department for a grant and he says:

'I liked the concept, I liked John Bird, who ran it (and who used to live in my constituency). So we tried to give it a push. It was a positive solution to homelessness.'

Sir George offered to fund a post from his Department for one of two housing workers. Many government ministers, MPs and opposition MPs also pledged their support to *The Big Issue* in various ways. Some regularly bought the paper, others promoted it in their interviews or wrote for the magazine. The self-help philosophy appealed right across the political spectrum.

Both the support services and the distribution methods of *The Big Issue* have been refined and diversified over the years. Some sort of in-house support was necessary even if only a small percentage took up the services if and when they felt they needed it. However, when the company began support services, it had to consider two things: how far it would go to duplicate the work of other agencies and how would the company finance the staff. This was an issue for the fledgling social business. If it had been a charity, grant applications would have been rushed off for the cost of support staff. But this was a business. Only when the money came in could staff be recruited, and this was very random at the beginning. The work was supplemented by a growing number of partnerships within the voluntary sector.

The housing workers' advice for the vendors then was very much crisis driven, referring homeless people to emergency, medium and permanent accommodation, unlike its present agenda of resettlement work. An average of 30 vendors were seen each week and since most of them were rough sleepers, it meant phoning round hostels to see if they could be placed for the night.

Working with rough sleepers made the team realize very quickly that homelessness is not just about housing. Getting someone somewhere to live is just the beginning of the problem. 'Homelessness is an identity problem,' explains Lucie Russell. And:

> 'You have to help them find a new identity which isn't just about a house. It's about new circles of friends, a new community, jobs, training. It's really trying to help somebody into a different stage of their lives.'

This is borne out by vendor Eric (36). He started selling in early 1992 when he was desperate for money to survive. Graduating from university with a business degree, he had had various jobs before his family situation disintegrated:

> 'My relationship had broken down, my father had died, I had to relocate with no finances. I was finished and didn't have anywhere else to turn. I ended up in homeless places, like hostels. I was mental.'

He came down to London from Luton. He says, 'I didn't have anyone, or anywhere to have a cup of tea. I didn't speak to anyone. I was mad. You don't ever forget it.' His feelings about The Big Issue's support service at the beginning are mixed however:

> 'I didn't get much emotional support from The Big Issue. It's only now I am picking myself up that people are being friendlier to me. When I really needed it, I didn't get it.'

But he concedes that the staff probably did not have the resources at that point and did not realize how ill he was. 'I'm not blaming them. I'm grateful to them being there and saying you can buy papers,' he says.

Eight years on, the ability to earn an income from *The Big Issue* has meant that his life has stabilized. He is in his own flat and the differences between now and then are immense.

'When I first started selling I was homeless and I looked it. I smelt it. I was really ill. I was really thin. Couldn't string a sentence together. Everyone said I was losing the plot, and I didn't even know it. Now I sell in Covent Garden. Most people say, I couldn't stand in the street and talk to people. But if you are homeless you've got no choice. I was very angry at first if people didn't buy it. I'm not a violent person at all, but I still feel like that sometimes.'

Eric recognizes the issues that staff at *The Big Issue* were continuously dealing with:

'Fundamentally when you are dealing with homelessness, you are dealing with people who have no sense of integration about themselves, to others or to anything. It is a very agitated sort of state and that is why people just dump themselves on whoever they meet.'

Ex-street people continued to be employed on the distribution and outreach teams. There were still the original problems of boundaries. John and Lucie had decided that this informal policy should be part of *The Big Issue*'s attempt to help ex-vendors move on. John had thought about this in his original study when he hoped homeless people would begin supporting each other. However, it turned out that there was a high turnover in this area.

Patrick Dennis remembers the work as very different from today. Patrick, now vendor training and relations manager, was doing vendor training. There was an obvious need to establish a set format for vendors to introduce them to the company and to train them how to sell. Patrick expanded the 'inductions', developing vendors' sales techniques and how they should present themselves.

He remembers the early days working with no rigid structures in place, with almost a family atmosphere. Since many of the team had been vendors, there was a comradeship between the staff and vendors because it was guys they had vended with.

However, at that point, remembers Patrick, the staff were not really conscious of the kind of problems that were brewing. Whilst creating a friendly and trusting atmosphere, it also created other difficulties. At that time 90 per cent of the vendors were rough sleepers and had drink problems. The staff weren't equipped to deal with this, which made the street work a lot harder, so they referred them to outside agencies.

Paul Felts, who became distribution manager in 1993, started at *The Big Issue* in September 1992 as a volunteer. Many of the staff whom Paul managed were also part-time vendors. Some went on to other things. At other times they returned to vending or just disappeared. This became a pattern. One ex-vendor who was the assistant distribution manager suddenly disappeared off to Brighton. 'He marched into *The Big Issue* office and said "I'm John Bird, give me some money",' remembers Paul. 'So the staff gave him the petty cash tin and never saw him again.'

The staff began to be more aware of how careful they must be not to put people in a position where they could fail. There is a difficulty with homeless people who get off the streets but who do not break from their street values. John says:

> *'One of the problems is that if you pick somebody off of the street and they say all the right things, and then you put them in a position of authority within the organization, all sorts of problems come up. Are they abusing their authority, can they handle working with or relating to people they have known or slept in doorways with?'*

This has been, and continues to be, a very big challenge for *The Big Issue* staff. Over the next few years, more professionally trained people were employed in the area that dealt directly with the homeless.

Employing people who were vendors is something *The Big Issue* has never got to grips with. Even today, the company still does not know whether it is an organization which offers sheltered employment or not. Many organizations have a rule that people they have worked with have to be out of touch with the organization for a year before applying for a job within it.

By mid 1993, up to 500 vendors were regularly working across the capital. By now, there were around eight people working both in distribution and outreach support. When *The Big Issue* started, all staff in the distribution and vendor support services worked directly with the vendors. Whilst distribution staff were technically in charge of selling the paper to the vendors and organizing pitches, in reality their jobs criss-crossed with the support workers.

The support workers provided the link between the vendors and the public. They were troubleshooters and dealt with vendors' problems, badging up and training new recruits. They provided an extensive welfare service and followed up complaints from members of the public. They networked homeless services whilst developing contacts with other organizations working in this area. Outreach workers were on call to deal with crisis situations on the streets and were especially concerned with the safety of women vendors.

In the Victoria office, vendors could just drop by, not having to make an appointment to see the housing team or one of the support staff. Vendor Jon Gregg says that in the early days it seemed more down to earth. He would go into the Victoria office and see the housing team mingling with the vendors: 'Lucie and John would pop in. I'd be rubbing shoulders with everyone. I could ask if I could pop in for a quick chat with the housing team.'

Jon ended up on the street after suffering redundancy and was unable to pay his rent; he came to London from Hayes.

> 'I was down in Green Park two weeks before Christmas in December 1992 and I met a guy outside the tube station selling The Big Issue. I remember that the main thing I kept asking was "what's the catch?" I wondered was it like a religious organization, and would they want you to go to church on Sunday? I thought he was trying to enrol other people and he got commission or something. It's just the way the mind works when you've lost everything.'

Sleeping on the streets, he had nothing except the clothes he was wearing.

> 'I was in dire straits. So it came at the right time. I went to the Victoria office, got badged up just before Christmas, went out with my friend in Green Park and Knightsbridge. So for 1993 I was just selling, not very much, but taking it steady trying to get back on my feet mentally and physically. I was still on the streets on and off. If I had some money, I could get a cheap room

somewhere. Then for my new year's resolution for 1994, I thought I am going to do something about this and went to see the housing team. They got me some temporary housing.'

Jon's experience shows how *The Big Issue*'s presence was a personal lifeline:

'One of the most positive things about The Big Issue *is that the first thing you want is money in your pocket. And that can be instant, by the end of the day you have some money. That makes you feel a lot better to start with. There are agencies which are more structured but you can't get anything straight away. And you might be fobbed off. At the end of each day I just kept feeling better and better. And I knew there was other help available.'*

Women

Women have always made up around between 10 and 15 per cent of the vendors. They are a more transitory group with different needs and experiences from the male vendors. Homeless womens' difficulties have much to do with violence, either inside the home or in hostels. Consequently, women who have experienced domestic violence sometimes feel insecure about selling *The Big Issue*; this is compounded by the fact that women are often propositioned or attacked on the streets. Domestic violence is the biggest cause of homelessness amongst women in the UK, causing 55,000 women to run away each year.[3]

As a woman vendor D used to get violent responses from men, come-ons and guys asking her back home for sex. She believes it is very important to develop confidence out on the street and once she did, the propositions declined. Staff are continuously trying to find out how selling can be made safer for women, as well as countering the very male image of homelessness that may be intimidating to homeless women. There are still a large number of women who are homeless but have children, which is not conducive to selling a magazine on the street.[4]

Female staff at *The Big Issue* have on occasions held drop-ins where women can come for an afternoon to relax and discuss issues. Mel Hooper, who worked in sales support, started a second women's group in mid 1997 after the first one had ceased.

At first only a few women attended; she says, 'They are not the type to hang around in this building, they're in and out people. It's a very male atmosphere.'

Activities were arranged, such as talks about natural remedies and how to ward off colds, or arranging massages. But because the women's circumstances are continually changing, many just disappeared. Mel found it very difficult to keep the enthusiasm of the group going. Now, however, many of the women vendors are regulars in the writing group and use the facilities of JET (Jobs, Education and Training) (see Chapter 6).

THE PAPER – EDITORIAL AND BUSINESS DEVELOPMENT

John Bird was in overall charge of the paper but Phil Ryan ran it on a day-to-day basis. The paper was immediately visible on the streets because of its stunningly colourful, eye-catching covers. It was put together by a host of freelancers and volunteer writers found through contacts or word of mouth. Both experienced and wannabe writers sought out the new *Big Issue*. In 1992, three young journalists, Ollie Tait, Fiona Macdonald Smith and Lucy Johnston formed the core editorial team.

Interviews were obtained with celebrity writers, comedians like Eddie Izzard and Arthur Smith, writers Douglas Adams and Ken Follett and bands such as Pulp and the Asian Dub Foundation. *The Big Issue* had had such an immediate impact on the media and the public that famous people wanted to be in it. There was never a shortage of celebrities agreeing to appear on its pages.

The Pulse reviewed London's cultural scene, in particular the more inexpensive and alternative end of the market. There were reports on initiatives for homeless people, a jobs page, Missing Persons, and articles covering subjects such as the election of 1992, international issues such as the 'restaurants du coeur' (places where homeless people in France could eat for free) or the sad state of the Docklands Light Railway. It was all rather haphazard and unplanned, but the basic premise was that the general interest stories should be as unusual as possible, funny and interspersed with articles on social issues and homelessness.

The tabloid-sized paper was deliberately not printed on glossy paper. The first issues have a kind of roughness, a streetiness about them, a sense of being a combination of a student and an enthusiast's publication. 'Coming up from the street' was the first strapline followed in the third edition by 'Helping the homeless to help themselves'.

It was important that homeless people should use the paper as a voice, either to report on issues of direct relevance to them, or to use the pages for creative writing. *The Big Issue* is the only mainstream media outlet for homeless people. From the first issue, the Capital Lights page provided this opportunity and has been one of the most consistently popular sections of the paper with readers. The writing group, which provides much of the material for this section, was started then (for more detail, see Chapter 6).

The writing group met once a week and was run by Lucie Russell and a literacy tutor. There were workshops on creative writing and guest speakers were invited to address the group. Initially, getting copy in on time from homeless people was difficult as they tended to be unreliable. However, as the group became more established a team of writers regularly published poems and stories on the squats and hostels they were living in.

Jo Mallabar, editor from 1994 until January 1997, started as a volunteer at *The Big Issue* in April 1992. She had been books editor on the recently defunct *20/20* magazine. She liked the paper and thought it was funny. 'There were so many fundamental errors in the way they were doing the journalism, I thought I could improve it,' she remarks. But when she first arrived at the office she had to sit in John's office, 'because he thought I might be a plant from one of the tabloids trying to get some dirt on him!'

Jo's first task was to launch a books page, with a view to looking at the whole magazine. Phil Ryan left in the summer of 1992 and Jo became deputy editor, in charge of the day-to-day running of the paper. Her first major task was to prepare taking *The Big Issue* to appear fortnightly. At that time there was a core production and editorial team of six, assisted by freelancers. Emphasis was put on setting up a much more structured environment than had previously existed.

The press agency Reuters strongly supported *The Big Issue* from its launch. Through its Foundation it agreed to train journalists on weekly courses, free of charge. It also paid for *The Big Issue* to receive a set of daily newspapers as the company had no cuttings service.

National Missing Persons Helpline

The Big Issue and the National Missing Persons Helpline (NMPH) have been inextricably linked since their inceptions (see page 31). When *The Big Issue* moved out of its basement office in Richmond, the NMPH moved in and launched itself on 1 July 1992. Having started with missing children, the organization developed into the only charity that looks for and helps both children and adults. As co-founder Janet Newman says:

> *'If an elder person goes missing who has Alzheimers, or people who are mentally ill go missing, or people with stress, we take that just as seriously. If something happens to the family unit in any shape or form it affects the children.'*

Of the estimated 250,000 children and adults who currently go missing every year (although nobody really knows the real number) a small proportion end up on the streets. The NMPH answers an estimated 100,000 calls a year, 'many from families whose loved ones suddenly vanish without any explanation'. Staff also provide a discreet message service for people who prefer to remain out of touch. Missing people are reported to the Helpline in two different ways: by families who want to find a missing person or by police who may get referrals from hospitals or hostels.

From the first issue of *The Big Issue* four missing people have been featured in each edition. Janet explains:

> *'We have had lots of cases where people have seen themselves in* The Big Issue, *whether they are selling or whether they have bought it. It's a brilliant way. They are often so pleased that someone is looking for them.'*

The staff write the text, incorporating a message from the family, in a 'gentle and subtle' manner. Janet and Mary Asprey used to receive phone calls from vendors who had noticed missing people in the magazine. This happened a lot in the early days and it was the best way to find missing people when it first started.

Mary emphasizes that *The Big Issue* has been useful because it is a low key way of publicizing people:

'It's effective for getting the right message across. It's important that people don't feel in any way intruded upon, but at the same time knowing they have a choice to get back in touch with their family.'

The volume of calls from *The Big Issue* hasn't increased over the years, but the quality of calls is very good. People call the NMPH who don't want to speak to the police and it is very rare that people complain about being in *The Big Issue*. Janet recalls one man who was angry, but once she had told him why he was in the magazine he burst into tears and couldn't believe his luck.

RUNNING A SOCIAL BUSINESS

The contradictions involved in running a social business raised itself constantly. *The Big Issue* was one of the first social businesses in the UK and had no blueprint to follow. It had to do two things: firstly, become an economically viable company, make a profit and continue its expansion; secondly, stay true to its social objective of helping homeless people to help themselves. *The Big Issue* therefore has a dual bottom line to which it continuously aspires. It needs to make a profit if it is going to continue to help homeless people, but cannot let the profit motive impinge too heavily on its social mission.

Where *The Big Issue* differs from traditional business is that it starts from a social need, not a mainstream consumer need. Traditional business is solely monitored on its profitability and shareholder's return. It must increase bottom line profit to increase its financial value.

One definition of social business is:

'Operating at the intersection between the voluntary, government and business sectors, social businesses are well placed to activate change. They operate by building a business solution around a social and/or environmental problem or need. Like traditional business, they bring a product to the marketplace in order to meet consumer demand, whilst also competing for market presence. There is a profit motive, but it is driven by the social and environmental objectives. It is their raison d'etre that differentiates them from the traditional and socially responsible business sectors.'[5]

The Big Issue's capital was not raised by issuing shares. Initial start-up capital came from a socially responsible business. Crucially, unlike a traditional investor, The Body Shop didn't expect a return on its investment. It was an example of venture philanthropy. A bank would not have considered the idea of a business dependent on a homeless work force. Bank loans would only come later when the business began proving itself. And in a more traditional business, any surplus would have been used as assets for business development or paid to shareholders.

How does *The Big Issue* view money? Differently from banks, certainly. 'We create money in order to oil the wheels of social change,' comments Maria Clancy, who formerly worked in *The Big Issue* international department (see Chapter 7). And she says:

> *'It is not so we can be piling it up in the bank and getting more interest on it. It's what you can do with it that has a meaning. And yet, if the money is not piled up in the bank, we run into problems.'*

She describes the circular mechanism of *The Big Issue*:

> *'We create a product which can be a mechanism which embodies social change by sheer virtue of what it does. We don't just create a product to satiate consumer demand. Yes, we have had to create consumer demand, but we started differently. We could say, in pure business terms, that* The Big Issue *had a consumer demand amongst people who weren't even consumers, essentially homeless people. There was a latent demand, which* The Big Issue *brought out, for a product that they could bring to the marketplace.*
>
> *'We have two levels of consumers. The first is homeless people and the second is the public. If the socially excluded group aren't buying the product, then we're not going anywhere. We created a consumer demand amongst the homeless and then they demanded it by coming in their droves. Then we have to go on to the marketplace and create consumer demand.*
>
> *'When we started we were selling social change; homelessness. We were selling the opportunity to engage in social change. That we will continue to do as the product becomes more refined. Selling the opportunity to become engaged in social*

change has become a secondary issue as the product has become stronger.'

The fact is, though, that social businesses, and this applies to *The Big Issue*, tend to be under-resourced.

As an accountant from a traditional business background, former *Big Issue* finance director Jonathan King discusses the difficulties of running a social business:

'It's the difficult job in any anarchic, creative enterprise to be the person who is trying to be what John calls the Jeremiah of the organization. The one who's trying to put on the brakes, not very successfully sometimes, but sometimes successfully.

'Sometimes we agree not to spend money and sometimes the social imperative might override what makes the financial imperative. We then decide that we might have to spend some money in one area and wait to see whether we can get that money back, or get a return later on.

The financial projections John had originally given Gordon proved to be way out. John thought the preparation and initial launch budget – which included salaries for four people, commissioning editorial and printing – would be around £30,000. He would then try to move quickly into a situation where the business was financially viable, and that might take another £30,000. What surprised him was that the response of both homeless people and the public was so enormous that it threw all the figures out.

The Body Shop invested £500,000 in the first three years. Half of this was spent in the first year to get the magazine up and running. It also financed the growing support services. Initially, these hadn't been allowed for, but were soon considered an essential part of *The Big Issue*'s development. Ironically, the main problem was that the appetite for the paper by homeless people and the public grew bigger and bigger. John recalls:

'What we thought was going to be a very small organization working with 50 or 100 vendors turned out to be working with ten times that within the first year. We had also estimated that the print runs would not be so big.'

By May 1992, the paper was selling 150,000 copies a month and had increased from 28 to 32 pages.

The cost to the vendors was set at 10p a copy. This was both a social and a commercial decision. Firstly, this was the price it was felt the vendors would accept. Secondly, it whetted the appetite of the sales force. However, it was a bad business decision because the company underpriced the magazine. It was actually costing the company 25p to produce each copy. The more papers that were printed, the more money the company lost. Consequently, the more successful the company became, the more it moved into debt. By June 1992 the company was losing £25,000 a month because it lost 15p for every copy that was sold to a vendor. This was a major crisis. The importance of having The Body Shop as a financial backer until the company could sustain itself cannot be underestimated. If it had not been for the financial underpinning of The Body Shop, the company would have gone under.

To resolve the financial crisis, John decided to go fortnightly in September 1992, meaning they had two publications a month. He reduced the cost of the paper by using cheaper newsprint. (The recycled paper, an initial attempt to commit to an environmentally friendly policy, had to be abandoned after a few months as the increased print runs made the paper costs too expensive.) He doubled the price to the vendors to 20p, whilst maintaining the price to the public of 50p. He also changed printers, to Wiltshire Ltd, near Bristol, which printed the magazine for the next eight years. Within two months, these policies bore fruit and the company moved into a healthier financial position.

In order to make it more attractive and saleable it moved from being an A3 paper to an A4 magazine. Vendors preferred the smaller size. 'You couldn't carry a hundred of those papers, but you can of the A4 ones,' remembers vendor Len. The increase of the price to the vendors was offset by the logic that with a monthly publication, the vendors had two very good weeks, followed by two poor ones. With a fortnightly publication, virtually the whole of the selling period would be profitable. In other words, vendors sold more for a longer period of time.

Another solution to the company's financial difficulties was to cut staff numbers. When the paper went fortnightly, the company just about managed on the editorial and production staff it had. By August 1992, there were around 30 staff in the

Hammersmith building working in production, editorial, accounts and advertising. Some had already planned to leave as the wages were poor, many were part-timers. Ten went.

Just as the staff were preparing to celebrate *The Big Issue*'s first birthday in September 1992, one of the ex-homeless staff stole £12,000. Money from sales to the vendors was put into a safe in the Victoria office, but only taken to the bank every few days. 'We had this low, but we learnt a lot from it because you don't put temptation in the way of the disenfranchised,' John points out. A security firm was then hired to take the money on a daily basis to the bank. Gordon Roddick was exasperated because he viewed the incident as a lack of care in straightforward procedures. John then offered his new printers a two year contract if they would replace the stolen money. 'They did, and Gordon was happy. But he insisted on the most stringent security,' John says.

Gordon's business expertise and mentoring were crucial to the success of the paper during the first years. John, he maintains, was appalling at financial management at the beginning. He learnt it very quickly because he recognized that it was his survival. Gordon comments:

> 'There were several crossroads in the spending and funding where I said 'sorry, there's no more if you don't get to this bit and keep it under control. So you better do it or else because neither I nor the company will fund you any more. As long as we can see you growing and nothing is being spent that is out of order, that's fine.' I'm too savvy to see if he was sitting there lining his own pocket and the paper going nowhere. The atmosphere was never like that.'

There was a long sense of business experimentation in the formation of *The Big Issue*. During the first couple of years Gordon and John met frequently. Gordon had to decide whether this was a project worth supporting that would grow at a rate that would seem sensible:

> 'We put in £500,000 over three years. If you looked at it as a business even with all the mistakes and errors, we probably wasted £100,000, I would guess. It's not that bad if you are looking at supporting a business that is growing into what it grew into.'

The changes worked. Staff numbers were controlled, the paper was consolidated and *The Big Issue* became stable. 'Gordon had put a gun to my head. He said "get the thing right or that's it". I did, because he gave me no choice,' adds John.

WORKING WITH A FOUNDER

What is it like working with a founder? John Bird fits neatly into the characteristics of 'the founder's syndrome'. These are normally those ambitiously unconventional people who set up businesses and organizations, sometimes against all odds, whether personal or commercial. When business management expert Charles Handy[6] depicted the characteristics of such founders (whom he called 'The New Alchemists'), he could have been talking about John.

Some of Handy's points are that, in terms of character and history, founders are experimental people. Some come from dysfunctional families, many did badly at school but were continuously trying different things early in life. They work very hard, they get their best ideas in the bath, when they are drunk, or in the field. And they don't turn up on time.[7]

Founders have a dedication, commitment and obsession towards their work. Creating new businesses is their love, although money itself is rarely the driving passion. Most have a low tolerance of boredom, and find it less exciting running businesses than starting them. They have what the poet Keats called 'negative capability': the capacity to keep going when things are going wrong, or when they are in the midst of doubts and uncertainties. Their creativity is not guaranteed to work at all times, but they persevere nonetheless.

In terms of working practices, none would fit easily into the ranks of a large organization. In their own business, they need to be in control, even if much of the day-to-day responsibility is delegated. Power and control are essential, at least in the early stages, but they do not appear to reach further than their own creations. This means that they are not often hankering after political power or building huge corporations.

These tendencies have created testing times for both John himself and the staff at *The Big Issue* and have caused clashes. Some staff have been unable to work in the chaotically charged organization run by a social entrepreneur who has the vision:

someone who is himself chaotic, constantly runs late, doesn't turn up for meetings and at times isn't there when people need him. This is not exclusive to running a social business, however. It is, for the founder, difficult to let go, to delegate and allow other people to take the organization in another direction.

Anita Roddick has talked about her role in the company she founded, now that The Body Shop has grown so huge:

> 'I have had to constantly reinvent the role of the founder-entrepreneur. That's tough when your natural tendency is towards a gleeful anarchy. There are no road maps, no instruction manuals. Passion is your guide. Instinct tells you where to go when a challenge arises.'[8]

Sue Hollowell, formerly director of personnel for *The Big Issue* (see Chapter 8), was one of the people who helped implement the structure of the company. She talked about the challenge of working with a founder as she almost forcibly pushed through structural developments within the company. Sue had been seconded from The Body Shop in June 1992 to manage the office. She had to set up internal structures, sort out contracts of employment for the staff, as well as looking after John as his PA. She was supposed to stay only six months, but did not leave until March 2000.

Sue found John very motivational as he kept everyone's spirits high but he was chaotic. A team of three, herself, Lucie Russell and Jo Mallabar, along with John, initially formed the directorial team. They met regularly to discuss the direction of the company. But part of the difficulty was that they had little of this kind of experience. She says:

> 'He used to call us the Three Witches. He said we used to "piss on his fireworks". We three women tried to harness him, which was quite a challenge – and a laugh. He had all these ideas, and we would say to him "OK, who is going to do them? How are we going to do them? What are the timescales? How much is it going to cost and can we afford to do it?" And that's why we "pissed on his fireworks" because when it came down to it we might not have been able financially to achieve what he wanted.'

The growth of the company affected John, and he was more interested in the dynamics and the ideas as opposed to the mechanics. Sue remembers:

> 'He had fantastic ideas. He was full of them. Very rarely was he on a low and if he was it was because of frustration because he wasn't as hands-on as he could be. He couldn't go out and talk to vendors as much as he wanted to, because now he had to be out there raising our profile and raising the money to keep us going.'

He had to be prepared to adapt to the changing needs of the company, and how Sue and the other directors steered the company at this time. John also had to begin sharing responsibility otherwise he would have burnt himself out.

Many organizations, such as *The Big Issue*, can be described as an extension of the personality of the founder. They want to work with people they like, so they staff the organization with complementary extensions of themselves. Charles Handy believes this is both natural and probably right as a management strategy. It makes the place feel like a family and is a recognized feature of successful small family businesses. This is the kind of 'corporate culture' that *Big Issue* staff have remarked upon. Many of the original staff of *The Big Issue* were recruited through personal contacts, people who could fit into the newly created chaotic environment. John also employed members of his family at various stages: myself, his son Paddy, daughter Diana and brother Peter.

Gordon Roddick's view on the complexity of having a visionary at the top of an organization that is growing so fast is that it creates difficulties, but is the only way to go:

> 'John is mercurial. If he were not that, The Big Issue *wouldn't be here. Those were the qualities that got the thing to happen. It was his drive, his unpredictable behaviour and temperament that got him the entrée into everywhere that he needed to get the thing to happen.'

This same behaviour, however, is what people see as being inappropriate. 'What they have to realize is that John will never change or modify his behaviour. So what they have to do is to change their attitude towards him.'

It is a classic entrepreneurial problem, believes Gordon. How the initial behaviour that got the business and everybody their jobs is then viewed as inappropriate. Staff have confronted Gordon saying '"John is fucking impossible. We can't deal with him. He's driving me mad. What are we going to do?" And I would ask "who do you want me to sack. John or you?".'

Anita Roddick has talked in an interview[9] about the difficulties of operating as a creative entrepreneur within a business that has to become more efficient and structured as it grows.

> 'What I'm missing is almost painful to me; I'm missing the intimacy we used to have in the early days like I'm missing my child. I believe Ben Cohen [co-founder of US ice-cream company Ben & Jerry's] feels like this also – because what we've got now is nothing that we invented. It's big! And entrepreneurs don't want bigness. We want to polish, control, and shape something constantly. And when we've shaped it, developed it and passed it on, it's great, yet we often lose our place in it.'

Lyndall Stein, *The Big Issue*'s first head of fundraising (see Chapters 6 and 8), describes John as a 'classic founder'. She believes that it is not possible to separate *The Big Issue* and its success from John.

> 'When I first was there I didn't fully understand how important his role was and how important his qualities were, partly because of my own irritation with some of the other sides of those qualities – which you might call faults. Founders are often charismatic, intelligent, unreasonable, pig-headed, single-minded, have a vision they often don't share, all of which is true of John.'

But Lyndall also spots a disingenuous streak. The other important part of the picture, she asserts, is about John's life that he hides:

> 'John is one of the only people on the planet that celebrates his wicked past – boy going to approved school – and hides his respectable life, with however many years it was he was quietly getting on being an art publisher. He doesn't ever talk about the

*fact that he was an art publisher. I thought he had emerged from
borstal boy straight into* The Big Issue!

*'John is very passionate about art, ideas, writing, knows
about publishing. Most people don't know this about John. He
was a self-educated man, but very educated and knew all these
professional skills. That combination – yes, he had that rough,
tough, identification with people on the street which he could
either switch on or off, and did shamelessly – but the other part
of John is this highly cultured and refined man.'*

Lyndall also points out that without the team of people who
worked 18 hours a day building *The Big Issue* alongside John, none
of this would have happened.

*'It goes back to team qualities, in how people's personalities are
so important in forming a creative work. How certain skills at
certain times are relevant and necessary, and how you have to
move outside for the organization to develop.'*

No founder can carry everything, and many suffer from more
than an average dose of hubris. As Handy suggests:

*'No one person can be the fount of all the creativity needed by a
growing entreprise. One feature of growing firms is that the
founder often turns out not to be the best person to build the
business once it has got going.'*

At this point, the style of management that is needed has to
become more formal and regulated, 'less an extension of the
personality of the originator, more formally professional'. This
transition is difficult. 'Yet if it isn't done, the organization will
wither and die when the founder leaves or loses interest.' Can a
powerful personality hear discordant voices? asks Handy.[10]

Ruth Turner, founder of *The Big Issue in the North*, extends the
argument to leading a social business. She believes that a social
business depends on the integrity of the person who runs it. She
points out:

*'Are we trying to take the moral high ground? Where is the
dividing line between a plumber who takes on people locally*

from his community to find some decent employment, and doesn't charge his customers too much. There are not many differences.'

The definition depends on not exploiting either the employee or the consumer. 'And what's to stop John not taking any dividend but putting his salary up quite a lot? Nothing,' she adds.

The company was growing very fast but it didn't have the money to employ the staff that were needed. Sue Hollowell remembers:

> *'You had some very, very committed people at the beginning because they were prepared to work for a ridiculous amount of money to help take it forward. We used to work till midnight. We lived in that Hammersmith office. Everyone was really focused on what we were doing. There was no hierarchy. You were just mucking in, doing anything to make it work.'*

But that couldn't last very long, for efficiency's sake. Sue set up the office and management team with representatives from across the company. Sue asked a friend, Colette Youell, who was training to be a PA, to work for her, and she would train her to work for John. Colette came to work for six months. She stayed on and was John's PA for five years.

The Response of the Media and Business

From the beginning *The Big Issue* rode on a high wave of media support. The press were both surprised and fascinated by the new initiative. It did, however, take years for the media to understand the exact nature of the paper, sometimes referring to it as a homeless people's paper, a charity paper or a paper written and edited by homeless people.

John Bird immediately became a celebrity, and was invited onto major radio and TV shows, such as the Jimmy Young programme, and in a TV version of Anthony Clare's *In the Psychiatrist's Chair*. The mention of *The Big Issue* became commonplace on radio, TV and in the printed media.

The Guardian ran a long feature in its weekend supplement on vendor Robert and (his dog) Lady Muck.[11] It was a type of article which became the norm as journalists began publishing life stories of people selling *The Big Issue*.[12] As the first year wore on, the press continuously discussed the publishing phenomenon of *The Big Issue* and the spectacular rise in circulation over the first nine months. A piece of bad press, though, appeared in *Management Week*[13] which reported the 'disarray' existing in the organization of the company and how John was 'incompetent'. It left the staff feeling disenchanted. There was certainly more than a grain of truth in the allegation of disorganization, and management issues were not at the top of the agenda. But the article appeared to be an unnecessarily vicious description of a company which was only entering its third month. A year later, the same magazine, without any prompting, wrote an article praising John, and apologizing.

The first major documentary on *The Big Issue* was broadcast only seven months after its launch on 13 March 1992. Channel 4 commissioned the half hour programme. The film was a sympathetic and realistic portrayal of the issues involved in setting up the street paper. Between December 1991 and January 1992, director Viv Taylor Gee and crew filmed vendors being badged up and selling. They showed the production and planning of the paper and interviewed many homeless people about what selling the paper meant for them, one of whom was Ray Gray.

There was also enormous interest from the business world and PR companies following the launch. Many approached *The Big Issue* because they were intrigued and wanted to be associated with the new company. Companies donated money and full page advertisements. As already mentioned, PR company, Still Price: Lintas had helped with the launch and had made a short TV ad. Robert Triefus of Timms Triefus Maddick helped on the promotional side. Posters advertising *The Big Issue* went up in tube stations and on billboards, paid for by PR and advertising companies and fundraising gigs starting taking place in clubs and student unions. The payback was that their connections with *The Big Issue* reflected well on themselves.

John Jackson, then managing director of The Body Shop, brought in many of its UK suppliers to contribute to *The Big Issue* on a grant basis. By doing this he not only made a positive contribution to the beginnings of *The Big Issue*, but laid the foundation for a relationship between business and organizations helping marginalized people. Gordon Roddick remembers that they did this willingly, proving the vast amount of social impetus within companies can be tapped into.

The Big Issue began to take root in the public consciousness. It was taken seriously by the media, had a businesslike approach and thus attracted the support of the corporate sector. It was even being praised and supported by members of the Conservative government during its first year.

Over the first year many of the vendors got off the streets into employment, although it is not known how many. Many stayed with *The Big Issue* until they were ready to leave, others sold for short periods of time and left without saying anything. Some are still selling. But the ultimate success was that homeless people were not prepared to put up with their circumstances. They were motivating themselves to do something about their lives. By the time the paper went fortnightly in September 1992, an estimated £1m had been earned by homeless people through selling *The Big Issue*.

CHAPTER **4**

GOING WEEKLY

BY MID 1993 the Audited Bureau of Circulation (ABC) figures were up to 143,000 per fortnight.[1] The next important business step was to go weekly nine months after launching the fortnightly edition. This decision was driven both by the needs of the vendors to increase their sales as well as to increase *The Big Issue*'s revenue. Not only would vendors be assured of earning a regular daily income over a shorter time span, but the increase in revenue via advertising and sales would provide more surplus for expansion.

The Big Issue went weekly in June 1993 with a redesign by *The Guardian*'s David Hillman incorporating bigger graphics and adding a listings section. To celebrate, a party, sponsored by Carlton TV, was held in the House of Commons.

The impact of going weekly on the company was immense. The weekly schedule was incessant, as the then deputy editor Jo Mallabar remembers. In order to keep up, the editorial and production departments had to invest in more staff, put them on more competitive salaries and almost doubled the departmental budget. They worked very long hours and the initial wave of enthusiasm upon which the editorial staff were riding soon broke under pressure of work. Staff became exhausted.

What happened in the editorial department was typical of what was going on in the company as a whole. This was the period, 1993–95, when the company was going from its meteoric rise into its consolidation period. Staff numbers were increasing and new departments, such as personnel and administration, were set up and had to be managed. The directors had to spend more and more time on organizing the structure of the company.

By April 1993, there were 40 full- and part-time staff of whom around ten had been homeless. Within two years staff numbers had doubled.

Many of the people who had joined *The Big Issue* in its initial stages were enthusiastic and willing, but not necessarily skilled and many learnt on the job. When the paper went weekly, more skilled journalists were needed because there was less time to train people. Journalists also started joining because the magazine was considered a good career move. But this brought its own contradictions. Jo remembers:

> 'What we had built to date was exciting enough, because the change was so rapid. Young journalists now saw their Big Issue jobs as the first step on the rung to a national. They had an interest in homelessness but it was career-edged.'

An Innovative and Subversive Journalism

The aspiration has always been to produce a magazine that people would not buy simply out of pity for the vendor. The journalism had to reflect this need. The aim was to build up a core readership, but the general rule is that the more specialized a publication, the smaller the readership. Consequently, if *The Big Issue*'s editorial had concentrated solely on homelessness and social policy, the readership would have been small. Hence the deliberate policy to concentrate on producing wide-ranging popular editorial, increasing the numbers of buyers substantially.

The Big Issue was described by *The Guardian* as 'the only refuge of honest, angry, investigative journalism'. It has also been labelled an anarchic, streety, current affairs youth publication. In fact, it has always sat in a niche of its own. It combines the essence of British radical magazines, which have a long tradition of campaigning on behalf of the dispossed, with the 1990s life-style magazines. This combination of radicalism and 'street-chic' within *The Big Issue* was unique at the beginning of the 1990s, and was what appealed so profoundly to the readers.

The radical press in Britain is littered with commercial casualties. Whilst retaining a campaigning stance, *The Big Issue* has managed to go beyond a small niche market into a mass market. Young people in particular concerned with a different type of social change in the 1990s, responded to the *Big Issue*. They also wanted to go clubbing, read about celebrities, films and books and generally have a good time.

John Lloyd, associate editor of the 90 year old left-wing magazine, *The New Statesman*, noted the similarities and differences between left-wing magazines and street papers.[2] The similarity between a street paper and a magazine like *The New Statesman* is that:

> *'you speak more directly to a constituency which is pushing for change in conditions of living and politics...* The Big Issue *explicitly does what it was designed to do, make a difference actively. To sell it, make money, and put pressure on society and politicians through things that it writes about.'*

He stresses the importance of the right editorial mix:

> *'You have to use some of the techniques of the mass press. You have to find out what your readers want. Provide a balance between giving the readers what they want and producing a magazine which is what you wish it to be. I have been on some papers which tried to tell people what they should want, but failed. This is suicide.'*

One of *The Big Issue*'s greatest advantages is that it is independently owned and therefore free to experiment. John Bird is owner and editor-in chief, and although he has the final say and exercises it as and when he believes necessary, the journalists generally have a free hand. Politically, it is radical but non-party political.

Jo Mallabar believes that the journalism was daring from the very beginning. That it was sold on the streets by homeless people affected how it was put together. This was the novelty factor. It was new, and the readers felt it was informing them about something quite crucial that was happening in London. It was also the only voice for homeless people in the media.

To capitalize upon this, the journalists had to find stories that no one else could. At that time, no other magazine had such an extraordinary and bizarre combination of editorial. *The Big Issue* investigated and covered stories involving all social and cultural groups. There was social debate, coverage of environmental issues and the emerging eco-campaigns around the country. The magazine promoted a certain type of lifestyle. And there were investigations which uncovered tragic, humorous and serious stories. There were reviews on art, dance, clubs, celebrities, bands, books, CDs, videos, fashion and film.

The gathering of editorial in the first few years was random and somewhat haphazard. The journalists never followed a mainstream agenda. 'In the early days we never bothered, which was quite reckless,' claims Jo:

> 'If something wasn't of interest to The Big Issue, then we said sod it. If it was, and it came into our own agenda, then we'd go into depth on it, do what we want.'

In July 1994, former deputy editor Andrew Davies postponed a plan to live in Russia when he was offered a job at *The Big Issue* as chief sub-editor. He had followed the development of *The Big Issue* from its inception. Was *The Big Issue* as groundbreaking and innovative as it believed? He believes:

> 'We were definitely in the forefront of the eco-protest, the tunnelling and tree tops protests. Then the mainstream picked up on it. It was something new and exciting, young people doing weird stuff, good photos, good copy. I think we were significant but I wouldn't like to claim a big credit for it.'[3]

Whilst following the political activism of the 1990s, it was in the area of homelessness that the news could be developed. The journalists talked to homeless people and involved them in finding out what was happening on the streets. *The Big Issue* can take the credit for being the initiator of the streetwise form of reporting which has subsequently become mainstream journalism.

Lucy Johnston was headhunted by *The Observer* in 1996 because of her ability to uncover contacts at a level where no other journalists had access. This became a trend. Many of *The Big Issue*'s young journalists have subsequently been poached by lifestyle magazines and the nationals, *The Guardian* being a particular favourite. This is to *The Big Issue*'s credit to have established itself as a feeder to larger publications. It became a kind of academy for new journalists.

The Guardian reported that some of the country's best journalists, like Germaine Greer and Zoe Heller, were writing in *The Big Issue*. Celebrities and famous people were buying the magazine.

In 1994, American actor Jack Nicholson was snapped by *The Mirror* newspaper buying a copy from a vendor whilst on a shopping trip to London.

Jo remembers discussions with broadsheet journalists who said what they liked about *The Big Issue* was that it was totally different, refreshing and unexpected:

> *'Open the magazine and you could find an eclectic and bizarre range of things that surprised you. When people thought they knew what they were going to find in any other magazine, they didn't in* The Big Issue.*'*

This approach could last whilst *The Big Issue* was still seen by the public as whacky and new, and whilst the homeless issue was very important to them. But this was to change from around 1995.

Winning awards is one of the most effective ways of raising the profile of a magazine. In 1993, John Bird won the Editors' Editor of the Year Award (from the British Society of Magazine Editors). Two years later, the magazine won the Commission for Racial Equality Race in the Media Award 1995, followed by being a runner up in the Best Environmental Coverage 1995.

Articles from *The Big Issue* began to be picked up by the mainstream press. As John Lloyd remarks:

> *'to have people talk about you is important, an expectation that the magazine will answer certain needs and will be exciting. This is difficult to develop, but it's a determinant of success if you are being talked about.'*

Magazines lose their edge, so people have to have a determination to struggle against it. What the mass of papers do is fire their editors and go in for reinvention. What *The Big Issue* did was to have a relaunch on its fourth birthday in September 1995, with a redesign. This remedied a rather 'messy' magazine. 'It was all over the place,' remembers Simon Rogers, features editor from January 1995 until he left to join *The Guardian* in 1998. 'No one knew where anything was. There wasn't that positive predictability which you need with a magazine.'

The redesigned magazine was sectionalized, incorporating a section for the newly formed Big Issue Foundation in the middle. The news pages were printed on blue paper. The redesigned cover

echoed the first cover: 'Why didn't the homeless all go home?'
Sponsored supplements, such as summer festivals or students
returning to college, were launched in 1995. This was an incentive
to attract new readers, generate more advertising revenue and
give a better value-for-money feel to the paper.

The magazine's new confidence started, Simon maintains,
with the world exclusive interview by Gary Crossing with rock
band the Stone Roses in December 1994. The Stone Roses wanted
to announce their return from the wilderness and they chose *The
Big Issue*. Even though the week's print run was extended by
around 60,000, it sold out. Music papers from around the world
offered increasing sums for the article, battling for second rights.
Big Issue journalists had more and more access to celebrities and
began to be seen as a forum for new happenings.

The cultural coverage focused on the new and dug out
unusual and curious events. The popular short story season, initiated in 1994, encouraged new writers, and in the first year
included Will Self, Nick Hornby, Esther Freud and Julie Burchill.
Singers, actors, comedians and artists were interviewed along
with interesting people who were not so well known.

The arts section built up a strong freelance team at this time,
comprising such staff as Gary Crossing (music), Erik the Viking
(clubs), Helen Sumpter (the arts), Xan Brooks (film), Paul
Sussman (books and Front of House) and Lena Corner (arts assistant). Tina Jackson arrived as arts editor at the end of 1994 to give
the arts section more direction. Both Paul Sussman and Xan
Brooks were recognized for their talent, with Paul being
Periodical Publishers Association (PPA) Columnist of the Year
1995 (Runner Up) and Xan being PPA Writer of the Year 1996
(Runner Up).

Tina Jackson came to *The Big Issue* from the alternative press.
She joined because of the magazine's social mission, and because
of its journalistic strengths, which she saw as outside the
mainstream, independent, and unafraid of dealing with topics
in the way they needed to be addressed. Tina sharpened up the
16 page arts section, with a what's on guide and mini features
across the arts, concentrating on new cultural phenomena. She
says:

> 'What we were doing then was reasonably unusual, which was
> looking at arts based issues as they came up from the street,

rather than just tackling the mainstream, the big voices. Now everybody is looking for the next thing to come up from the street.'

One example was dance music culture, which kicked off in a big way at the end of the 1980s, operating outside the constraints of mainstream activity. She says:

'At the end of the eighties and early nineties the people who had been players in that scene suddenly got record company jobs and became part of the media, turning their lifestyle activities into their work activities. That was very revolutionary[4] and had a knock-on effect for many other kinds of music.

'We were always looking for something that was new, was about people giving voice to their concerns, people who were at that time not necessarily getting a voice in the mainstream press.'

Tina adds that this was made possible by the journalistic team:

'They were young, keen, very clued into other kinds of culture outside the mainstream scenes because they had been students. They were very bright, very focused, most of them were very aware of what was making waves in their particular areas.'

One of the young journalists was Lena Corner. Her time in editorial is typical of the way many of the staff there have gained experience at *The Big Issue*. Lena arrived as a volunteer in June 1994, straight from six months on the *Richmond and Twickenham Times*. She was excited by the kind of stories in *The Big Issue* and had regularly bought the magazine from Martin the vendor at Richmond station, subsequently doing a couple of stories on him for the local paper. One of Lena's first tasks was to do an interview with DJ John Peel:

'Someone had already done it but hadn't tape recorded it. They were too scared to ring him back and say sorry, so they got me to do it. He was alright-ish. He was in the middle of writing a column for the Radio Times *and didn't really need to be reinterviewed by a girl who didn't seem to know what she was doing. I had never done celebrity interviews.'*

But, having been dropped immediately into the middle of things, she became a feature writer and expert on the London street scene.

Lena, later deputy editor of *I-D magazine*, believes that one of *The Big Issue*'s greatest strengths is how members of the editorial team spend time and energy training new young journalists:

> '*I was learning how to write. That was a good thing about* The Big Issue, *that someone would sit down and go over it with you, what to do, where it went wrong. They are really good at teaching you. You get a lot of support.*'

Humour and whackiness has always been an important ingredient of the magazine. The magazine was more irreverant and more flippant then than it is now, largely due to Paul Sussman who edited Front of House. This involved obtaining comments on various subjects from celebrities and generating the infamous 'mad world' stories. These were so popular with the public that they were published in book form *Death by Spaghetti*[5] which has sold over 20,000 copies (the proceeds going to *The Big Issue* Foundation). Paul's take on social issues was unique and sometimes very close to the bone.

He commissioned a 700-word column each week, written by a celebrity and says: 'I got a few refusals. A nice one from writer Iris Murdoch, a hand-written 800 word refusal which was actually longer than the original column would have needed to have been.'

Other features investigated a wide range of social issues – from the pensioners who were prepared to break the law to draw attention to low pensions, to deaths in police custody.[6] Articles highlighted children who played truant and the increasing instances of women behaving violently. Over a period of four years, Lucy Johnston delved into the drug culture and wrote a series of investigative articles on the physical and cultural effects of heroin, E, crack or methodone. Her feature on cannabis, which contradicted popular mythology that the drug is harmless, drew great interest and was picked up by some of the nationals.

From the eighth issue in May 1992 there was an international dimension added to the editorial. This was in tune with the belief that homelessness and social exclusion were not simply British issues, and *The Big Issue*'s mission should be international. The page, which I wrote and edited, was used as a forum for human rights campaigns, reports on self-help projects around the world, cultural and political events and book reviews. Launches, conferences and gatherings of street papers were covered so that the British public could be aware of the phenomenon and follow their progress.

The Big Issue in 1995 joined The Body Shop's campaign to release Ken Saro-Wiwa and the other Ogoni campaigners held in custody in Nigeria.[7] It reported on such diverse issues as homelessness in Iraq in the aftermath of the Gulf War, Madrid's gypsies, and a campaign to save baby girls in China's 'dying rooms'; NGOs wrote on their specific areas of work. Noam Chomsky, John Vidal and Mark Tully were just some of the more celebrated writers who contributed. An international supplement, Brave New World, which was part of an issue of New Internationalist magazine, reported on global housing and homelessness.

Street culture had credibility with The Big Issue's young readers. As time went on it also interested advertisers who knew they were getting through to a young readership that went out and about in London. The July to December 1994 ABC figures indicated that the public approved of this editorial approach. Weekly circulation in London and the South East was now up to 102,142. The National Readership Survey (NRS) figure was 2.5 readers per copy which meant an audience of over 250,000 a week.

The average 1995 Big Issue reader was identified as young (33 per cent of the readership aged between 14 and 24 years), professional (86 per cent in full-time employment), urban and active; 56 per cent were female. The quintessential Big Issue reader was interested in health, political and social issues, with a strong interest in the arts.[8] Simon Rogers sums up their prevailing attitude:

> *'Our readers are socially informed, but they don't want it shoved down their throats. They want to go out and have a good time as well. They buy* The Big Issue *because they want to know what is going on in the world. But taking into account* The Big Issue's *unique distribution system they will buy it for that reason as well.'*

Covers

Unlike shelf magazines, *The Big Issue* gets direct feedback from the public via the vendors. This applies particularly to the covers. They have dramatically changed over the years from the original abstract, collage-style, liked by the then art director Lawrence Bogle, to the current celebrity slant.

Carolyn Roberts (Caz), *Big Issue*'s art director before she was headhunted by the *Independent on Sunday*, worked directly on the covers for three years. Caz knew it was difficult to keep the edginess. She says:

> *'As the magazine grows in circulation and it isn't as one-off and unusual as it was before, it's bound to look more professional and more polished. It is hard to recapture that youth of the product.'*

Caz always had a mixed feedback from the vendors about the covers:

> *'A really good example is when I put the goldfish on the cover and the vendors went mad because there wasn't much on it, it was just a goldfish in a bowl. It was a little bit of a tease into the readership survey. But for me and quite a lot of people who mentioned it to me it was just intriguing, "why is that on the cover now and what does it mean?" That would make you buy it.'*

The goldfish issue turned out to be a good seller. Caz tried to stick to the recommendations that vendors made – that the colours have to be clean and bright, and it has to be a positive image. She says:

> *'You have to think about the relationship between the vendor and the cover because you don't have that with normal magazines, so you have to be really careful because if it was violent or aggressive or too negative then you associate that person with it at times.'*

In 1994, the 'Learning to Kill' cover, relating to an article on how to kill in ten easy lessons was not popular with the vendors as the public complained about it.

Now, there is the policy of having celebrity faces on the cover, which has drawn in a new set of buyers but has made *The Big Issue* a little indistinguishable from other publications. Buyers see, for example, American actor Will Smith on the cover of *The Big Issue* along with Will Smith on many other magazine covers. Says Andrew Davies, 'People still want to read about him, and you can't deny that. Celebrity magazines have been a huge success story during the 1990s and people are obsessed with celebrity. It helps the vendors too.'

Vendors writing involvement

Many vendors were initially involved with the editorial team, providing them with stories directly from the streets, but this dropped off in the mayhem of getting a weekly out in June 1993. Before that, Jo Mallabar remembers, the atmosphere was such that vendors would come into the Hammersmith office and chat with staff who had more time then.

It was important that homeless people should use the paper as a voice and the most productive way of accomplishing this was through the writing group. Originally, the idea was that lots of homeless people would write for the paper. What actually happened was that the writing group wrote one or two pages each week for Capital Lights (now Street Lights) and this continues.

Jo and her team were not always happy with Capital Lights. If readers were not acquainted with *The Big Issue* and suddenly came across Capital Lights, they might not see it as good writing but as just another sob story. So Jo insisted that editorial became involved in some of the writing groups. Many editorial staff took the groups. Paul Sussman took three or four: 'Vendors found them very rewarding. I am perpetually struck by how talented and quirky some of these people are. Wonderful, bizarre, surreal, enriching and exciting stuff.' Arts journalist Lena Corner talked about interview techniques and film editor Xan Brooks discussed how to review films.

The Capital Lights page in this period not only ran poems and creative writing but reports on the concerns of homeless people. Such subjects as conditions in hostels and which ones were about to close, what it was like for women living in hostels, the annual commemoration for those who had died on the streets, the on-going benefit issue and how it affected homeless and ex-homeless people.

Vendor Aileen took a group regularly to the theatre and wrote reviews on the Capital Lights pages. She wrote about seeing poet John Hegley.[9] The Gulbenkian Foundation ran a competition for homeless and recently housed writers, 'Voices from the Heart', with prize money of £3000.[10] Writers and poets gave readings at a joint English Speaking Union/*Big Issue* event.[11] The writing group also attended Opera Factory workshops at the South Bank.[12]

Some vendors expressed an interest in working in the editorial and production departments but this has always proved difficult. Training requires time and energy. People who have been homeless need extra support and encouragement. Everyone is so frantic in editorial that, so far, it has had varying success for the half dozen or so people who have been employed in that department.

REPORTING AND CAMPAIGNING ON HOMELESS/HOUSING ISSUES

A particularly busy year for government legislation concerning homeless people was 1994 and *The Big Issue* took it head on. The government's welcome Rough Sleepers Initiative (RSI) was combined with two other major pieces of legislation. The Criminal Justice Act 1994 and the Green Paper on Housing (which became the Housing Act of 1996) were perceived as assaults on both homeless and young people in particular. *Big Issue* journalists, vendors and homeless people regularly reported on both the positive and negative sides of the legislation and the possible consequences for both homeless people and the readers.

With the Criminal Justice Act, the government planned to criminalize squatting, leaving 50,000 people (one third of them families) under the threat of immediate homelessness or six months in prison. When Home Secretary Michael Howard said, 'Thieves already face tough criminal sanctions – squatters should too,' homeless organizations were outraged that the government was equating homeless people with criminals. As Sheila McKechnie, Director of Shelter said, 'The real crime isn't 50,000 squatters, it's the 600,000 empty homes in Britain. Criminalizing squatting will result in homelessness.'

In March 1994, *The Big Issue* reported on the Green Paper on Housing, part of which dealt with access by homeless people to council housing. *Big Issue* journalist Anthony Middleton interviewed Housing Minister Sir George Young about the new proposals. Local authorities would no longer be bound to

provide permanent housing for homeless people but only temporary accommodation. This meant that homeless familes were
excluded from council housing, except if they become eligible
through the normal waiting list. The definition of homelessness
would also be amended to include only those who are literally
roofless, rather than those who are living in insecure or temporary accommodation.

Sir George told *The Big Issue* that he wanted to rid people of
the 'perverse incentive' to make themselves homeless in order to
get to the top of the council and housing association waiting lists.
This new proposal in effect put the legal situation of homeless
people back 20 years, to before the 1977 Act. The 1977 Housing
(Homeless Persons) Act had for the first time responded to
homelessness as a housing problem, with homeless families given
statutory rights to permanent, secure accommodation by local
authorities. With the new Act, this duty would end.

Organizations and charities working with homeless people
believed that the homeless would be plunged into a merry-go-
round of temporary accommodation, reminiscent of conditions
pre 1977. Sheila McKechnie remembers:

> *'George and I always got on extremely well until he said he was
> going to change the Homeless Persons Act and I said, fine, you
> try it. It's war! And it was.'*

Despite protestations, this legislation was incorporated into the
Housing Act 1996. It has subsequently been modified by the
Labour government.

On the other hand, the government's successful RSI 1 was
followed by a second initiative and welcomed by the voluntary
sector. Then, in April and May 1994, Prime Minister John Major
made two public attacks, firstly on beggars and secondly on the
homeless. Major denounced people who beg as 'an eyesore' in an
interview with the *Bristol Evening Post* on 27 May 1994. These
people, he said, drove visitors and shoppers out of city centres
and persistent beggars should be fined and imprisoned. He
encouraged the public to report beggars to the police and wanted
tough laws used against them. He believed, 'it is not acceptable to
be out on the street. There is no justification for it.'

In April 1994, John Major had told the German magazine *Der
Spiegel* that:

> 'They [the homeless] are not on the streets because they have to
> be on the streets. There are empty places in accommodation
> units across London and in other areas where people could go if
> they wished. But they choose not to stay there and that is a
> cultural point. It is a strange way of life that some of them
> choose to live.'

He added that in the UK there is a surplus of homes above the
numbers of families.[13] *The Big Issue* immediately responded by
running a campaign in the 7 June 1994 issue. On the front cover,
the words 'Dear Mr Major...join London's homeless in answering
back' presaged an article inside with an additional 'Dear John'
letter and the public were asked to sign and send the letter to the
Prime Minister, suggesting that '...your recent observations
suggest nothing other than that you have no interest in looking
for solutions to the social problems that have multiplied over the
last 15 years'. John Major's stance was contradicted by homeless
people themselves; vendor Mary suggested he try living on the
streets for a day, even a week.

John Major's remarks were also out of line with the statistics
of one of his own government departments. A Department of
Environment report in 1993, 'Single Homeless People', found that
only 4 per cent of people who slept rough did so because they
preferred the way of life. The rest were on the streets because they
were unable to find themselves accommodation. Based on interviews with 1346 homeless people across the country, the
Department's report also found that many people slept rough
because of bad experiences in hostels. It also discovered that only
19 per cent of homeless people had begged and those that did
made an average of only £10–£20 per week.

Looking ahead to winning the general election, Labour's Jack
Straw, Shadow Home Secretary, also attacked beggars in
September 1995. He attacked 'winos' and those who were making
the streets unsafe for 'decent' people.

In an article in the October *Big Issue*,[14] 'Begging for it', journalists reported that a recent government consultation paper said that
'aggressive' beggars were 'distressing for members of the public
and visitors to the capital' and set out plans to review the vagrancy
laws. *The Big Issue* turned the argument on its head and did the
opposite of what the mainstream press was doing with their scare
headlines. Some beggars are intimidating, agrees the article, but

life on the streets is a frightening experience – so imagine what it is like for them, subject to daily harassment and distress. People who beg were interviewed and their experiences chronicled.

Apart from these major pieces of legislation, and John Major's attack on the homeless, there were the ongoing more localized attacks on people's lives reported in the magazine: the government threatening soup-runs in the capital, accommodation agencies ripping people off, landlords letting out dangerous flats. Features and news stories covered dodgy landlords, homeless kids, seaside homelessness, 'hot squats', the rough guide to soup kitchens, London's top ten empty residences, hostel closures, a teenager who was jailed for being homeless and a *Big Issue* vendor who died in police custody. On the 50th anniversary of D Day in 1994, *The Big Issue* told the story of old veterans who live on the streets. A report called 'Falling Out', published in May 1994 by Crisis with support from the Department of the Environment, had suggested that 25 per cent of people on the streets had formerly been in the armed services.[15]

CAMPAIGNING ON SOCIAL POLICY

The Big Issue dipped its toes into social policy from 1995. Sinead Hanks, who had worked as a researcher in the House of Commons, suggested that *The Big Issue* needed a department which would inform the company not only about what was going on in Parliament, but also the general trend of social issues. There was discussion on whether it was *The Big Issue*'s role to lobby and research into homelessness when there were experienced organizations such as Shelter doing it so well. John Bird had been reluctant to get involved in such activities, saying that he wanted *The Big Issue* to be 'the force outside of Parliament'. Lack of finance put a stop to the whole discussion when Sinead left in 1998 but she had helped to run two campaigns, the Empty Homes Campaign (EHC) and the Right to Vote for homeless people.

The EHC, a joint inititative with The Empty Homes Agency (EHA), began in February 1997.[16] The EHA had been launched in 1992 to bring homes back into the housing market and claimed that through its efforts 6000 people had been housed in its first five years. There were then an estimated 790,000 empty homes in Britain. They targeted five examples of empty homes and campaigned, with *Big Issue* readers, to fill the properties.

In an article launching the campaign, *Big Issue* editor Jo Mallabar wrote:

> *'all sides agree that no one benefits from empty homes, yet we live in the midst of a homeless crisis: 53,860 households according to Government statistics, which have on average 2.5 members. A recent survey by the YMCA put the figure for young people who had experienced homelessness in 1995 at between 200,000 and 300,000.'*

The first property to be profiled was the huge Tower House, in Fieldgate Street in the East End of London which, at the time of writing, is still boarded up. Now owned by the London Borough of Tower Hamlets, it was built in the late 19th century to provide bed and breakfast accommodation for homeless people. It was here that Russian revolutionaries Joseph Stalin and Maxim Litvinov stayed in 1907.

Readers of *The Big Issue* were invited to send a form to Tower Hamlets Council, saying 'Tower House has stood empty since 1989. It is one of the 790,000 empty homes in England. Please will you ensure that this empty property is put back into use for those in need.' Readers were encouraged to report a long-standing empty home to their local authority. *The Big Issue* continued the campaign for a few months. It was then restarted in October 2000.

The Right to Vote campaign was initiated in 1992 by CHAR, the Housing Campaign for Single People. In *The Big Issue*[17] CHAR reported on their homeless citizens charter, in opposition to the government's recent Citizen's Charter, pointing out that homeless people would not be able to vote in the 1992 general election. Tens of thousands of homeless people, said CHAR, were denied the right to vote, as people sleeping rough were not allowed to put their names on the electoral register. Even those spending a short stay in hostels, bed and breakfast hotels or shelters were not accepted in many areas.

The campaign demanded that the Representation of the People Act (1983) be changed to enshrine the right to vote for homeless people. This would mean that homeless people could register at a contact point like *The Big Issue* offices or a day centre. The hope was to get a Private Member's Bill through Parliament in November 1995.

CHAR continued the campaign and *The Big Issue* became actively involved a few months before the 10 October deadline for electoral registration in 1995. Ruth Turner, founder of *The Big Issue in the North*, initiated this because in Manchester rough sleepers were allowed to register shop doorways as their 'home'. Just before the local elections, *The Big Issue in the North* worked with Manchester City Council's electoral registration officers to ensure homeless people were able to register. As reported in July 1995[16] Carol Hawthorne, who had been homeless for three years, had registered her address at the Manchester *Big Issue* office. Ruth remembers:

> 'We had a letter in from a member of the public in February 1995, saying I don't understand why homeless people are not allowed to vote. It was because they haven't got an address. So I contacted Manchester City Council and they said, interesting you should ask, it is actually legal. And there has been a Home Office Working Group report which has just said that it is actually lawful for homeless people to vote because they have defined residence as not necessarily meaning bricks and mortar.'

The Big Issue in the North carried out a big electoral registration campaign in Manchester and got people to vote, linking up with CHAR. Although the law still has not been changed, and so is still not enshrined as a right, the law does not forbid it. The Home Office recommendation is that electoral registration officers do not necessarily define residence as having to include bricks and mortar. It is down to the discretion of the individual electoral registration officer.[18]

ADVERTISING

Trying to sell advertising space in a publication sold by homeless people was the biggest challenge for the advertising team. It was a first for the advertising industry and media buyers just did not understand the concept. It was not a sexy, glossy publication and the circulation was unknown. But as sales increased, companies gradually saw the rewards for buying into *The Big Issue*.

Advertisements had initially been obtained by hard graft and through contacts. The expansion of advertising revenue was crucial to the financial success of the magazine and by the end of the first year moves were made towards establishing a professional team.

Paul Sussman's entry into *The Big Issue* was similar to the random way most staff joined in the early days. He was badgered to join by someone he had previously worked for who was now setting up the ad department at *The Big Issue*. 'I had no desire whatsoever to join *The Big Issue*,' he says.

He also found complete and utter chaos:

'which in part I was responsible for. It was absolute bedlam. No organization. Very fly by the seat of one's pants, as indeed I think most of the organization was in those days.'

He remembers a lot of volunteers. Many people from various backgrounds joined in for the hell of it. By the May 1992 edition, the paper had been relying fairly heavily on goodwill advertising. The team was very keen to move on from this because the income was limited. Full-page advertisements were obtained at cut prices from such organizations as the Terrence Higgins Trust, The Prince's Trust, the Royal Society for the Protection of Birds, GrandMet Trust and bookstore Dillons, almost as an act of solidarity by the companies that wished to support the new paper.

The team's main success was to get major banks on board throughout the autumn of 1992. Although initially these adverts were financed from their community budgets, which was based on goodwill and only short term, the team realized that with a sustained effort they could be brought in regularly on a commercial basis. This had the roll-on effect of other companies taking the paper more seriously and coming in with advertising themselves.

In the first Christmas edition of the A4 magazine in 1992 Sally Stainton, who had joined earlier in the year, remembers 'her' ad on the back and she felt the magazine had finally arrived in the advertising world. Helping to unpack the van which had arrived from the printers at six in the morning, she remembers the vendors seeing the ad on the back, and being impressed, saying, 'Wow, what's fucking Persil doing on the back cover?' She says, 'To see it being sold in the streets with your ad on the back was just a knockout.'

In order to professionalize the advertising team, Dermot MacPartland was hired as advertising manager in September

1992. Dermot inherited a magazine which was selling about 140,000 copies per fortnight. Although the circulation figures were healthy, the problem was that the business community, and hence advertisers, would still not take the magazine seriously. They thought people bought it just to help the vendor and were not reading it. So the first challenge for the advertising team was to convince advertisers that the growing circulation meant that people were buying it to read.

Dermot and his original team, Maria Clancy, Silvia Johnson and Sarah Beal, turned the department around. Silvia Johnson, who became the deputy manager of the team, was responsible for developing *The Big Issue* as a successful advertising medium in the music and entertainment industry.

In 1993 the magazine was pushed into the commercial arena by obtaining an ABC figure and an NRS figure. This was crucial for *The Big Issue* since sceptics were saying they did not believe so many people were buying it. The first ABC figure (January–June 1993) was 143,000 copies per fortnight of which 125,000 were sold in London and the rest in Brighton and Manchester. By November 1993, the circulation was 100,000 per week, a 35 per cent increase on the fortnightly sales.

The reasons companies advertise in a magazine are threefold: good editorial, good circulation and information on the readership. There is no point having one or two, declares Dermot, you have to have all three. Ostensibly advertisers were buying the editorial, the circulation and the readership. But initially they were getting this extra fourth thing from *The Big Issue* that no other magazine could give them, which was the 'feel good factor'. This was a new development of the 1990s. It was seen as a big swing for clients to be putting something back into the community, sponsoring events for young people, for instance, and being branded alongside.

Dermot believes that *The Big Issue* was one of the main instigators of this new attitude amongst business. To get the business community to accept a street magazine like this was in itself revolutionary. He says, 'For example, for a bank to put an ad in a magazine sold by homeless people had never been done before.' His belief is that media buyers do not really care about society's ills, but that they have a need to reach a certain number of people:

> *'If you can help them do that cost-effectively, then they will advertise with you. Even if* The Big Issue *was to get bad press it would probably affect the [fundraising for the] Foundation, but as long as the ABC figure kept rising and the NRS was healthy, advertisers will still use the magazine.'*

The Big Issue was perfect for brands that wanted to be part of the youth culture. Many advertisers used the magazine during 1993 and by 1994 big names were on board. Corporates such as BT, Lever and Mercury Communications, consumer companies like Pepsi, Coca-Cola, Bacardi, Bennetton, Boddingtons, Calvin Klein, Virgin and Levis joined the major banks, with many from the entertainment industry: Fox, Warner Bros, EMI, Columbia Tristar and Polygram. Major charities such as Oxfam, Shelter, Greenpeace and the Terrence Higgins Trust also reaped the benefits of advertising in *The Big Issue*.

The question of having an ethical advertising policy has been a constant source of debate. Many staff felt that the magazine should be socially responsible and not carry ads such as those for cigarettes. Dermot remembers the arguments:

> *'We got one ad from British Nuclear Fuels early on and we immediately heard from Anita [Roddick]. We got told off. We ran it because we needed the money. So we were to turn away money which we were desperate for.'*

John Bird at the time authorized the advertisement. 'No one reading *The Big Issue* would see it as an endorsement by us,' he believed. 'Our readers knew that like *The Guardian* we might take ads from companies we did not believe in.'

There is a contradiction between needing the money and taking an ethical line, as John Lloyd well knows:

> *'Almost all newspapers have a black list of advertisers they won't take. But it is mainly the small and poor magazines which take the ethical line but need the finance most of all. The temptation to take a large amount of money is huge. The principle has to be thrashed out, but be flexible enough to incorporate new ethical issues as they change.'*[19]

The Big Issue has carried cigarette ads, although not often. There was pressure from some staff and public to stop them. The issue will be resolved when cigarette ads are banished from the press. Dermot says:

> '*My feeling was that this is a sizeable amount of revenue. We felt it was the devil's money, that they're awful people, they're killing people, but we thought "take the money". We always felt we could spend the money better than other newspapers.*'

The magazine has always taken advertisements from drink companies too, posing another dilemma. Dermot adds: 'If you don't take cigarettes maybe you shouldn't take beers, if you don't take beers, you shouldn't take liquor because a lot of our vendors have got drink problems. So it becomes a minefield. There we are trying to be a business, competing with other magazines.' The argument was resolved by accepting the fact that it was not the advertisements in the magazine that would increase vendors' drinking habits and that the ad revenue would help them in other ways.

There are advertisements that the paper would obviously never take – sinister right-wing groups promoting eugenics and racial purity, for instance. Generally speaking, a charity with a Charity Commission number can be trusted. Classified ads are more problematical and all of them have to be methodically checked out. All ads for hostels are checked through the local council's housing officers. Phone lines or sex lines are not taken because it lowers the tone. Chat lines were for a short period, but were discontinued in 1999 due to pressure from staff and the public (losing income of around £960 per week). Advertisements from fertility clinics are checked with the British Medical Council.

Occasionally advertisements which have proved to be deceitful have been run, but there have not been many. 'We had an ad once that encouraged homeless people to move to Norfolk and live by the sea in a hostel. We found out it was dodgy, the guy was exposed by the council in Norfolk and we apologised immediately.' The concerns are twofold: not to leave either the vendors or the readers open to any potential exploitation.

As more advertisers came on board, the editorial to advertising ratio switched from 67:33 to 60:40 over 40 pages, which was considered a good balance between copy and revenue. *The Big Issue* had initially turned over in the region of £80,000 in advertising. By the third year, 1993–94, the team were up a massive 400 per cent and turned over £420,000. The advertising department in 1995–96 was generating 42 per cent of the total income of *The Big Issue*.[20]

The Business

By mid 1994 the company had turned round and was making money, due to the continuing rise in circulation and the increase in advertising revenue. But there had been a major hiccup when the magazine went weekly which had not been predicted.

Going weekly nine months after going fortnightly meant that, although it increased the vendors' selling potential, there was a dip in both sales and income from advertising. The public took time to realize that it had gone weekly, and advertisers also took time to respond to the weekly schedule. John maintains that the company lost £150,000 by going weekly over a period of about six months. So business-wise, going weekly looked like a wrong move. Eventually, though, the company started to reduce the gap by upping the circulation and increasing advertising.

By the end of three years, had The Body Shop asked for its investment to be repaid, *The Big Issue* could have paid it all back. Gordon responds:

'We said keep it and make the business develop, then we have really contributed in a major way. The point is that you have to take risks. Risk means that you inevitably do a lot wrong.'

But Gordon was happy enough with how things were progressing. The Body Shop accountants went into *The Big Issue* on a regular basis and looked at the books. He remembers:

'They used to come back pale and shaking sometimes, saying do you know what that son of a bitch is doing? This is out of control. I used to say, calm down, it's not like that. Things are going wrong. But we wouldn't have known they would go wrong unless we tried them.'

By 1993, many big businesses were supporting *The Big Issue*'s work with donations, from the NatWest Bank, to Laura Ashley, Lloyds Bank, GEC and Midland Bank. The Co-operative Bank had been a major supporter of *The Big Issue* since its inception and holds the company's account at its Ealing branch.

By 1994, it was necessary to move once again. With the growth of various new departments, the Hammersmith office was overcrowded, and the Victoria office was due to be demolished. The investment company, 3i, came up with a sponsorship deal. They owned an ugly 1960s building in Clerkenwell Road which they had been unable to sell and offered it to *The Big Issue*, rent free for five years with a six month break clause written into the lease. *The Big Issue* only had to pay the rates, insurance and upkeep of the building. The new office was opposite Clerkenwell Green, previously home to many radicals.[21]

Sponsorship was raised from the Swiss Bank and many other corporates and organizations to pay for the renovation. Housing Minister Sir George Young opened the building in May 1994. At last, all staff and vendors were now in one building.

But Clerkenwell was becoming a trendy area and the property prices were rising. In September 1995, an offer of £1.4m was made to 3i by a developer who realized the potential of the area. Having invested a lot of time, energy and money in the building, it was felt that moving again at this time would be detrimental to the company's development. The Co-operative Bank was approached and agreed a £1.4m loan repayable over a 12 year period with no capital repayment required in the first year. As from 30 January 1996, Fleet House, Clerkenwell, belonged to *The Big Issue*.

The negotiations with the bank and the auditors raised a number of interesting issues for the social business. Chairman Nigel Kershaw remembers:

> *'The bank asked us what collateral we had. We said, none. What about trading? Not very good. We said, that's because we give all our money away. We spend it on the social initiative.'*

The bank refused a mortgage.

> *'Our argument then became, what happens if we strip out the social initiative from the budget? This will show you that the magazine, which is our core business, is making a 12 per cent profit on turnover equal to other magazines. We are asking you to invest in our core business. We are not asking you to invest in what we do with our social dividend.'*

This worked. What was important, states Nigel, was that *The Big Issue* brought a new financial model to the bankers and the auditors. He says:

> *'If another publisher had asked them for a mortgage and they had the same kind of profit margin, the bank would not be refusing them. They would not be saying to them we're not going to lend you money because we don't like the lifestyle that you spend your profits on.'*

The fact that *The Big Issue* gives the money to the social initiative is not a concern of the bank's.

Buying the building gave the business some financial stability. However, one effect was that it forced the directors of the company to focus on budgetary and strategic planning with the cost of buying the building and the interest paid to the bank. Previously, insurance and rent had never been paid. Owning the building meant that not only the refurbishment but annual maintenance would have to be paid for.

One of the issues that having two sites had highlighted was that of the social divide between staff. Sinead Hanks, who initially worked in the Victoria distribution office, puts it quite bluntly:

> *'I think this was quite integral. It was like the working classes in Victoria dealing with vendors and the middle classes in Hammersmith working on the paper, and they don't understand us and we don't understand them. I never got to meet anyone in editorial until we moved into Clerkenwell. I found it quite strange because I was never quite sure what camp I fell into.'*

She believes this divide still exists: professional journalists are going to be more middle class, with those who work with vendors seeing themselves as working class. She believes there doesn't seem to be much of an understanding that everyone has their own part to play.

This is the contradiction of having people working both in a business and with homeless people, in the same organization. But, John believes, this is natural. When there is one set of staff confronting homeless people on a day-to-day basis whilst others are running the administration, selling advertising and producing the paper there is bound to be a certain degree of distance between them all. At times, getting people who work away from the homeless to spend time in distribution has helped. But it hasn't been an unmitigated success. It is still a struggle to break the divide.

In the midst of all the negotiations on the building, John Bird went to Buckingham Palace to receive an MBE for his services to homeless people.[22]

SETTING UP THE COMMUNICATIONS DEPARTMENT

Primarily, it is the vendors who are the magazine's best PR, the most visible as they are out on the streets. But PR and advertising companies have given their services for free for cinema, radio advertisements, and billboard posters. *The Big Issue*'s marketing activities started with the launch advert in 1991 which introduced the essential *Big Issue* concept of self-help.

In 1994, the advertising agency Gold Greenless Trott (GGT) organized the cinema adverts for *The Big Issue*'s fourth birthday. In the spring of 1996, GGT organized celebrities Mariella Frostrup, Eddie Izzard, Katie Puckrick and Martin Clunes to do radio ads. Later in the year, *Campaign*[23] reported on two new *Big Issue* cinema commercials 'Cake' and 'Taxi' by directors Graham Fink and Chris Palmer, again by GGT. John Hegarty of BBH has also been a great supporter of *The Big Issue*.

The other side of the PR work is the communications department which was set up in 1993 as press interest in the new company increased. Due to the company's financial limitations there has always been limited resources available for press work. Due to the unique nature of *The Big Issue* this did not impede the company's public profile and a healthy and regular press interest was maintained.

The brief of the communications department – or press office – was to sets up press engagements, mainly for vendors and John Bird. It also filtered unnecessary press, TV and radio calls, and negotiated with film and TV companies that wanted to feature *The Big Issue* in their programmes. It monitored relations between the vendors and the media to ensure that the vendors were not exploited. It developed a good working relationship with the media and warded off bad coverage, as well as processing hundreds of enquiries from students and the general public.

Sally Stainton's heart was not in advertising and she moved over to head up the press office when it started. She found that the *The Big Issue* concept was so new that the press, although mostly supportive, was continuously giving out the wrong message (such as '*The Big Issue* is a charity newspaper, produced by homeless people'). Many times mainstream journalists did not bother to check these facts when writing stories. Journalists were also preying on vendors for stories and this became worrying for two reasons: what were the vendors saying and how were the press treating the individual vendors.

Her first Christmas as press officer, Sally was inundated with requests from television and radio, and women's magazines wanting to know about the 'traditional homeless person's Christmas'. It enraged Sally that people suddenly became interested in homelessness only for the period of ten days around Christmas. She says:

> '*I always said we don't involve ourselves in projects that exploit homeless people for your ends. We will provide you with images of vendors who are improving themselves by selling the magazine. But they will be positive images of change taking place, which is what* The Big Issue *is for. We will never use or provide pictures of pathetic people with blankets because we are about changing the face of homelessness to the public.*'

The calls coming into the press office at first were invariably magazines or tabloids wanting studies of individual homeless people. Increasingly, it was difficult to get vendors to do that, particularly when the media did not understand that many did not want publicity. Part of homeless people's regeneration is a process of severing themselves from their previous existence. However, there are some very 'media friendly' vendors. Sally says:

> '*Sometimes when I am coming to work, I am mobbed by people who are looking for the chance to get on telly. One vendor in particular who sees me every day, gives me a contact number for any work.*'

Since a huge number of homeless people have mental, drug and alcohol problems, it is a process of educating journalists. At times, their requests are offensive, such as asking for 'a pretty, white, 17 year old girl in the West End who has got three A levels'. They cannot begin to understand why that girl would make herself vulnerable because she has placed herself in the public's eye. Sally was unwilling to meet a lot of the requests.

She now sees her main job as protecting the vendors, in a damage limitation role. If they are involved with the press, then she will be with them, to brief them and make sure that they appear to their best ability. Or that they are not drunk. She is protecting them against themselves in some cases because she does not believe that journalists understand the damage that subjecting vendors to a moment's fame can do:

> 'We've had a history of intelligent and capable vendors who have been used by the press and then discarded. They find it very difficult to readjust to going back on the streets and selling.'

Many journalists think that by giving them £50 and expecting them to be grateful, it is a worthwhile experience. In fact, she believes, it can be very destructive.

Another of Sally's roles has been educating the public about homelessness and what *The Big Issue* has done to combat it. Many members of the public have never understood what a contradictory process social reintegration is, nor what self-help is all about. More ask why their vendors have been selling for years. Why have they not moved on? She explains:

> 'Very often it's a case, particularly if I know the vendor concerned, by talking about what he (or she) was like before selling The Big Issue, what he was like when he first started, what he is like now. Pointing out the change that has taken place in that person's life and that we don't ever say we have got all the solutions.'

Mary, 55, used to play the harmonica every weekend at Hyde Park, but gave up when the police started harassing her. She started selling *The Big Issue* in 1992 at Bond Street station, in London's West End. '*The Big Issue* was a godsend for me. I was sleeping in cardboard boxes, in doorways, on doorsteps, anywhere, stations.' Mary left home when she was 14 years old because of disagreements with her parents. She explains how the public behaved towards her:

'I used to just wander about. Find something to eat. Carry on the best I could. Mostly to get away from the weather and to be near people so as you don't think you are some sort of disease walking about. Otherwise you get inferior and think that nobody wants to come near you and you mustn't go near them. Even up here you see people come near you and jump back like they're going to catch something off you. You can't catch homelessness. It's just one of them things that happens in life. I get that reaction mostly from women. Once a woman threw a £1 coin at me. She said here you are, this is for you and threw it up in the air.

'When people come and buy a magazine, it really surprises people that you've got manners. They think you are just going to grab the money and say "here's your magazine". They think that's your attitude. They don't realize that you must have a lot of self-discipline at the end of the day. They are constantly surprised that you're just a normal human being.'

Mary obtained a one-bedroom flat which she shares with her two dogs. She has a more stable life, but understands how other homeless people have difficulty settling after years on the streets. 'I can understand why people have trouble in their flats. Everybody gets lonely.'

Sally therefore has to inform the public – and the media – that most homeless people are not on the streets, they are in hostels, in squats or staying on friends' floors. When she first started in the press office, it was an almost daily task to explain that most of the vendors were attempting to be housed permanently. That was the need, not just the need to get off the streets.

While she is happy to promote positive stories about vendors' lives, Sally also continuously challenges the public's belief that the only thing that vendors are going to do with their money is 'piss it up the wall' or buy drugs, or cigarettes. She says:

'Sometimes people say I'm not buying The Big Issue *anymore because I gave someone the money and they went and spent it on alcohol. They expect you to go, oh my god how awful! I feel like asking how many bottles of wine did YOU buy last week? I still get so angry that people can be so stupid about what it's like to be homeless. It's prejudice and ignorance.'*

The nature of homelessness has changed quite dramatically during the 1990s. Sally finds it challenging to make sure that people know that even though there aren't so many people sleeping on the streets, it is not a pleasant option to be put in a hostel. Consequently, there is still just as much of a need for *The Big Issue* as there was when it started. Also, because, for all sorts of reasons, people are excluded from the possibility of making an income through employment.

THE SUN STORY

There was bad press about certain vendors periodically in the press and there was a feeling in the company that at some point a tabloid would do a nasty job on *The Big Issue*. On 28 October 1996, *The Sun* ran a front page story headlined 'The Big Earner' about a vendor selling in the suburb of Kingston-upon-Thames. *The Sun* called Mark 'greedy' and accused him of boasting that he took home 'pocketfuls of money every night'. The press office had a huge damage limitation job on their hands.

Sally Stainton was furious that the two *Sun* journalists, who had pretended that they themselves were homeless, had treated someone so contemptuously. She says:

> 'They relied on Mark's goodwill in directing them to The Big Issue. They relied on him believing that they were decent and honest, and he told them lots of things about himself, which he exaggerated. The Sun was horrified that he was living in a flat. We had to take his badge away and say, sorry mate, you've been found out. He said, "well I've never lied about it. I work bloody hard – 12 hours a day".'

It was highly unlikely, however, that he was earning the reported £1000 per week. Some staff and vendors were upset at what the incident had done to the vendors' image; Sally says:

> 'Because it suggested that all vendors could be deceiving their punters, because it suggested that it was too easy to earn money, because it suggested that we are hoodwinking our public.'

John Bird issued a statement, part of which read:

> 'The "exclusive" published in The Sun *this morning tries to highlight the problems of a vendor earning too much money. Of course to some people it is offensive that homeless people should earn lots of money… Of course if* The Sun *wanted to run a true story about* The Big Issue *it could have highlighted all the people who sell the paper, struggle and gradually win control of their lives. Those who have been improved. But it doesn't sell newspapers to describe those that have benefitted from selling.* The Sun *by it's nature as a scandal sheet can only look for scandals.'*

In the following weeks, there was a backlash, with reports of members of the public spitting on and insulting vendors. The article had a very bad effect on Mark and he reportedly disappeared out into the countryside. Lucy Johnston in *The Observer* newpaper (3 January 1996) reported on problems *The Sun* had caused vendors in an article entitled: 'Attacked, robbed, pelted, abused: *Big Issue* sellers run the gauntlet'.

The staff's belief that Mark made quite a lot of money but nowhere near what he said was echoed by Victor Adebowale, formerly of Centrepoint:

> 'The article in The Sun *about the very, very, infrequent case where a* Big Issue *seller is making a good living, hinted that someone is on £60,000 a year selling the magazine. My response to that is yeah, what of it? It's as relevant as earning £600,000 a year gambling in other people's shares.'*

On 9 November 1996, *The Sun* excelled itself by somehow obtaining and then printing part of an exclusive interview with singer George Michael, due to be printed two days later in *The Big Issue*. (It was his first media interview for six years and was a huge boost for the magazine, which was a sell-out.)[24] *The Sun* also praised *The Big Issue*, whereas weeks before it was damning it. A writ was fired off to the tabloid and many months later an undisclosed settlement was reached.

CHAPTER 5

THE MOVE OUTSIDE LONDON

IMMEDIATELY AFTER THE launch, there was pressure to extend outside London. Gordon Roddick recommended to John that any expansion should be with local partners. John says:

> 'We had to offer a kind of franchise relationship. We didn't have the manpower, the skills or the money. The Big Issue was loaded down with activity. I had to meet all the contenders from around Britain, and also from around the world. It was dispiriting, as many of them demanded more than we could deliver.'

The first experience was a disaster. Milton Keynes, some 30 miles north west of London, was the first town outside the capital to have a distribution centre in early 1992. John recalls, 'We had a vendor who got himself a girlfriend in Milton Keynes. We opened there and had a little launch and some press interest.' But there was no one locally able to carry on the organization and they pulled out soon after. Further expansion was left for a while until they were approached by a small group working with homeless people in Brighton during 1992.

However, the people who were keen to work with *The Big Issue* did not fully understand the concept and had different ways of working. When the working relationship broke down in 1993 staff were sent down from the London office to continue the work in Brighton. Vendors there have successfully sold the London edition of *The Big Issue* since, moving along the south coast towns. Brighton has the highest per capita rate of homelessness in the UK, twice that of London, and a significant level of heroin addiction, which is the main problem facing *Big Issue* vendors.

At the first birthday in 1992, John met Mel Young and Tricia Hughes. They had come down from Scotland to talk to John about starting in Glasgow and Edinburgh and numerous meetings followed. Meanwhile, Lifeshare, a street action charity in Manchester, wanted to start up *The Big Issue in the North*. In December 1992, *The Big Issue* was launched in Manchester in partnership with Lifeshare. The London issue with a supplement was sold in the city centre. John remembers:

> '*It was a great idea to partner with local people. But soon it became apparent that there was a problem. As Lifeshare was largely made up of volunteers, there was little continuity. It seemed that the responsibility for the paper was picked up and put down. It was most frustrating. It was yet another problem for us.*'

In the new year, a group came down from Lifeshare, which included volunteers Aidan Forster and Ruth Turner. John says:

> '*They told me the problems. But they had a solution. They wanted to run the paper, with us employing them to do so. It was great. Another weight off my mind.*'

Over the next few months, though, it became obvious that the person who would drive it forward was Ruth Turner.

Also in 1993, the discussions with Scotland turned into a programme for the launch. John remembers:

> '*We got a fundraiser and Mel and Trish worked their butts off. There was a real enthusiasm to bring* The Big Issue *to Scotland, although there were some snidey comments. One Scottish journalist suggested to me that the only reason I wanted a Scottish* Big Issue *was to get rid of troublesome Scottish vendors in London. One of our initial fans from over the border was a friend of both Mel and myself, Jimmy Boyle.[1] Jimmy was great and supported Mel and Tricia's endeavour.*'

The Big Issue in the North

Ruth Turner had produced a magazine whilst deputy president of the student union at Salford University.

> 'I wanted to do some campaigning, and not particularly to do with homelessness, just poverty and things that were unfair generally. Shelter put me in touch with Lifeshare, another charity where I went and did three evenings training about homelessness.'

It was the inability of charity work to offer solutions that worried her. She continues:

> 'I did a soup run and stood in Piccadilly Gardens with the most disgusting soup. You had to hand that to these funny people who were looming at you out of the bushes in the dark. And I thought this is horrible. I then went to a phone box with an experienced volunteer to try and get someone some accommodation. And there wasn't any. And I said, "what do you mean there isn't any?" And I thought, I've been politically interested, involved in the community, a student activist. I was a bit disgusted that they didn't tell anyone. They knew all these awful things about homelessness, but didn't say anything.'

Ruth suggested to Lifeshare that she could run their campaigns for them, but someone else suggested doing a *Big Issue* and after the visit to John Bird and Lucie Russell in London, they started 'without very much thought at all'. In early 1993, Jane McRobbie introduced Anne McNamara to the Manchester *Big Issue*.

For over a year, the Northern office developed the paper but there were problems. Ruth and Anne increasingly felt out on a limb. Ruth remembers:

> 'We always felt a nuisance! A lot of it was about perception. We thought that because there were loads of staff and computers in London, that it was quite a big organization and they were being really snotty to us! Looking back, they were probably only about one step ahead in terms of being as shambolic as we were.'

As the team learnt, and *The Big Issue in the North* became a force to be reckoned with, frustrations increased. After its relatively short experience, London could teach the North nothing new. In fact, Manchester was proving that in a short time they would soon be showing London. Ruth and Anne asked John if he had any objections to them setting up their own company. John says:

> *'I didn't. They were more than capable to be their own people. We continued to support them financially and with editorial copy. But they needed a sense of ownership. Added to this, contact with them was proving tortuous. I though much of that would disappear. As to some extend it did.'*

So Ruth and Anne planned to go independent. Working with the vendors during the day, on the magazine at night, they spent the evenings with the accountants from the Co-operative Bank.

> *'We drew up a fictional business plan to keep John, the accountants and the bank happy, which showed that in the first year of trading as an independent operation we would need a £20,000 overdraft for cash flow purposes. So they asked us to put our houses on as collateral. At that stage, I was in a council flat in Salford and Anne was in a rented flat, so we said OK, fine, we don't own anything!'*

However, Ruth and Anne then did their real 'back of an envelope' business plan:

> *'We didn't think we needed an overdraft at all. Out of pride, we were determined that we would be ruthless about getting rid of two things. One was the volunteer, voluntary sector mentality which we had inherited from the charity in Manchester where we had been told that volunteers are a good thing. They just cost us time and money. Then we needed to get rid of London to start taking control of what we were doing.'*

It was for the best that the London office was too busy to help develop the fledgling *Big Issue in the North*, because it gave them that vital spirit and self-sufficiency. In April 1994 the independent edition was launched, and the company set up in February 1995. *The Big Issue in the North* had initial sales of 4000 per fortnight, sold in Manchester, then Liverpool, Leeds and throughout the North West. The circulation did not mushroom in Manchester as it had done in London or Glasgow. It has been a fight to sell every magazine, but the circulation has always steadily increased. Ruth says:

> 'We know where every extra hundred increase has come from. We have never suddenly sold an extra 4000. We know that's because of where we placed a vendor or because we did Granada TV news.'

In cities like Liverpool, for example, some customers earn little more than the vendors. Ruth believes that, as well as often not having a pound to spare, this makes people feel more judgemental about the vendors. They are closer to having to make those kind of moral choices themselves.

Ruth and Anne were very definite about not wanting to start a charity for the support services. However, the first time the business made a profit, about £4000, the company employed a vendor support worker, Joanne Moores, with a further grant of £10,000 from Crisis. The position was then changed to vendor development worker, signalling that the job was to move vendors on, rather than just support them.

Having received some money from a charitable trust, the trust discovered the magazine was not a charity. Ruth explains:

> 'We didn't realize we had to be a charity to get the money. Everyone – legal advisers, accountants, people from trusts, fundraisers – wanted us to turn The Big Issue in the North into a charity. Or set up a charity that could then own the magazine as a trading arm. And we just said no.'

They went down another road, setting up a charity reluctantly as a separate entity from the business. It was for tax purposes only, enabling them to apply for grants. The charity, originally called The Big Step (now called The Big Issue in the North Trust), would operate in a businesslike and entrepreneurial fashion, taking the business as its role model.

The Big Issue in the North has gone from strength to strength. In 1996 they had to move from their offices and received £150,000 of lottery money for a new building. But their present headquarters in Oldham Street cost £800,000 to buy and develop and much of the sum was raised by fundraiser Liam Black. In September 2000, they received a further £175,000 from the National Lottery to help fund refurbishments of the trust's new building in Leeds. This will house a GP and health unit as well as an employment training and IT unit for vendors.

In five years, the magazine has won awards, produced research studies on vendors and homeless people, created 66 full-time jobs and has an annual turnover of £1.5m. The magazine sells 54,000 every week. Since its inception, it has helped more than 6000 homeless people in 60 towns and cities across the North of England to earn a living. In 1999, Ruth and Anne were awarded the Ernst & Young Community Entrepreneur of the Year Award for the northern region. In the summer of 2000, Ruth Turner left to pursue other work, leaving Anne at the helm.

Ruth comments:

> 'We didn't know what a social entrepreneur was at the beginning. Years ago, I wrote policy documents about what type of business we wanted to be. I look at them now and think, "no we don't". That's not because we have given up on ideals, but because we were hidebound by certain models that we thought we ought to adopt. You just learn. Also, when you've done something, you look around and say, what next? Your horizons expand, what you think you can do expands, what the vendors tell you they want expands, so it just changes.'

THE BIG ISSUE SCOTLAND

Mel Young had bought a copy of the *The Big Issue* in London. At the time he was working in a publishing company and both he and Tricia had had experience of community work on housing estates. At their meetings with John in 1992 and at the beginning of 1993, they were asked to do a business plan. They then set up a separate company, *The Big Issue Scotland*. The agreement between the two companies was based solely on trust, something which John called a 'social franchise'. As *The Big Issue* had no spare money, Tricia and Mel raised money from various sources in Scotland, including Mercury Communications.

The speed with which the Scottish paper was set up proved that a businesslike approach based on short-circuiting the problems experienced by the London office was the key. They copied the formula; they had expertise in magazine production, but not in distribution and vendor support so they learnt these from the London office:

'We had been advised by people in London, although we didn't believe it, but of course it was right, that when you are doing a plan, you need to have your vendors ready.'

They visited hostels and went round the streets talking to people who were begging and sleeping rough. Mel remembers:

'They said to us. "Sounds OK. Where's the magazines?" "It'll be out in another month." "Could be dead by then," they replied. So it was all a bit hit or miss.'

Two or three days before the launch a dozen vendors were badged up in Edinburgh, where they were more organized but in Glasgow they were recruiting people off a bench and ended up with four.

The Big Issue Scotland was launched on 25 June 1993 as a fortnightly in both Glasgow and Edinburgh. Mel recalls:

'The launch went extremely well. We got really good PR out of it. We had the Lord Provost of Glasgow. John came up. It went like a dream. We'd been in touch with an advertising agency beforehand and some of our posters went up for free. So off we set and never looked back.'

But, similarly to the London experience, they were not prepared for the huge number of vendors and the volume of sales. They had not expected to sell more than 25,000 copies per fortnight, with around 120 vendors. The first 25,000 sold out immediately and the print run was increased a little on issue two.

Mel believes that the whole business could have imploded:

'Most businesses that go bust do so in the early days because they have overestimated their revenue and underestimated their costs. Our case was completely the other way round. We had

completely underestimated the potential revenue. So we had queues of vendors arriving in Glasgow to get badged up and we were continually running out of papers.'

By the fourth issue, they printed 50,000 (up from 40,000) but sold out in four days. Reprints were costly, but they eventually got the print run right. Mel says:

'In the very early days the Scottish people just took to it, just loved it. They have a real sense of fair play. They hate to see people homeless, so they were wanting to support homeless people. At the same time they like people doing things for themselves, particularly amongst men, it's a macho thing. It's actually against dependency. And for respect. So the whole philosophy of The Big Issue *appealed wonderfully to the Scots' psyche.'*

Because of mass poverty on the housing estates, in Glasgow there are many people on the streets. But there is a great community atmosphere, Mel says:

'You find this at Christmas time, it's staggering. Vendors get Christmas presents all the time. The vendors respond and give their customers Christmas cards. You see them going out with wads of cards all written to their customers.'

One year in Glasgow, a vendor brought in a box of chocolates as a Christmas present to the staff. Suddenly everyone was bringing them to the staff. Mel remembers:

'And we thought, what is going on here? And of course, they wanted to be part of Christmas. They were receiving things, but they didn't have anyone to give anything to, so they started to give us boxes of chocolates.'

Initially, there were four staff doing everything, working 18 hour days, seven day weeks. Tricia worked with the vendors and Mel edited the magazine but there were crossovers. John had originally wanted a pull-out Scottish supplement within the London edition. Mel, though, was sure that this would not work as the Scots would want their own editorial, reflecting their own Scottish mainstream media. And he was proved right.

They could learn from London's mistakes. Mel adds:

'We were in a wonderful situation because we were nearly two years behind London. But at that point, for our first three years, London were always ahead of us. If they made the mistake by perhaps going up a cul de sac, we could avoid it. That was the advantage of being in the group. We got a lot from that.'

The circulation grew continuously, peaking around 1997. The sales are now slightly down. There are a number of possible reasons for this, believes Mel, but nothing conclusive:

'Part of it is the drug problem. There are 12,000 injecting drug users here in Glasgow. We are sometimes associated with them in the public's mind, but we have managed to come through all that and are seen as part of the solution.'

Also, people used to buy the magazine more than once, but now only buy it once a week. He adds:

'I don't get the impression that there was a sort of burn out factor. It wasn't a fashion accessory up here like in London, so it hasn't gone out of fashion. We do get vendors who are selling still after seven years, so that is an issue. And it is not politics, either. It was not the election of a Labour government as we have always had Labour here in Scotland.'

The Big Issue Scotland also received lottery money for their Glasgow building. In the summer of 2000, they won the Journalist Team of the Year Award. Mel adds:

'In the commendation the judges said that The Big Issue in Scotland *was now a magazine which all other people had got to read. It set the agenda, groundbreaking, top in investigative journalism in Scotland. We have managed to create something new which people want to buy. Current affairs, social affairs. Now we have to sustain it.'*

The Big Issue South West

Five months after the launch in Scotland, *The Big Issue* made its first appearance in the West Country when vendors sold 200 copies of the London issue in their first week on the streets of Bath. It was originally an initiative of Shay Withnell and Bath City Centre Management (BCCM). BCCM was interested in the magazine as an alternative to begging. It was sold from the City Centre Manager's office, where Shay set up in the reception area.

The local supplement appeared at Christmas 1993. Nine months later, a distribution centre was opened in Bristol. Bath's circulation was to become one of the highest in the UK, relative to its population. Subsequently, they developed a presence in Taunton, Exeter, Plymouth and Bournemouth with drop-off points in Truro and Gloucester.

The Big Issue South West (TBISW) was set up as a company from the outset and launched as a separate edition in April 1995. Former editor and now MD of *The Big Issue* in London, Jeff Mitchell, remembers the launch:

> 'We were working with a local PR agency. We had lots of press coverage, and our sales went from 13,000 to 17,000, a 40 per cent rise, in one week. Between eight and ten pages of editorial and advertising was devoted to the South West. The reception was phenomenal and it reinforced the need for a regional approach that local communities can buy into.'

He concludes:

> 'Local journalists are not known for their insight into social issues and they were saying, "this is great, when are you going to be doing more?" And it's gone from strength to strength. We have become more confident in what we are trying to do with the magazine, so that in any week we could do a special edition on a South West topic. More recently still, we have done more scoops, more investigations, exclusives. With the rates that we can pay journalists we can expect them to be quality and well-researched articles that would be worthy of a national Sunday paper.'

TBISW Jeff believes, has great potential to achieve positive change in the South West. Like Wales, there is the issue of rural homelessness to contend with:

> 'When we started, there was a lot of begging and street homelessness in Plymouth, for example. I think now most towns throughout the region have some visible effect of homelessness. There are different kinds of problems created by the drift into market towns like Taunton, which were ill-equipped to deal with an influx from rural areas. Whereas people might have gravitated towards London say, 15 years ago, and London has got the economy of scale to provide a number of services, that doesn't happen in somewhere like Taunton or Barnstaple in Devon.'

TBISW's coverage is not comprehensive enough to have a presence in all these towns. But they are endeavouring to keep an overview of developments for future action. At the moment round 350 vendors sell from seven West Country offices in Gloucester, Truro, Bournemouth, Exeter and Plymouth, with the main offices in Bath and Bristol. From there the vendors travel out to small towns, such as St Ives or Stroud.

The South West has a large transient population, mainly because of festivals and travellers. Travellers follow the traditional routes that either end in Bournemouth, Plymouth or Cornwall. Also, organizations such as the Soil Assocation, Triodos Bank in Bristol, the Ethical Property Company and cycling and transport lobbies are based in the region. Thus, the character of the South West is influenced by this predominance of social responsibility and environmentalism. This has partially shaped TBISW's current philosophy. As Jeff says:

> 'We are TBISW, a social business; ethical concerns are our concerns. All the subjects that we have covered in the past – Shell, Nestlé, McDonald's – now surely, this is the time to bring them to the fore of what we are fundamentally about as an organization.'

TBISW has started a new contract publishing project called Streetwise Publishing which will operate differently from other companies. Jeff explains:

'It is going to take an ethical approach. It won't be "commission us to produce your annual reports because the money will go homeless people", although that is where the profits will go. It's going to have an 11-point ethical charter attached to it, stating what we believe in and stand for, environmental concerns and social regeneration, for example.'

They will not be working with anyone with a questionable ethical record. In the long term, they are looking at whether the Big Issue Foundation can be involved in setting up placements for employment and training. At the time of writing, Streetwise Publishing was looking for support to get it going, a grant rather than investment. Jeff was concerned about investing money from the core business in case it went wrong. He is hoping to work with Aspire, the social business employing homeless people to sell goods from catalogues, also based in Bristol.[2] Jeff says:

'They have got something that we haven't had yet in terms of wrapping up a complete business system that still manages to fulfil a social brief.'

THE BIG ISSUE CYMRU

In May 1994, *The Big Issue* was launched in Wales, first in Cardiff then later in Swansea. On the first day there were six vendors in Cardiff selling the London edition. It had a local eight page supplement, and in the first week 1875 magazines were sold. *The Big Issue Cymru* was started by Su West and a group of volunteers in an office donated by Cardiff City Council. Su recalls:

'I wrote to The Big Issue *in London saying I was in Cardiff, doing a social work course, and that we should set up* The Big Issue *here. This must have been around the end of '92. I got the response 'go ahead and do it, we haven't got any resources, no one knew how long it was going to last. Great idea, off you go!"*

John remembers the difficulties too:

'I went down to meet with Su in Cardiff to talk about the expansion. At the time we were supporting the North, and Brighton. It was the same old story. A lack of time and funds meant we

*could not stretch ourselves. Su's tenacity kept the idea alive and
the launch was a great success.'*

The Big Issue Cymru was run entirely on volunteers for a year. Su
remembers:

> *'The money that we started with was various bits and pieces
> from charitable trusts and companies. We only had a couple of
> thousand pounds in the bank when we started. Cardiff City
> Council gave us space in the Housing Help Centre and allowed
> us to use their premises. When we launched we just got cheap
> premises across the road. The money was just coming in and
> going out the next day in terms of rent and printing costs. So
> we never had any substantial money. It was always hand to
> mouth.'*

Sales increased with each issue after the launch and by mid 1995,
14,000 copies a fortnight were being sold. By this time they could
afford to put the four staff on a salary. Demand for greater Welsh
content increased, and the sales were high enough to warrant an
independent 32 page edition, which was launched at the end of
July 1995. However, *The Big Issue Cymru* has constantly battled
with the difficulty of not having enough resources. Wales is probably the most geographically disadvantaged of all Big Issues. Su
says:

> *'The population of Wales is tiny compared to the whole of the
> UK. A large percentage of the population of Wales is based in
> Cardiff, so in terms of expansion and places to grow – like there
> are all these untapped areas in the South East that* Big Issue
> London *can move into – we've exhausted them. We've got
> Newport, Cardiff and Swansea, the three biggest areas.'*

Cardiff only works with around 40 vendors at a time. This has
meant the involvement of *The Big Issue* in London in helping
Wales to become self-sustaining. John Bird comments:

> *'Wales is the most difficult area for* The Big Issue. *Therefore we
> have had to offer it more support. However hard they work, they
> have this problem of a vast area, a destroyed industrial
> landscape. And a poorer urban community.'*

The Big Issue Cymru has a presence in north and mid Wales, but the returns are minimal and the business cannot afford it. But they are areas of great need. As Su maintains:

> *'We work with only six vendors in Aberystwyth, for example, but there is absolutely no other service provision, so there is the argument – if we pull out, what happens there? It's not a perceived need, it's rural, it's hidden, with no other provision and we are quite often dealing with people who really are the bottom of the ladder.'*

There are offices in Newport, in Bangor and in Aberystwyth (in north Wales) as well as satellite distribution places. A record shop in Wrexham, a tattoo parlour in Llandudno and an independent record shop in Haverford West have all distributed *The Big Issue* but they tend to come and go.

The situation in Wales highlights the hidden problem of rural homelessness. Su explains:

> *'To be mobile in these areas is the answer. There is also a lot of work to be done raising awareness. Many homeless people are forced to leave areas where there is a lack of provision and non-local homeless people aren't as welcome.'*

The challenge is also the size of the area they are working in. Su says:

> *'We are working with less resources than anywhere else, yet we need more resources because we are working up and down the country and we need to employ staff in these remote areas. But we are not getting the sales to back it up, so there are a lot of people working in isolation, with a higher staff turnover.'*

Currently, the circulation is around 13,000 a week and the magazine is popular with the public. With the arrival of the Welsh Assembly, Su and co-director Alex Hinds have been active in campaigning. 'In 1998, we launched a group called Rough Sleepers Cymru , consisting of ourselves, Shelter,[3] the Cyrenians and a couple of other organizations. The Welsh Assembly was now running and it was a good time to start lobbying, asking why we hadn't had money for rough sleepers in Wales.'

The Welsh Assembly has been very receptive both to the group and to the problem of homelessness. It has announced funding for homeless projects in Wales. It leads Britain in tackling homelessness after members voted in the summer of 2000 to extend the categories of homeless people in priority need to care leavers, 16–18 year olds, people fleeing violence, and people leaving prison or the armed forces.

AROUND THE COUNTRY

Editions were also tried in the Midlands and Newcastle, carrying four fifths of London copy and eight pages of regional copy. These 'metro' editions were managed from the London office. By 1994, the Midlands area was covered by the opening of a distribution office in Birmingham, now run by Mair Edmunds and Bob Tulk. A year later a distribution point was opened in East Anglia in Norwich, run by Jim Graver.

The Big Issue's north eastern edition started in Newcastle in 1995, as a joint venture between London and Scotland. This has always proved a difficult spot and sales have been erratic. Sales were originally projected at 30,000 a week but never went beyond 10,000. Vendors were not allowed to sell in the huge shopping mall outside the city where potential readers could be accessed. The experience has proved different from London, Manchester or Glasgow. Paul Felts, from the London office, was sent to Newcastle when the edition launched and remembers:

> 'I went round to all these young people and said, "if you sell this magazine you get 50p for every copy you sell". And they all went, "Why?" "Because then you'll have loads of money." "But that'll take all day. No mate, I might as well just go and steal a car." It was a poor area. Most of the vendors up there were jack the lads who can make a fortune doing other things. If only we could channel what those guys were doing on the streets into proper jobs. They'd probably make a really good living on the stock exchange floor, they can bullshit! It was funny to see how* The Big Issue *was received up there.'

By 1996, *The Big Issue*'s presence in Britain seemed almost total. The national ABC sales figures for November 1996 were a healthy 258,263, and the national NRS figure for July 1995–June 1996 showed 825,000 people across the UK were reading it. However, there were, and are, still many towns where there are homeless people but no *Big Issue* distribution points. The challenge has always been how to balance the costs of a distribution centre with the income from sales. The cost of rent and staff when sales are not high enough has to be weighed up: solutions are either to partner with another organization working with homeless people in an existing office, or to encourage homeless people to pick up the magazines from the nearest centre.

Steve Lawrie, circulation and sales manager for London and the southern region in the London office, started with *The Big Issue* in Brighton. He comments that *The Big Issue* overstretched itself in the past, opening offices with three or four year leases, without knowing whether they were going to sell enough magazines there:

> *'And three or four years down the line we found that we weren't and couldn't sustain that. We have actually got to a point in the last year when we have had to draw things in, consolidate what we have got and think about the whole area.'*

Southampton is an example, Steve continues:

> *'I ended up managing Southampton, an office which opened in September 1997. But people hadn't taken account of the fact that people who were selling in Southampton had been coming to Brighton to buy the magazines. So we actually lost a lot of sales out of Brighton. We had opened Southampton on the basis that we would sell 7500 magazines, but it has never sold more than 3500. So it was completely overstretched.'*

The lease on the office in Southampton was not renewed. In effect, the London office had committed itself to managing offices in the regions without having the ability to do it. Now, it has learnt lessons and has consolidated, putting in place clear management and structures and some of the satellite offices now manage their own regions.

Partnering with other organizations, such as day centres or homeless foyers, does work. Steve says:

'The new way of looking at it is that we need to cut back on our costs. We want to give people the opportunity to sell the magazine, and we also want to provide other services. The ideal thing is to go to places like day centres, or hostels that already have resettlement workers, drug and alcohol counsellors, the whole set up. We work with them, rent some space and sell the magazine from there. And our vendors will still get the support that they need.'

As well as the support work they need people to sell the magazines and do cash reconciliations each day. Steve remarks:

'By and large it's been OK, but there's been hiccups. We partner largely with day centres. There's the foyer project in the Isle of Wight, Winter Comfort in Cambridge and a church organization running a day centre for homeless people in Peterborough.'

BRIGHTON

The situation in Brighton has changed over the last seven years. The sales are significantly down, at least one third less in the year 2000 from 1998. From a peak of 13–14,000 a week, they are now selling 6500–7000. But, as Steve says:

'There are the same numbers of vendors. Brighton as a town has been exhausted by The Big Issue. *It has seen vendors come and go. It has a reputation for having lots of vendors for the size of the town.'*

One reason, like Glasgow, is that the vendors have particular types of problems, some of which members of the public are not going to be sympathetic with. In 1999, Brighton had one of the highest number of deaths due to drug abuse. Steve adds:

'Thirty-nine people died from heroin overdoses alone. We knew 24 of them, and they had been vendors. A lot of vendors go to Brighton for the same reason everyone else goes – it's a nice place to go to. They go down for the lifestyle, the environment, the sea, especially in the summer. In a week in winter we might badge up five or six, in a week in the summer maybe 30 or 40.

> *'Secondly, there used to be a travellers' community, but that packed up and went. The travellers were good sellers and used to cover towns around the area, like Tunbridge Wells, Portsmouth and Hastings, keeping the circulation up. So now we are back with people only selling in Brighton. The sales also go up around Christmas and when it is colder, so the sales balance out. If you've got ten vendors in town you're probably not selling any more if you've got 50, because public sympathy doesn't increase because there are more vendors, it just means the money is spread more thinly.'*

Five staff work in the Brighton office as well as a whole team of volunteers. They do everything from working behind the counter to mentoring and literacy courses for vendors. Brighton has always worked strongly on the creative side and has a vibrant writers group, run and developed by Neil Ansell, who is the manager of the office and also writes for *The Big Issue*. A computer project for the vendors has been running since the beginning of 2000 and provides access to computer technology for those who normally would not have the opportunity, with PCs and almost constant internet access.

IRELAND

A partnership was established in Ireland between *The Big Issue* and a group in Dublin, led by Niall Skelly and *Big Issues* was launched in June 1994. Originally sold by both the homeless and unemployed in the capital and towns across Ireland, the magazine's circulation rose quickly to around 40,000 per fortnight. However, the model created in Ireland didn't catch the imagination of the people in the same way as in the UK. When the Irish economy went into a huge uplift from the mid 1990s, with unemployment substantially decreasing, it did not keep pace with the changing situation. Now called *Issues*, it is sold mostly by refugees across Ireland, providing hundreds of socially excluded people with a financial lifeline. But there is no relationship between the new magazine and *The Big Issue* in the UK.

The Big Issue proudly notes that it is the only national media organization, apart from the BBC, with offices up and down the country. Its experience has much to teach social businesses. The principle lesson has been that 'stand alone' offices work better than expansion from a central office. This has been Gordon and John's philosophy with the development of the social franchise. *The Big Issue* could never have successfuly expanded beyond its own areas without local partners.

6

THE FOUNDATION AND SUPPORT SERVICES

'IT IS MUCH easier to get people out of the street, than it is to get the street out of people.'

LAUNCH OF THE BIG ISSUE FOUNDATION

Until 1995, the support services for vendors were financed by an annual donation from *The Big Issue* with additional contributions coming from the corporate sector and other charities and foundations. But there came a point when the business was unable to fund all the support services it wished to offer in order to help vendors move on.

There were early discussions on launching a Foundation but, originally, Lucie Russell maintains, they were very anti-charity because *The Big Issue* was about business and self-help; they had to ask themselves why they were going to set up a charity when traditionally it was against all those things *The Big Issue* was striving to overcome – handouts and the dependency culture.

But the need for a Foundation became more apparent. It was difficult to fundraise for a business. Lucie Russell was going to charitable trusts, requesting money for a training unit or to develop the housing team and, when trusts saw that *The Big Issue* was a business, asked why the company could not fund these support services itself. The needs had to be explained over and over again. The trusts, though, had a point. A traditional business would have put money aside for such activities, or would only have allocated funds as and when they became available. But *The Big Issue* had to date either invested in the business or had supported the fledgling support services. *The Big Issue* was dealing with hundreds of people every day who needed an instant network of support and access to training and jobs. Staff working in the support work needed more finance available for their work. Therefore, the non-commercial support work was being held back by funding constraints.

The decision was made to keep the magazine as a business and to launch a charity arm. All profits from the business would subsequently be gift aided to The Big Issue Foundation,[1] and a fundraiser would be brought in to raise the necessary funds for the support services. There would also be tax advantages to having a charity. Thus, The Big Issue Foundation was launched in the House of Commons in November 1995. It consolidated all the support services – vendor support, the housing unit, drug and alcohol workers, a mental health worker, Jobs, Education and Training (JET) and the writing group. The Foundation operates across London and the South East, East Anglia, the Midlands, the South West, the North East and Wales. *The Big Issue in the North* and *The Big Issue Scotland* developed their own charity arms.

There is an overt, unresolved tension between the business and the charity. The business continuously tries to maximize sales, bringing in as much revenue as possible. Vendors are encouraged to sell as many papers as possible, not only to maximize their own incomes but to keep the whole operation going. Some vendors in prime pitches are very good salespeople. If they move on to jobs or training, which is what the Foundation encourages, then the pitch has to be filled quickly in order not to lose sales.

This was highlighted in Wales, recalls founder Su West:

> *'In September 1998, 13 of our vendors went back into full time education, meeting our objectives of moving on. They had built up the confidence to go back, they had developed skills and a work ethic. But they were also our best vendors. We lost 30 per cent of our sales. So it was difficult to weigh up: business versus move on.'*

Rory Gillert, deputy chief executive of the Foundation, sums up the conflict between the commercial imperative on the one hand and care and support on the other:

> *'If the company's financial health is dependent primarily on the sales of the paper sold by homeless people, and the advertising of the magazine, then in effect the financial health of the company is held to ransom by fluctuating factors, the fluctuating homeless population for example.'*

When in a time of financial difficulty, the pressure on the staff to increase sales becomes greater, then it is more likely that, for example, people will be badged up inappropriately. He adds:

> *'They are not homeless, or it is questionable whether they are, or people who are very young and vulnerable are badged up, and the last thing you should do for them is to put them out to sell a paper. So if the sales are going down, what are you going to do to get them back up? Whereas it might be a good thing if the sales are going down because the support staff might be doing a great job in moving people on.'*

The conflict between the business and charity is also reflected in the different methods of working with the vendors in London: those in distribution and sales work on the business side and do not necessarily have experience of working with homeless people whereas those on the support side are professionally trained support workers. It has created a division. An example of this is given by Steve Lawrie. When jobs were advertised for, say, cashiers (staff selling magazines to vendors) the advertisement asked for 'some experience in dealing with homeless people, a caring attitude, ideas about how to work with other agencies as referral'. He says:

> *'But what actually happened was that the people who ended up coming in became fed up with the job, because all they wanted to do, especially in London, was serve papers over the counter. The Foundation did all the support work. So we ended up changing the job ads saying "the ideal example of the type of job would be working behind a busy bar on a Saturday night". But that's not right either, because it means that the kind of people*

*you get in aren't interested in working with the Foundation and
talking about vendors needs. It's a difficult balance.'*

Then, there is the conflict that sometimes occurs between editorial coverage in the magazine and the Foundation work, for example writing a profile of a vendor who had been selling *The Big Issue* for a number of years. As editor Matthew Collin explains:

*'We have to realize that the Foundation does have work to do
which long term is much more important than a single story.
We write a story and move onto another story next week. The
Foundation has to deal with long-term consequences. We have a
very good relationship with the Foundation. When we are covering those sorts of things, we always let them see it because it
could affect their work.'*

This conflict is also visible to outside organizations. For David Warner, former CEO of Homeless Network, the tension need not necessarily be a problem. Maybe, *The Big Issue* is at the cutting edge of, or the merging of, the private and voluntary sector into a quasi-voluntary-private sector. He says:

*'In terms of the rest of the world it stands out very starkly as an
oddity and therefore working within it there must be quite a
tension managing the different, and ultimately conflicting,
demands of the two sides of the equation.'*

There was also an argument for not setting up a foundation at all. Former *Big Issue* head of fundraising, Lynn O'Donoghue, remembers:

'When I was at Homeless Network I said to The Big Issue *do
not set up a charity, you don't need to… There are already 200
registered charities in London. Why do you want to employ
people when you can contract with others. For instance,
Centrepoint or London Connection could come into your offices
and deliver services to homeless people.'*

But she concedes that at that point *The Big Issue* was not tapped into the homelessness scene and:

'We decided that where we identified a demand, we called it a need. So a demand for something turned into a need for our services. We automatically decided to provide a service. It is because when we set up nobody understood homelessness and the homeless sector in London, and did not realize that other organizations could come in. We do an awful lot of duplicating.'

A survey of vendors was conducted in 1996 and Lynn states that they discovered that 80 per cent of vendors were tapping into other services anyway. There have been two surveys commissioned by *The Big Issue* to find out from vendors about their circumstances and whether they use the Foundation's services. These two surveys have helped with formulating the move-on policies and were also important in showing how the vendor base had changed during the 1990s.

The first was conducted by consultant Kath Dane,[2] an independent researcher and specialist in homelessness issues, and was funded by the Barings Foundation. Kath interviewed 100 vendors, randomly selected from the 400 or so active London vendors, over four months in the latter part of 1996. She looked at demographic information about the vendors, identifying their support needs, and finding out the level of uptake and satisfaction with the support services offered by *The Big Issue*. The survey represented around 25 per cent of the vendors regularly selling in London at any one time and was therefore considered a representative cross section.

It showed that the circumstances of the vendors had changed substantially since *The Big Issue* was set up in 1991. Most of the vendors were now staying in temporary accommodation, hostels, bed and breakfasts or squats, whereas in 1991 they had been rough sleepers. This had partly been the result of the RSI. Lucie Russell said, responding to the report:

'There is now a problem with the "hidden homeless" who, because of changes in local authority housing, are increasingly being pushed into temporary accommodation. When you look at the standard of some of the places our vendors are in, sometimes the street looks like the better option.'

More significantly, the most positive outcome of the survey was that selling *The Big Issue* had a profound effect on people's lives, by giving them a sense of independence and self-respect. The two main benefits of vending were earning an income and meeting people.

> 'Many vendors described the significance of being able to talk with people from all different backgrounds and lifestyles as an opportunity that they would not have anywhere else. These clients were often described as "friends" or "regulars". Some vendors reported how they were needed by their regulars and missed when they took time off from vending. The importance of this social contact and breakdown of the isolation that is often an adverse effect of being homeless cannot be underestimated.'[3]

This worked both ways between vendors and the public. Actor Maureen Lipman tells of how she could always rely on finding out what her daughter was up to through chatting to her local vendor. 'She always told him what she was doing', Maureen recalls.

The majority of vendors said that their financial situation had improved and over 60 per cent said their confidence had gone up and they felt more independent.

Whilst the survey confirmed what everyone believed, that *The Big Issue* was doing what it had set out to do, it also pointed out that five years on the issue of move-on needed to be readdressed. John Bird commented:

> 'There are signs that people are getting clogged in our system and it is incredibly difficult to resolve this. I was encouraged by the fact that there was no surprises. It confirmed a lot of our gut feelings. We still haven't got it right. We recognize that we are part of the problem as well as part of the solution and we're not going to gloss over that. Having the honesty to face up to those problems is the first step towards solving them.'

The second survey during the annual rebadging of vendors at the beginning of 1999[4] was a more in-depth study of the vendor profile. It also showed that more vendors were accessing the support offered by the Foundation at about 40 per cent. The survey also identified that more Western and Eastern European people were now selling *The Big Issue*.

MOVE-ON – THE ARGUMENTS

The Big Issue can only work with people initially motivated enough to sell the magazine. Not all homeless people are able to do so, due to mental health or other problems. And even then some do not manage to reintegrate or move on.

One of David Warner's criticisms is that *The Big Issue* initially simplified the complexity of the debate, although people subsequently did acknowledge that the problems weren't just ones of lacking accommodation. He says:

> *'By making the case that the vast majority of vendors were sleeping on the streets, it made it appear that their only problem was lack of accommodation, that they were all entrepreneurs and able to get up and go. Whereas the reality was quite different. There were still probably a good 20 per cent of those on the streets at that time who were very damaged, confused and difficult individuals.'*

But this is a criticism he would make not only of *The Big Issue*, but of a number of other high profile organizations. They present complex issues very simply and therefore the message gets lost. The issue of street sleepers, who are only a minority of the homeless, is an example.

> *'I think all of us have been guilty to a greater or lesser extent in perpetuating some of those myths because they make easy messages, easy soundbites, easy campaigns. It's a good fundraising campaign to do hundreds of mailshots saying there are hundreds of people on the streets every night, and that you are the only organization doing anything about it. And what that creates in the public perception is that that is the only homelessness problem.'*

As the company expanded and the Foundation became established, a certain amount of formality took over. The numbers coming into the London office were huge. Many vendors remarked on the change and Lucie comments:

> *'I used to know every vendor. Everybody had a chat with everyone. Everyone helped each other out. It was like a big club and*

*family, very supportive. Now what the vendors say is that they
don't know the staff and the staff are too busy to sit and chat.'*

More and more members of the public are still commenting that
their local vendor has been selling for years and ask why have
they not moved on. If a vendor moves into accommodation and
has rent and bills to pay, income from selling *The Big Issue* cannot
simply be cut off. It would create an immediate financial crisis.
The Foundation has continuously grappled with the process of
how people move on and stop becoming dependent on selling
the magazine. It is a very complex issue and each individual is
different. Should the policy be flexible and individually tailored
for each vendor? Or should vendors only be allowed to sell for a
specific period of time and then have to move on? Can all vendors
move on and is it possible, for instance, for a 55 year old ex-
homeless man with drink problems to move into a full-time job?

All the *Big Issues* and regional offices have tried and tested
different methods of move-on over the years. In London, vendors
have always been able to stay as long as they wished. At *The Big
Issue in the North*, there is a strict and monitored time limit. *The
Big Issue Scotland* is similar to London, but has just initiated a new
policy in Glasgow in response to the drug problem (see p151). *The
Big Issue Cymru* has a less strict time limit than the North, and *The
Big Issue South West* tried the time limit, but changed back to a
more flexible approach. In London, after nine years , the move-on
policy is changing. *The Big Issue* is now being advocated as a
stepping stone, as opposed to a career path, for those who are able
to move on.

Staff in *The Big Issue* have had, over the years, many different
ideas as to what should constitute move-on. These opinions have
helped formulate the flexible policy. So what is the definition of
successful move-on? Lucie maintains:

*'I always say that someone who cuts down on their drinking
after 30 years, that's as much a move-on as getting a house or a
flat or a job. For that person that is the biggest thing that they
have done in their whole lives.'*

Patrick Dennis believes that when someone comes in through the
door of *The Big Issue* that is a huge achievement in itself. They
have decided to do something. Patrick's philosophy is twofold.

He believes the staff can provide people with options. He says:

> *'If people want to use the paper as a stepping stone to get to a*
> *particular place, a place of stability, that is OK. If, on the other*
> *hand, you come into* The Big Issue *and see it as a full-time job*
> *then that is OK also.'*

It is how the particular individual sees their solution and, either way, he says they are not going to be burden on the tax payer.

Robyn Heaton, former manager of JET, believes it is very difficult to have a blanket policy. Selling, she believes, needs to be tapered off. She doesn't believe that people should be selling *The Big Issue* four years after being housed. However, there are the exceptions – the people who either through their age or ill health will be unable to get a formal job. They supplement their income so they can have decent food to eat by selling *The Big Issue*. *The Big Issue* has to recognize there are always those who could never move on.

Then, there are those who are not employable, or who get a job but cannot hold it down. Many are no longer committing crimes and are keeping themselves out of prison. If they were back in prison, it would be costing the state thousands of pounds per year.

The choices for move-on exist. But, as vendor Jon Gregg admits:

> *'If you are left to your own devices it is the easiest thing in the*
> *world to come into the office, pick up your papers and get out,*
> *putting off sorting your problems until tomorrow, next week or*
> *next month.'*

Jon sees many of the old faces still around who have not got themselves much further forward. He thinks that it is a shame because, he believes, more vendors could move on than have:

> *'It's very tricky, because the whole hypothesis of* The Big Issue
> *is self-help. They don't force vendors to do anything. The help is*
> *there if people want it and you couldn't ask for a better place to*
> *come to if you needed help with drug and alcohol problems. But*
> *because they let vendors do it in their own time, some will take*
> *longer than others. If people seriously worked their pitches they*
> *could get quite a long way in six months.'*

Mel Hooper, who worked for five years in sales support, saw many people simply disappear, only to return at a later date. Many go into hospital or prison and then come back. There is a group of vendors who have been selling *The Big Issue* from the very beginning. They are people who personally know John, and when *The Big Issue* started it was an immediate answer to what they needed. He says:

> *'I think they are the hardest group. All of them are contradictions. You couldn't move them on. It would be heart-breaking to say to people that's it. They started from a different premise. What are you going to tell Alfie?'*

Alfie, now 76, sold the *Evening News* before being called up in April 1943. As a member of the Pioneer Corps at the age of 19, he was one of the 156,000 troops taking part in the D Day allied invasion in the summer of 1944. Both his parents were killed in January 1944 by German bombs in Islington. When he came back from the war, he had nowhere to go. Anna Moore wrote in *The Big Issue*:[5]

> *'According to* Falling Out *[see Chapter 4, p81], "70 per cent of the servicemen surveyed said they'd suffered physical or mental health problems including depression, stress and nerves, and over one third had never managed to settle". Alfie had no "post-trauma counselling, no careers advice, no professional help". He never settled. On his return, he went back to selling papers.*
>
> *'He "stayed with friends" for the next 50 years. He never married, retired in 1989 and started selling* The Big Issue *in 1992. He'd been spending his nights walking up and down the Strand, refusing to lie down, and he'd been mugged three times. "I see people in the doorways fast asleep, but you wouldn't catch me lying there", he said. "London's a madhouse now".'*

He now sells at Highbury and Islington tube station and was pictured in *The Big Issue* cutting the cake with John Bird at the magazine's ninth birthday party in September 2000. 'I sold three hundred of that issue,' he remembers. 'All my regular customers wanted copies, especially the women!'

It is important to catch people before they get into bad habits on the street, asserts Mel Hooper. She says:

'Particularly with younger people who are not used to being homeless, you can see their demise quite quickly. Within three or four months they look like hell. They've got a habit. They're culturally suddenly in a situation where they are meeting all these people they've never met before. Everything's available and we've given them revenue. If you don't catch people as they come in, especially younger people, then it is more damaging for them to stay here longer. I think they get caught in a culture that can take them down a slippery slope quite quickly.'

Drugs

Drugs are now a major problem on the streets, something which was not so pronounced when *The Big Issue* started. It is currently one of the biggest challenges for organizations working with homeless people. John Bird commented in the ninth birthday editorial in September 2000:

'Now our streets are awash with cheap, readily available narcotics. Today, the new people who come to start selling The Big Issue *show signs of neglect unparalleled in the past. Drugs have brought such damage to street-people that it has rewritten the problem for us.'*

He called for all the agencies to work together to fight this pernicious influence and continued:

'Most drug users have homes and jobs. It is easier to hold down a habit if you are in secure surroundings. But if you have drug problems and live on the streets, then it is to the streets that you bring that problem. Unless we can tackle the increasing social dislocation that drugs bring, then we are fighting with one hand tied behind our back.'

The drugs problem was one of the issues raised at the Vendor Working Group, set up in September 2000. Vendor Jim Lawrie was adamant that:

'One of the biggest problems is that of drugs and alcohol. It's not a very nice subject but it has got to be faced because there is

*so much rubbish thrown around about it. Now let's hit back,
which means that we can take that question on through the
pages of* The Big Issue.'

He argues that the drugs problem must be openly discussed. Also,
the public must understand how people have got into such
problems and he says:

*'We've also got to be honest with ourselves – are people using
the magazine to feed a habit? Some are.'*

An important impact on crime from the police's point of view is
that *The Big Issue* has employed drug counsellors or made referrals. As Inspector Steve Dyer[6] remarks:

*'Much statistical information today suggests that a lot of street
crime is drug-related, so anything that can be done to break the
cycle of dependency on drugs is, of course, most productive.'*

Because of potentially dangerous situations, there is an obvious
fear amongst police officers when they are dealing with people
who are mentally ill. Michelle Benham, formerly *The Big Issue*'s
mental health worker, spoke to students who were training to be
police officers. Michelle explained about reading signs and
symptoms. Basic things, like adopting non-threatening postures,
are often something lacking in police training.

Steve Dyer's gut feeling is that *The Big Issue* has had an impact
on crime figures in London, but there are not enough statistics to
back this opinion up. Kath Dane's survey found that vending
broke the cycle of crime. Many vendors said that since vending,
they had stopped all criminal activities such as begging, theft and
robbery. Some said that vending was the only legal means that
they had ever had of making money. It also had an indirect effect.
According to Westminster Safer Cities Project, *The Big Issue* helped
cut crime. The Project talked to police officers who confirmed that
the public feels safer with vendors around and that *Big Issue*
sellers often act as witnesses to wrongdoing.[7]

London's Services

Currently in London only, a more comprehensive induction programme is being established. Lucie explains:

> 'There will be four half hour inductions. You can't get a temporary badge until you've gone to the second one, and the full badge until you've been to the fourth one. They will explain how to sell the magazine, but also how to access the Foundation services. This will be followed up with regular reviews.
>
> 'This is saying we aim to have helped people move on within two years. No compulsion, but we will do everything we can to do that. We will be saying to people when they come in, this is not for ever. I have always felt that it isn't wrong that selling The Big Issue *is a job for some people. But there are others who could do so much more.'*

The next stage is to set up smaller offices around London which staff believe will provide a better service to the vendors. It has already worked well at the satellite office in Clapham, South London, which opened in the summer of 1997. Situated near the railway station, it provides easy access to those vendors in the South and West of London. The office has the advantage of having a small number of vendors with whom the staff can work on a one-to-one basis. The King's Cross office was sold at the end of 2000 (see page 208), and the company moved to Vauxhall in South London. King's Cross, in North London, was a difficult area for vendors who had to run the gauntlet of drug dealers in the short distance between the station and the office.

The nature of the support services in London probably does not differ much from other agencies. There is no pressure to use the services, although vendors are encouraged to do so. Vendors will never be 'clients', nor will they be 'service users'.

Unlike in Manchester, the London office has always, despite requests from vendors, decided against providing such services as showers. It is partly to do with lack of space, but mainly because there are so many other day centres providing that service. *The Big Issue* did not want to develop a 'day centre' culture, where people would hang around all day. The purpose of *The Big Issue* was to get out and sell. It also wanted to limit the duplication that is so preponderant in the homeless sector.

Manchester is poorly served with services for homeless people and there is a logic to creating a one-stop shop there.

The Vendor Services Team (VST), managed by Fiona Kirkman, provides housing advice and referral to emergency, temporary and permanent accommodation. It also offers resettlement support and welfare rights advice. There are referrals to specialist agencies on a range of issues including alcohol, drug and mental health issues.

For the past three years, generic support workers have been employed who have a knowledge of drug and alcohol issues, and housing, and can refer people on, under the umbrella of the Vendor Services. In 1999, *The Big Issue* worked with over 1000 vendors of whom at least 600 used the Foundation's services. The team helped to rehouse 120 people and helped 220 to secure specific drug, alcohol or psychiatric help.

Since Crisis research has suggested that 23 per cent of the homeless people who die each year take their own lives, other staff who work with vendors are equipped to deal with mental health problems. Befriending people, listening to them and allowing them to talk is a vital part of the work of the Foundation. The Samaritans gave all the foundation staff in London a training course in crisis intervention and basic counselling skills. The training included working with people suffering from minor depression right through to those who were suicidal. Training with the Samaritans was extended to include area development workers, vendors who represent and assist all the vendors in their local areas.

The violence expressed towards homeless people on the streets sometimes results in murder. Violence between street people themselves, combined with the ill health that they suffer due to drug and alcohol addiction, has resulted in the deaths of hundreds of homeless people throughout the country, many of whom have sold *The Big Issue*. Many have only been in their twenties and thirties.

Ill health is the biggest killer when it comes to those *Big Issue* vendors who have died. Kenny had been the first vendor to receive a flat from the Key Issue Appeal (see page 130) in 1994. A popular Scotsman who sold *The Big Issue* around the Oxford Street area for years, he died on 10 March 1998. He was in his early fifties. His friend, Mary, also a vendor, remembers him:

'Little Kenny was a great friend. I was really sorry when he died because he was like a daddy to everybody. If you had any problems, you could come and cry on his shoulder. But he never came and cried on anybody else's. He must have had problems himself... I went to the memorial service. There were quite a lot of people there. At the pub on the corner, the fellow put on a nice spread after the memorial.'

Big Issue staff and vendors attended his funeral and a bench was erected in Cavendish Square, near his pitch, by the nurses who treated him in hospital. This reflected the deep friendships that have occurred between the general public and vendors. Anne O'Donnell, who had been a vendor before becoming a part-time typist in the editorial department, also died suddenly in 1998. Many who have died have their farewells put on the Street Lights pages of *The Big Issue*.

Vendor services offers a resettlement package, visiting a new tenant for up to six months after they have moved in. It is difficult keeping some people in their flats once they have moved in and the proportion of people going back onto the streets is quite high. And this is not only at *The Big Issue*. This has not been resolved by any organization. Dee Meertins, former housing manager, explains:

'Lots of people whom we have housed are back out. They'll do the circuit, hostels, squats, street. They can't maintain a tenancy. You wonder whether you are not giving them enough support, or it is the fact that they weren't ready in the first place.'

The numbers and demands of the vendors seeking housing has changed over the years. By 1998, the percentage seeing the housing team was smaller than previously but was still mostly single vendors, between 25 and 40 years old. With the RSI taking hundreds off the streets, more were in hostels, squats or some form of temporary accommodation so there was not such an urgency. The problem still exists. But with temporarily accommo- dated people becoming the biggest group visiting the housing team it becomes a harder task to move them into more permanent accommodation.

The Key Issue Appeal, an initiative between *The Big Issue* and the Notting Hill Housing Trust[8] (NHHT) was launched in October

1994. It was initially supposed to run for one year but was extended and was targeted at single homeless people. The NHHT had a number of one-bedroom flats which needed improvements at a cost of approximately £25,000 per flat. The appeal was launched for £400,000 in order to renovate around 15 flats over 12 months. *The Big Issue* then nominated vendors to become NHHT tenants. An additional benefit was to the young unemployed, who were employed by the contractors to train in the building trade. The initiative contributed to urban regeneration through improving the flats and established a blueprint that could be used elsewhere. By March 1996, eight homeless vendors had moved into permanent accommodation, with *The Big Issue* helping to raise funds for the refurbishments.

JET

Vendors identify lack of formal qualifications as one of the major barriers preventing them moving on. JET helps vendors identify their training and educational needs, working closely with vendor support services. Intensive work has to be done with people to help them become training or job ready. In 1999, JET helped 98 people into jobs, 3 set up their own businesses, 15 took up voluntary work and 122 secured places on external training courses.

JET was set up in 1994, by Bernard McGee and Robyn Heaton, and was originally called the Publishing Unit. Money from the Swiss Bank Corporation was raised to buy the original equipment for the unit and Levis came in with a grant of around £40,000 to enable it to carry on the work.

Bernard and Robyn developed training for vendors in office work, computer skills and desk-top publishing to help them build up a portfolio of their own work. The aim was also to find the trainees jobs and placements with companies. The working atmosphere was informal but structured, with a staff of three. Bernard was adamant that 'it would not be like a government training scheme', with a specific timetable, so trainees worked at their own pace. It also gave them an opportunity to be in a working environment and so begin to adjust to normal working hours.

The age range of the people coming to JET is between 20 and 60. Many of the younger women are interested in IT because of the possibility of office jobs at the end of training. Some may have a computer at home and want to learn to use it. In March 1998, between 100–120 vendors per month were using JET. JET was also offering careers guidance, and vendors were coming in looking for college courses, using the library, the telephone and newspapers for job searches.

Alex, for example, had been coming and going from *The Big Issue* for a number of years, having been sleeping in Lincoln's Inn Fields for nine months. Between vending he worked on sheep farms around the country. By November 1997, he realized he wanted to move on and was accepted onto a course to train to become a shepherd. But he ran up against a problem. 'Because I slept rough I couldn't get statutory funding for the course, so I had to raise £4000 to go to college. So I spent a week in JET writing letters, and raised £1000 towards the course.'[9]

Working with the vendors is a long-term commitment. Robyn explains:

> 'We have just got a guy into a computer job and when we looked at the records, we noticed we had been working with him for 16 months. That's dealing with all the housing issues, pre-vocational training, clothing, CVs, and finding an appropriate place for him. So it's really long term.'

She adds:

> 'There are a few vendors who can find jobs within two or three months because they are not so damaged. But for many, with their confidence down, damaged by the system and their family, it is long term. For job-hunting the issue is housing. If they live in a hostel, it is almost impossible to get them into employment until they get into affordable accommodation. So the JET staff work closely with the housing team, and sometimes with the [former] drug and alcohol and mental health worker to make sure there are no other issues that will stop someone moving on. The whole process is one-to-one.'

JET has established very good working relationships with other organizations, such as The Mary Ward Centre, that run creative courses. JET continues to build up its relationships with businesses which are, Robyn believes, now more community minded. Many vendors have been offered jobs over the years by customers who buy the paper. JET refers people to jobs only when they know that the person is suited and is going to be reliable and responsible. When such people have got into jobs, it has opened the eyes of employers. Employers are starting to understand that just because someone has become homeless doesn't mean they are a bad person or they live up to the classic image.

There is a demand for ex-vendors from those employers who recognize the customer service skills that vendors have built up. Many vendors do not realize how much they are learning while they are selling to the public. London Underground is one of the employers that consider some *Big Issue* vendors for jobs because they know they are consistent about their work and have good customer skills. If people are seriously interested in joining London Underground, JET will run a training course alongside an outside charity which takes potential recruits through all other steps of recruitment.

Many ex-vendors do not want to work in a formal structure as they have been their own boss whilst vending. Some have come off construction jobs, or are ex-service people and want to continue working outdoors. Many have started their own businesses.[9] But there is the ongoing problem of homeless people not being able to access financial services, such as a bank account, because they have no address. Many organizations have been lobbying for change. The Big Issue in the North Trust published a report detailing how banks discriminate against the homeless. The report showed how more than 1000 of the magazine's vendors have been refused an account because they couldn't supply appropriate ID and proof of address.

The British Banking Association (BBA) explained that the demands for ID are enshrined in money laundering legislation – and to break them would put bank counter staff at risk of being jailed. 'We're still awaiting a decision from the Financial Services Authority,' said BBA director Mike Young of the request to relax the rules,' wrote Rob Cave in *The Big Issue in the North*.[10] 'However, The Big Issue in the North Trust has pointed to a partnership between *The Big Issue Scotland* and The Bank of Scotland which allows magazine vendors to open an account with their sales badge, a letter of reference, a medical card and their birth certificate.'[11]

In April 1999, the London Borough of Camden hired two ex-vendors to work on the new kerbside recycling scheme. It was an innovative scheme between *The Big Issue*, Ecocentric Solutions, an environmental business, and the charity Oxfam. Camden is currently interviewing more vendors for this expanding environmental service.

A Vendor Support Fund (VSF) has been running for a number of years to give extra help to people moving on. This is for people moving into accommodation, buying clothes, moving into new jobs or onto a course. Vendors can apply for a small grant for items such as painting and decorating materials, items of furniture or equipment and are also expected to make a contribution. This is often waived in emergency situations, such as family illness or a funeral. In 1999, 704 people received a grant from VSF.

The Big Issue Foundation in London plans to develop a peer education project based on successful ones run in Brighton and the Midlands. Lucie describes the Brighton project:

> '*A series of workshops are held with homeless people, talking about health issues and homelessness. The people who take part in it become experts. They then go out to other homeless people and impart that information. They are also creating and writing a pamphlet on health issues, such as how to access GPs, or explaining hepatitis and TB. People on the web design course are designing the pamphlet.*'

The mentoring project, run by JET worker Waller Jamison, is also very successful. Around 12 people are being mentored, mostly by people from Goldman Sachs, and Lucie says:

> '*Waller has produced a mentoring guide book. We've started sending it out to other homeless organizations because it is very comprehensive. The mentoring relationship works well. One of the problems some homeless people have is that they have no one to talk to. Nobody cares about them. They are totally isolated. The mentor is someone who is there for them, encouraging them, giving them advice.*'

One vendor mentioned that he had never been to the theatre, and now his mentor has taken him a number of times.

WRITING GROUP

The writing group is as old as the magazine itself. Weekly meetings of a group of around 20 people have produced writing for the magazine, poetry books, public readings, articles and encouragement to pursue writing as a career or at college. Vendors have always wanted to get involved in creative projects and *Big Issues* around the country have initiated a number of art, music, writing and cultural events.

Joe Berryman came to the writing group by accident in 1996 whilst he was obtaining computer experience in JET. His inspiration to write came from a close friend who inspired him to write poetry. Joe tries to write pieces between meetings. As an enthusiast of Bertolt Brecht and John Betjeman, he took full advantage of the writing group's visit to join the Poetry Library. Joe has been living in a hostel for the last few years and says:

> 'I think it is important that you have something in the paper on a regular basis. It's part of recognition, a little remuneration perhaps, satisfaction, continuing to be creative even when you are under stress, even the stress of being homeless.'

Joe and some of the group have also been involved in acting. At the end of 1997 they rehearsed a performance with 'Daisy Chain', which was put on at the Riverside Studios, Hammersmith, with sketches by various artists, musicians, actors and poets. He enjoyed the experience but found the rehearsals stressful. The difficulty was getting into a routine of being there on time and doing his piece. 'Homeless people are hopelessly unpunctual. That's the way we drift because we don't see the point of being punctual anymore,' he explains. Currently, he is filming, learning video techniques, part of a group run in partnership with Notting Hill's Gate Theatre.

There is a constant resource of poets, writers and others with different skills who help run the writing group and do workshops. There are poetry events, competitions or plays to attend. Many of the writers have gone on to journalism courses at City University and writers' workshops, paid for through the VSF. Other vendors have attended courses in foreign languages, English and music.

Home is where?
Home is where the hurt is,
The smacks, screams and 'don't do thats',
Dictatorial lectures,
Daily whacks,
The sly looks,
And slinky adult hands,
Shame on you,
Hussy slag.
Where you must eat all your food,
Or be force fed,
Beaten every morning,
For a nightly wetted bed,
Indoctrinated into bowed headed ugliness,
Father fearful he knows best,
Home is where the hurt is,
At least that's what all the homeless,
I have met have said.[12]

Fee Jane caught the imagination of the audience when she presented this poem at the launch of *the big issue home book* in October 2000 in the offices of ad agency TBWA. A performance poet, Fee Jane has been involved in the writing group run by Neil Ansell in *The Big Issue*'s Brighton office, and regularly writes poems for the magazine. Fourteen members of the group were up in London for the launch and to see their work in print. Regulars at the writing group in London also contributed: D, Fabini, Gary Saxton, Joe Berryman, Fatma Durmush and Jeanette Ju-Pierre to name but a few.

Jeanette Ju-Pierre, now working for the Department for Transport, Local Government and the Regions (DTLR), found the writing group very inspirational. She explains:

> 'When I first arrived I was only writing poetry and then by joining the writing group I started to write articles. My first assignment was to review an art exhibition in Store Street. My article about Whoopie Goldberg went in. She was signing copies of Book at the Megastore in Tottenham Court Road and I went up to tell her how much I admired her.'

The writing group reminds her of a rehabilitation group because people are also able to vent their feelings. She explains:

> *'It's a safe place where they can do that. It's good that they can have a space they can call their own because if they went into other groups outside they might feel left out. Here they all share similar circumstances.'*

Jeanette participated in the Farrago Poetry Slam (at The Poetry Place, Covent Garden) composing on-the-spot poetry in a competition. With other members of the writing group, she has read at London's South Bank with poets Matthew Sweeney and Jo Shapcock. She has already had a volume of poetry, *Crushed Calabash*, published, and won a prize. She has read her work on stage with *The Big Issue* poets who have also performed on Radio 1 and Radio 4.

Kerbing Your Emotions, an anthology of poetry by *The Big Issue* poets who gave readings at venues around London, was published by JET in 1995. To raise funds for the cost of publishing the book, the poetry group performed in two poetry evenings, raising £400. Paul Wilson, a graduate of Glasgow School of Art, who found himself homeless when he came to London in 1992 and sold *The Big Issue*, illustrated the book, which sold very well.

Fabini's involvement in the writing group has been crucial to her reintegration after a long period of depression. Originally from Colombia, she has lived in London since the late 1980s with her now grown up daughter. At her local priest's flat in 1996 she met a man who sold *The Big Issue*. She found selling the magazine a life-saver but it brought up deep feelings. She says:

> *'I was very very sad because it wasn't my background. I sold papers a little and I caught bronchitis. I was doing these things here but remembering my work in Colombia working for the national airline. But I took it as a part of life, saying OK that happened to me. Now I am in a low position. But I accepted it and enjoyed it because I was meeting different people.'*

Fabini is adamant that it is only because of *The Big Issue* and the writing group that she has got back on her feet. She explains:

'Because I couldn't speak, I started to express myself in writing and I was very quiet. Also because of my English. I come here every week. What I love about The Big Issue *is that they listen without any judgement. They are there to help people who are in a very low level in society. I think* The Big Issue *has taught society a lesson.'*

Vendor Involvement and Concerns

Homeless people are not involved in the running of the company or the Foundation. The main focus is on practical issues, such as making sure that the opinions and ideas of those who sell the paper are incorporated into the decision-making process. There is no consensus amongst the vendors as to the success of their input, with some quite happy about their involvement and others believing that the company totally ignores their opinions. A Vendor Working Group held a first meeting with staff in September 2000. A newsletter, *The Bin*, is written and produced monthly by vendors for vendors in JET. *The Bin* includes helplines, adverts for services, short stories, news of what is happening at *The Big Issue*, crosswords and comment.

A book in the distribution area is available for vendors to put their views and comments about *The Big Issue* to the London staff. They ask questions or pass on useful information, or comments from their customers about the magazine.

There have always been vendor meetings with staff, but the nature of these has changed over the years. Originally, they were attended by Lucie and John. Later, they were held monthly, with the editor, communications director and support staff. Often, only between six and twelve attended. Vendors discuss a variety of issues from magazine covers to issues relating to the pitch system. In February 1998, a petition signed by vendors was presented to the meeting to claim compensation for the late delivery of papers on a Monday morning. The problem was subsequently solved by instigating a procedure where 20,000 papers are delivered on Saturday at an extra cost to the business.

A major issue with the vendors has been price rises, although very few over nine years. The magazine cost 50p until January 1994, when it went up to 60p, followed by a rise to 70p 14 months later. In May 1996, the price rose to 80p. Each time a drop in sales was expected, but any initial loss was recovered. When the world paper price went up in 1997, a decision was made to put the price up to £1.00. The vendors were very concerned as they thought that they would lose their 'drops' (tips) as previously many were given a one pound piece for the magazine. The sales did drop slightly, but the vendors ended up making more money. They bought the paper for 40p and sold it for a pound, making 60 per cent.

Rory Gillert comments:

> *'Sometimes vendors start saying "we're not involved, we're not listened to", so we have to get mechanisms to replace the "we're all family together" type ethos which was around in '92. Some of them do feel that they are doing the work in order to keep* The Big Issue *afloat. There's a core of vocal people. They complain about the way the pitch system is set up and in some areas there are too many vendors, and floating. But that's inevitable really.'*

SELLING PROBLEMS

Staff conduct an annual rebadge every January. Rebadges generally reveal that whilst over 2000 are carrying badges in the Greater London area, only 35 per cent regularly sell.[13]

The more organized the pitch system, the more papers are sold and the more money goes directly into the pockets of the vendors. It has been a continuous challenge for the staff and vendors to maintain an efficient pitch system and equilibrium on the streets. London is divided into five zones and vendors are given a corresponding coloured badge for each zone. This is a system that is replicated in towns and cities throughout the UK.

When a potential vendor comes to *The Big Issue*, they may be asked to provide proof that they are homeless, for instance a letter from a day centre. Normally, income is regular if a pitch is worked regularly. However, there are reasons beyond anyone's control that can cause sales to decrease. One is the weather: if it is very hot, very cold or raining, sales will probably go down. Selling is also seasonable, with sales dipping in summer because of the influx of tourists and Londoners going on holiday. Security alerts in the capital in the mid 1990s affected sales as do strikes by tube staff. All these factors mean that vendors can only estimate how much cash they are going to have in their pockets at the end of the week.

Problems constantly arise on the street, usually involving confrontations between vendors. Most commonly this is about who is supposed to be on which pitch. Most can be sorted out easily, referring to the pitch allocation and code of conduct. There are also confrontations between vendors and people who are begging. Vendors are encouraged to respect the established pitches of other street earners and talk to them to ensure there are no arguments.

As for the legality of selling newspapers on the street, Schedule 4 of the Street Traders Licensing Act covers *The Big Issue* right across the country. When certain city councils have disputed this, staff have to investigate the local by-laws as some councils maintain their street trading laws differ from the main Act. For London there are two different rules. In the City only, vendors sell under the City of London (Various Powers) Act 1987. In the rest of the metropolis, they sell under the London Local Authorities Act 1990.[14]

Problems with shopkeepers do occur. It often concerns vendors standing too close to their doorways or shouting too loud, and sitting down on the pavement outside. Personal appearance at times create confrontations. Through experience, *Big Issue* staff have usually successfully resolved these disputes through a face-to-face meeting. It can also be vendors' dogs, which sometimes are disruptive and behave anti-socially. However, dogs are many vendors' best friends and are a boon to people in crisis.

South Londoner Pete Webster was selling *The Big Issue* from 1992 to 1994 when the housing team found him a flat. He became a coordinator looking after the vendors in Ilford and was then employed as an outreach worker until 1999. On the question of taking someone's badge away, Pete says that they have always taken the same line: three or four verbal warnings for breaking the rules and then they lose their badges for a short period of time. But, he says, 'We give them loads of chances because we don't want to take someone's living away. However, if they carry on abusing that there is only so far you can take it.'

If the staff can see there is something going wrong they try to talk to them:

> *'But you can't force help on people. You can only do your best by talking and trying to get them to see maybe the drugs and alcohol or mental health worker. If they don't want to, that's it.'*

Only a small fraction of vendors are debadged permanently. Most of them are suspended for one week or a month, usually for being drunk and abusive to the staff or public. There is a process involved, which is sometimes long and drawn out. Pete explains:

'We try to say to them you're not allowed in here if you smell of alcohol or if you are drunk. We say leave the building. But mainly we are not too hard on that. It is when they start getting abusive and loud and starting fighting with other vendors, that is when we step in.'

A very serious offence (like a violent assault) will, of course, result in immediate debadging and the involvement of the police. Those who cause most problems tend to be the middle-aged ones who are upset with life, claims Pete. Sometimes they have a go at the other vendors who are quietly sitting down and having a cup of tea in the vendors' cafe, situated in the distribution area. Pete adds:

'We can't afford to have people like that in the building because vendors themselves are stressed out anyway. Particularly if they have been standing out on the streets for five hours and have only made a couple of quid. They're going to be really pissed off about it and the last thing they need is another vendor being drunk and starting on them.'

THE BENEFIT ISSUE

When vendors are badged up they have always been advised that, if they are claiming benefit, they should declare their earnings to the benefit office and they sign a statement to this effect.

The company had to deal with a major crisis in September 1994 when it was splashed all over the newspapers because a member of the public had complained to the TV programme *Crimestoppers* that some *Big Issue* vendors were claiming benefit whilst vending. This led to a visit by two staff from the Employment Service to *The Big Issue* offices.

The officials demanded, under Section 58 of the Social Security Act 1986, the names of *The Big Issue*'s 'employees', ie vendors. However, the two visitors had not done their homework. The vendors are not employees of *The Big Issue*; *The Big Issue* is the wholesaler and the vendors are retailers.

John's argument was simple. He says:

'As wholesalers selling to retailers, we had no rights or responsibility to demand the social security record of the retailers. If the law was changed, then that would be different. Mr Murdoch is not responsible for the tax or social security records of the people he distributes to. When Mr Murdoch is responsible for the records of retailers then, likewise, we would be. It was a simple case of the Employment Service wanting us to do their work for them. They said we were not unlike cab offices where employers needed to keep records of their drivers. I told them that they could not lump us in with employers, because we don't employ homeless people to sell.'

The law stated that recipients of Income Support can only earn an extra £5 a week before their benefits are reduced. It is not illegal to sell and claim at the same time, but benefit would obviously have to be adjusted in accordance with the amount of income from sales. 'We don't encourage signing on and selling at the same time,' said John at the time.

'We have had many discussions with benefit offices up and down the country. There will always be problems in and around people who are so abject they are taking benefit. The main discussion we are having with government at the moment is for them to support long-term projects to enable homeless people to come off benefit – that is the solution to the benefit issue.'

The visit unleashed a storm of protest from the press and public against the Employment Service on behalf of *Big Issue* vendors, pointing out the iniquities of the social security system. The mainstream press was very supportive. Even Richard Littlejohn in *The Sun* called for Prime Minister John Major to order 'an immediate halt to this vindictive operation'. He called for a review of the benefits system to allow people to earn a modest amount on top of their Giro until they get themselves back on their feet. Apparently, the case was even raised in Cabinet, as well as in Parliament. The possibility that John Bird would be jailed for contempt stoked up huge support from vendors who threatened to rally round if he was transported to the nearest prison.

The main concern of the staff was that if *The Big Issue* gave the Employment Service vendors' details, it would be a massive breach of trust. Many homeless people were trying to escape from one life and struggle to build up a new one. If their details were given to government many would disappear and the whole project would be in jeopardy, creating more beggars and people moving back onto the streets.

The Guardian leader entitled 'The Big Imbecility'[15] said:

> 'It is the rigidity of the rules – rather than the generosity of the benefits – that deters claimants from finding work. Ministers who genuinely wanted to end the "dependency culture" would not have waited so long.'

It also pointed out the difficulties of bringing the long-term unemployed back into the labour market – and the social dangers this generates. And, it was precisely this matter which was being addressed by The Big Issue.

The Big Issue subsequently campaigned for changes in the benefit system so that people caught in the poverty trap would not be penalized for trying to improve their situation. The magazine[16] carried an investigation into the benefits system and called for people to be given the opportunity to get back into work and not be put into a position where it pays better not to work. There needed to be a honeymoon period to move people from benefits and back into unemployment. The Big Campaign was launched at fringe meetings at both the Labour and Tory Party conferences in 1994. At the Labour Party meeting on 3 October, MP Glenda Jackson and editor of the New Statesman and Society, Steve Platt, called for changes in the benefit system. Since then, there have been cases where individual vendors have been targeted but not a blitz of the kind that took place in 1994.

WORKING WITH THE POLICE

The police have always been an important factor in The Big Issue's operation. There has been close contact between local police forces and Big Issues up and down the country. Rory Gillert says:

> 'Generally, the police are supportive. The police are generally likely to look on Big Issue vendors more favourably than, say, a beggar. They are not generally going to hassle Big Issue vendors unless their behaviour is completely out of order. The police probably would say that it actually makes their job easier if

people are selling The Big Issue *rather than lying around or begging.'*

When Inspector Steve Dyer came to *The Big Issue* offices to talk to the vendors, he did not get a very warm reception. He says:

> *'I wasn't applauded into and out of the room! But in fairness to them, they listened and gave some feedback, and talked to me about problems they have. I would say now that if some of the things that they say are true about the behaviour of officers and it was drawn to the attention of supervisors in the police service, it would be dealt with and dealt with quite severely.'*

The vendors suggested to Steve Dyer that if they were to report a crime to the police, they would not be taken seriously. They'd be moved on, and be less sympathetically treated than someone who had a house, a car and a family. But is this true? He says:

> *'The psychological point is that we all have value systems that impact on what we can or can't do. Whether or not it impacts on what we do professionally, it must do because we can't act outside it. I'd say that we would try to give people the same professional service regardless. I would say that, but then am I being too protectionist of my organization? I can only speak from a personal point of view. It's all very subjective.'*

After meetings with vendors, did he discuss it with colleagues and has it made a difference? He responds:

> *'It has made a difference to some people. I'm quite happy to accept a lot of the criticisms that they make which are absolutely genuine. I don't think there is any mileage for them to make up stories about the police.'*

Steve Dyer set up meetings with *Big Issue* staff members Jane Edwards and John McFadzean because they were involved in the Homeless Person's Forum in the City. He says:

> *'We got on very well. I gave some talks to the area coordinators and vendors saying, look, we're not that bad really. We are human, pinch us and we bleed. They came along and did exactly the same to the police officers.'*

CREATING PARTNERSHIPS

How does *The Big Issue* fit into the voluntary sector? How good is it at creating partnerships? Nick Hardwick, former CEO of Centrepoint and current CEO of the Refugee Council, does not believe that the voluntary sector is very good at working together, and this applies equally to the homeless sector, which he agrees he helped to create. He thinks that *The Big Issue* is slightly out at a distance and sometimes has rough edges in its relationships, which is a healthy situation. He remembers an occasion when he was at Centrepoint and he thought *The Big Issue* was about to write something critical about his organization. They became seriously worried, because of *The Big Issue*'s legitimacy. But, he says:

> *'I think there is a danger with the homeless industry, because you don't get much criticism. So I think that some voices that are slightly detached, are independent and a bit quirky. They don't necessarily take the party line and this is very healthy. I would take that* The Big Issue *doesn't work terribly well with the voluntary sector as a compliment, not a criticism. There need to be some voices outside.'*

Victor Adebowale, former CEO of Centrepoint, reacting to a criticism about *The Big Issue* not partnering with others in the sector, says:

> *'We get the same thing. You get a very high profile organization with a highly charismatic leader and you've got loads of money. The question is, yes, I suppose you could argue that you could do more partnership work. I wanted to do some partnership work with* The Big Issue, *but the problem with that is that you find yourself in a situation where anybody you partner with gets blinded by your PR.'*

To argue that one organization can do it all is verging on the irresponsible, Victor asserts:

> *'But there's a tendency for organizations to become octopus-like and do everything because they can. But what that does is take away from organizations that can do it really well but don't have the resources, and need the partnerships to develop those organizations.'*

He doesn't believe there are too many homeless organizations or duplication of services in London and says:

> 'I think people jump to that conclusion too blithely. Are there too many bars in Soho? My view is that it all depends on how the market is managed. The argument is not that there are too many, but what are they doing?'

Mark McGreevy of the Depaul Trust thinks it is strange that *The Big Issue* has always marketed itself much better to people who buy it than it has to the homeless sector. He says:

> 'In terms of the dynamic that John introduced, I think it has fundamentally changed the nature of charities. You look at them now and they are much more geared towards social regeneration, economic independence, skilling people than just providing bed spaces for people on a night.'

He believes that two innovative things have happened in homelessness in the last ten years: the Rough Sleepers Initiative (predominently within London) and *The Big Issue*. He says:

> 'I think it has been absolutely fundamental in shaping and raising public awareness of homelessness. It has demonstrated that corporate sector for-profit activities can serve well without patronizing. It has shown me that you can have an approach of risk taking and getting out and doing things. It doesn't require everyone to be a social worker. Sometimes it just requires someone to get involved in helping themselves. I think the hand up rather than a handout is probably the motif that the sector has learnt an awful lot about.'

FUNDRAISING

The Big Issue Foundation is unique from other charities because it has the magazine from which it can raise funds. Over 4000 individual donors have been recruited from the magazine in the past five years, making up 44 per cent of the total donations.[17] Also, the beneficiaries, unlike other charities, are immediately visible to the donees on the streets.

Lyndall Stein, head of fundraising 1996–98, and her assistant, Rachel Stewart, established a successful fundraising department in August 1995, just before the launch of the Foundation. Pre launch, quarter-page strip ads asked the public to help the new Big Issue Foundation. In return for financial support, donor's names were listed in the magazine as a founding friends Roll of Honour. It worked well because people identified strongly with the brand of *The Big Issue* and, within two months, the post brought in tens of thousands of pounds.

Lyndall had initially believed that she could bring in up to £60,000 in the first year but this was surpassed and around £250,000 was received in the first six months. The mailing programme (between four and six per year) to individual donors obtained through the magazine has subsequently developed into the cornerstone of fundraising.

In addition, there are information mailings, for instance, telling people about the main points around the Housing Act. When *The Sun* published its story about the vendor (see pages 95–96), the Foundation sent out a mailing telling the real story. During the 1997 general election, a mailing explained the key points around homelessness.

Lyndall comments:

> *'Finding the right "voice" in which you speak about the organization and what it does is absolutely essential. I could have done some very effective work in the short term by using images of homeless people as victims. It would work to bring in money, but would run counter to the central message of* The Big Issue, *which is all about independence and self-help. Fundraising has to build on and enhance the central mission of the organization, or it will end up clouding the message and hampering the work.'*[18]

Lynn O'Donoghue joined *The Big Issue* as head of fundraising in April 1999. With Penny Marshall and Shanthi Ayres, she has consolidated and expanded the work started by Lyndall, Rachel and Susie Turnbull. She says:

> *'*The Big Issue *has a brand so we have an opportunity to raise money from individuals in the way that smaller charities can't. The charities that don't have a brand, that you haven't heard about that do really difficult work, need the statutory money.*

> *We of all organizations should go to the government last because*
> *we have the opportunity to raise money from other sources.'*

Statutory funding stood at 11 per cent in the year up to 31 March 1999. This rises to over 20 per cent in the year up to 2001, with the grant of £200,000 from the Rough Sleepers Unit (RSU). The Foundation has also received two tranches of money from the National Lottery Charities Board. The first £143,000 was for a three year programme of expansion. This was followed by a second amount for the development of a regional management structure. John Bird caused a stir by commenting that unless more of the projects that had received money could be more economically sustainable, they would be returning to the Lottery the following year for more money. 'We should be teaching charities to make money', he said. 'I would like the rules to be changed so that we can have self-sustaining partnerships between the needy and business.'[19]

Besides government money for a housing worker, JET has also received statutory funding for its work. This will be a growth area in *The Big Issue*'s future funding, reflected by the RSU grant. 'The Rough Sleepers Unit is interested in jobs, education and training. No one is interested in anything apart from jobs, education and training,' comments Lynn. Grants for vendor support services are more difficult to secure (particularly in London where there are over 200 homeless charities) because, she explains, trusts expect the Foundation to refer vendors to existing services. Where there are no appropriate existing services it will be easier to secure help.

The Foundation advertises in *The Big Issue*. Lynn acknowledges the possible contradiction between an advertisement asking for money for vendors to move on, and editorial coverage. She cites the example of a piece in the ninth bithday issue where editorial had celebrated the fact that a vendor had been vending for nine years. 'We in fundraising didn't [celebrate]. He should have moved on by now. The difficulty is that the magazine has to sell itself. The foundation is more interested in quality of life for the vendors. The magazine has to produce copy to sell. So there is automatically a conflict of interests.'

Comparing advertising and fundraising, in terms of *The Big Issue* readers, Lynn also says:

> *'We in fundraising are appealing to those people buying the magazine who respond as donors. Advertisers are advertising for those readers who respond as consumers. We're constantly thinking: is that reader a donor or a consumer? Advertisers appeal to younger people. A donor is likely to be older.'*

Events such as concerts, often described as crucial for profile-raising, have been avoided unless they bring in a good return. Large scale events can prove very expensive and, without sponsorship, are unlikely to be cost-effective unless *The Big Issue* are the sole beneficiaries. A concert, given by the band Verve at the Brixton Academy for *The Big Issue* and NCH Action for Children raised £23,000 for the Foundation. Whilst successful, it was felt that more staff would be needed to work on such events in future.

However, a donor event held in the House of Commons, hosted by Foundation vice-president Mo Mowlem in 1999 was a great success. It launched The Big Gift programme, inviting people to donate a minimum of £5000 a year. The programme has since raised over £50,000.

The Big Art Issue, 'Putting homeless people in the picture', an innovative fundraising project, was launched in April 1996. Prints made especially for *The Big Issue* by well-known artists, such as Terry Frost, Peter Blake and Bruce McLean, are sold to the public through the magazine, with a percentage going to the Foundation. Martin Village who, with Clive Jennings, runs The Big Art Issue says:[20]

> *'The idea was that we pay the artists. Normally, for an artist, it's "will you donate one painting?" It's never a commercial relationship with a charity. We didn't want to get people to do things for nothing, as so often happens to artists, for charitable purposes.'*

The fundraising strategy is now being rethought. Lynn comments:

> *'Now, the magazine as a medium to raise money from individuals is becoming less effective. We are having to look at targeting individuals outside the magazine. So we are doing a cold mail to individuals who maybe don't buy the magazine.'*

It will focus around a story of someone who has successfully travelled through JET. It is also anticipated that the Foundation website will bring in thousands of pounds annually.

Very little advertising for the Foundation has been placed in outside media. This is because a high level of initial investment is needed to generate a reasonable return. Advertising agency TBWA (formerly GGT) approached the Foundation as they were interested in doing an ad campaign. Lucie Russell says:

> 'We felt it would be better to have an ad campaign for both The Big Issue *and the Foundation. They have now done a campaign and are in the process of getting their clients to donate free media space for it. That is why we are having a dinner in the Science Museum, hosted by Mo Mowlem.'*

St Luke's advertising agency will also be working with *The Big Issue*. St Luke's, established in 1995 by Andy Law, amongst others, is the advertising industry's only co-owned venture and is committed to 'total equal employee ownership and the pursuit of personal values'.[21] They have employed a community affairs person whose sole job is to work on how St Luke's can have an impact on its community. 'We have worked out a series of proposals working together, such as mentoring', says Lucie Russell.

Scotland

For a while the social support at *The Big Issue Scotland* was similar to London's. A charity was set up but on reflection Mel Young believes that this was a mistake. It was primarily set up because fundraisers said it was easier to raise money as a charity but Scotland has many organizations and charities in the voluntary sector working with homeless people doing exactly the same things. Therefore, in terms of support, the staff decided to work with outside organizations and refer people on in order to avoid duplication in the sector.

The Big Issue Scotland does not have any idea about how many people do move on to jobs. Scotland has never been in agreement with *The Big Issue in the North*'s policy of having a time limit on selling. They did discuss it but rejected it. Some vendors have been with *The Big Issue Scotland* since the beginning. Mel has been trying to find out why they stay around:

'One guy said to me, "this is the best it's ever been in my life. I have all these customers who I know, who speak to me. I have this wonderful rapport. I've now got myself into temporary accommodation. I make a little money. I love the staff, I love the blather. Why should I move on? Why are you pushing me away? I don't want to go into that world whence I came because I hate it".'

There is much anecdotal evidence like this. It is hard not to be influenced by such stories.

The Big Issue Scotland's view of support and move-on has changed over the years. Sometimes they would get very heavy with vendors, banning them if they were 'bevvied out of their head'. Then they would reassess the banning rules and the attitude would be more relaxed and supportive. Then something would go wrong, so it would change again. They were trying to develop an understanding all the time.

A number of vendors now identify *The Big Issue Scotland* as their family. If people do not have a family, then the magazine is creating one. Consequently the staff have to see what they, as a family, can do for the vendors who want to stay. Mel says:

'What I'm trying to do is a rather sophisticated thing. Rather than push them away, we give them an opportunity to come back. This gives them some reassurance that it's OK to move on. It's almost like trying to create a club atmosphere.'

He wants to create a similar opportunity for ex-vendors, too, so that they can always come back.

Currently, they are piloting a new move-on policy in Glasgow, based on the Grand Central Partnership's[22] methods of a step programme in New York. They needed a new approach because of the enormous drugs problem that homeless people in Glasgow are experiencing. Dozens have died over the past year from dodgy heroin, many of whom were *Big Issue* vendors.

Mel explains:

'From now on, just because they turn up at the door and want to sell The Big Issue, *doesn't mean they are going to be allowed to sell it, if they are on drugs. Before, they could. Now we are saying, you are out of your face with smack, you can't sell it,*

but don't go away. We will have the services that get you into a
state where you can be accepted to sell. The vendor will start
with a white card, then progress to a yellow card. They will get
a further card if they hit the criteria for each step. They do not
move up until they are ready. When they reach the top they will
have a CV and some training behind them. The most important
thing, though, is that they can go down the ladder, but will
never fall off the bottom. They will always have that white card.'

Jeff Grunberg, from Grand Central Partnership, has worked for
years with homeless people who have drug and alcohol problems.
As he pointed out, if someone in work has a drink or drugs
problem, either their colleagues or boss will talk to them, and they
are offered counselling and help. The key thing is that that person
is actually in work. Then, they are able deal with their addiction.
Mel says: 'Similarly, we are saying you can't keep selling while
you are in this state. But we will help you.' As well as doing referrals, a drug service will be set up by *The Big Issue* in Glasgow
because other agencies are oversubscribed.

Mel wants them working with other vendors who can mentor
them and provide support. They are setting up clubs for vendors.

'We have one here which is very successful. A lot of vendors
have nothing to do and are bored, so they go hill walking at the
weekend. But they can't become a member of the club until, say,
they have an orange card.'

The Big Issue in the North

The Big Issue in the North has always had a time limit on selling.
One reason was that smaller city centres, like Manchester, Leeds
and Liverpool, became full up with vendors. They needed a
policy to deal with this situation, as Ruth Turner explains:

'Also, what we found was that the longest serving, most articu-
late, best-off vendors were on the best pitches, but they weren't
spending very much time selling because they had their regular
customers and could make a bomb in half a day. But then
whenever a new vendor came and tried to stand on their pitch,
there would be a big fight about it.'

Ruth and the team had to shift some of the vendors out of town to prevent overselling, but then realized they had to move them on. She says:

> *'And it just became stupid when we said help the homeless help themselves, and there were people who hadn't been homeless for a year and a half. A time limit was put on those selling the magazine. They could only sell for a maximum of 18 months after they had been housed.'*

The other *Big Issues* did not agree. Ruth says, 'It wasn't an easy decision and we weren't 100 per cent sure at the time. We couldn't prove it but we were fairly convinced that there was no other option.' It also came down to expectations, too. Ruth felt there ought to be higher expectations than just selling the magazine. *The Big Issue in the North* realized that, since this was such a risky path to take, they would have to do it well. The idea was to try it for two years, and if it did not work they would do something else.

The Big Issue in the North has carried out a lot of research about where their vendors come from. It was interesting for them to compare it with that done on London vendors. Ruth says:

> *'We found that the skill level of our vendors was a lot lower, most of them hadn't had jobs. Most of them hadn't had their own tenancy agreement, never mind owning. Whereas there were some really great stories to be told in London about people who had had it all and lost it, our lot never had it in the first place. So we found that it was really important to recognize what the people who were selling the magazine had come out of – the Northern economy, and that it was about generational homelessness and unemployment which maybe you need to deal with in a very different way to someone who has had their house repossessed.'*

The Big Step – a registered charity – was established in 1996. They then told the first vendors that they would have to stop selling the magazine. Ruth remembers *The Big Issue* summits (where all *The Big Issues* got together a couple of times a year) where feelings ran high. She says:

'We almost had fights and chairs thrown across the room when we had Big Issue summits about this – it was ferocious.

'We were so adamant it was going to work and thought, my god, what if it doesn't? We did a workshop with these vendors and got them to talk about their hopes for the future, and fears for the future, what they were going to go on to, what they wanted from us, what they thought about us. It was really quite intense and difficult. They were so worried about moving, and so desperately excited. A yellow kitchen I remember one of them wanted. And a garden. So it was all about fear and hope.'

Every single vendor had to go through this process, 150 per city. Ruth says:

'We monitor all of that. Obviously it doesn't work out for all of them. Some will come back and start again. And we don't know what happens to all of them either. The monitoring now of the outcomes is so much more intense and thorough.'

They have found that the attitudes of the vendors have now changed:

'When you asked vendors what their ambitions were, then it was to sell outside Marks & Spencer's, to sell x numbers of magazines, or to get regular customers. Now their ambitions are not about being Big Issue vendors. Almost universally, and it happened remarkably quickly, their aspirations and expectations started to be raised.'

There was a core group, who were difficult to get housed and to move on. They kept coming back. Now, though, the work with vendors is much faster. 'I couldn't be more convinced now that it was the right thing to do about move-on.'

A subsequent programme called Big Futures combines, amongst other things, a doctor's surgery, an employment unit and showers, based in their Manchester headquarters.

'I think it's like an academy, you know. Our vendors can get involved in football, where the kits are supplied by Manchester United, or Leeds United in Leeds. They can get involved in music where the coaches are people from the Hallé Orchestra, art – top

*artists from the region. They just get the most phenonenal oppor-
tunities, and good on 'em. But they shouldn't be squandered.'*

Now, the second they walk through the door, there is a certain
expectation. There is compulsory accredited sales training for all
of them, called Learn to Earn. Then Learn to Live, about personal
development and skills for resettlement. And the third course,
also accredited, is Learn to Work, and that's about moving on.
Ruth says:

*'And the support given now is two years, like an academy of the
fast track, from the streets to something else. We can do that
now. It would have been wrong to do it when the services
weren't there.'*

The Big Issue's work was further boosted at the end of 1996 by a
report published through Liverpool John Moores University.[23]
This investigated whether homeless people selling *The Big Issue*
experienced any real benefits in terms of financial independence
or improvements in their health, welfare, self-image and percep-
tions of the future.

Between May 1995 and March 1996, approximately 70
Liverpool vendors between the ages of 17 and 45, mostly males
and all single, completed a questionnaire and a number were
interviewed in depth. The results were compared to a similar
investigation with a number of homeless people in Liverpool who
were not selling *The Big Issue*.

The summary of the report stated that one of *The Big Issue*'s
prime objectives, that of raising awareness of the causes, nature,
extent and consequences of homelessness in Britain, had been
massively successful.[24] The report also showed how *Big Issue*
vendors have become politicized and motivated to confront
public prejudice and official attitudes towards homeless people:

*'Although blaming the government for their situation, The Big
Issue helped them to understand their individual predicament
within a far broader perspective and look beyond their own
"weaknesses" as the causal base for their plight. The Big Issue
had led the majority of them to question, challenge and reject
the image which had been imposed upon them by public
attitudes and government policies.*

> *'Consequently many felt they were active in a campaign to raise public awareness about the life experiences, nature, causes and extent of homelessness in Britain. Also, they had more confidence to challenge "official" decisions which affected them eg.* Big Issue *vendors tended to insist upon registration with a GP, whereas virtually none of the non-vendors were registered.'*

Not only have public and governmental attitudes begun to shift. Now, homeless people are not prepared to accept these attitudes when they are thrust upon them.

WALES

Big Issue Cymru has developed a further variation. In Cardiff, a vendor receives a badge for two years with an expiry date. They also see a vendor development worker every three months to discuss their plans for the future. Su West explains:

> *'The idea is that people are thinking from the beginning, where do I go from here? If people are still with us at the end of two years, they will have a review as to whether they get a badge extension or not.'*

Many people will naturally already have moved on after two years. Su says:

> *'There are some people who have been with us for six years now, who will probably be with us until they feel they cannot vend any longer. They might be people who have mental health problems, some of the old guys we deal with who have alcohol problems, who are keeping dry but haven't really got a chance of getting employment. So we continue to work with people who will be reviewed regularly.'*

There are other people who are selling a few magazines every so often. They have no desire to move on and are not getting much out of the magazine and Su adds: 'Often, we might say we're not helping you, you're not helping us, we don't think we should renew your badge.'

It is built into the vendors' mentality that it is only for two years. More often than not, people will get an extension, because they still have drug and alcohol problems, or they are still not in secure housing. Su says:

> 'But we have people who are in secure housing and are more than capable of getting a job, but they just like the lifestyle. But we say, that is not what it's all about.'

The vendor profile in Wales has changed, with vendors younger than previously: 50 per cent are between 22 and 35. *The Big Issue Cymru* does not see many women, although there are more than when the magazine launched. A generic worker offers crisis support and puts vendors in touch with the relevant agency.

SOUTH WEST

Move-on in the South West is a combination of policy. Eighteen months used to be the time limit. Jeff Mitchell comments:

> 'The jury was out for a long time to see if it would work. And then we thought, hold on, there are people here who are never going to be able to do any other kind of work. For instance, women in their late fifties with partners who are heavy drinkers. You can't say you are going to have to go, you've had your 18 months. But for other people, we try and if they are capable of moving on after 18 months we would love to see that happen.'

Currently, it is case-by-case whilst trying to maintain the atmosphere of progression. 'We say to people it isn't about being dependent on *The Big Issue*. There are always other opportunities out there.'

The problems their vendors have now are very different from 1993. Many now have a more chaotic lifestyle than before, with more drug problems. Jeff says:

> 'What we try to do is to get them into other services. There is that pressure to have to provide more support for vendors who have a more chaotic lifestyle. They say, "the amount of magazines I am selling could get me sorted out with accommodation but that's not my problem. My problem is that I drink most of what I make in a day." We need to get new priorities, and work with the relevant agencies so we can continue to offer opportunities for people to help themselves.'

Over 18 months, a Foundation Training Awards Scheme was run in partnership with the University of the West of England. This was an NVQ-based, core skills orientated programme for people to learn basic numeracy and literacy. Twelve vendors at a time made short-term life plans, and gave weekly reports that would then provide evidence of their ability to communicate. It was phenomenally successful, but the funding ran out. They hope to be able to continue it in the future. Jeff adds:

> 'Around 30 did something meaningful. One participant last heard of was teaching English in Japan. The programme focused them and gave them such a confidence boost. We found a lot of people didn't want to go and work for anyone else. They wanted to go and set up a ceramic workshop, or van delivery service. They wanted to work for themselves, or go on a TEFL course.'

In the regional offices covered by The Big Issue Foundation, such as Norwich and the Midlands, there are generic workers who turn their hand to everything. The link with distribution is closer as there are generally far fewer staff. Many of the out of London offices use volunteers for jobs such as running vendors to the doctor. If there is only one Foundation worker, they build good relationships with local organizations. Instead of providing a drug service, for example, they will ask the local drug centre to come and do a couple of hours outreach in *The Big Issue* office. If they find they have too many people with drug problems, a part-time worker is taken on because that is where the need is.

'The magazine is dealing with demand and we in the Foundation are dealing with need. That is the difficulty', says former fundraiser Lynn.

> 'Where the magazine decides to sell is not necessarily the greatest need to help homeless people. In the past, people have said, we're selling the magazine, we'll go and put a worker there. Now we say, no. If you decide to open up an office, the Foundation may not deliver services from there because it doesn't necessarily fit in with our plan. It can't be led by the business.'

The business opens up in an area because they know they can sell magazines. The Foundation opens up where there is a need for homeless people to receive services. That is the contradiction.

CHAPTER 7

INTERNATIONAL DEVELOPMENTS

SOON AFTER *THE Big Issue* launched, people from continental Europe, North America and later South America, descended on the London office and wanted to know how they could start a similar street paper. *The Big Issue* was in no position to provide financial support, but it could provide advice, based on its own limited experience, on feasibility studies, funding sources or business plans.

Street papers hit the streets of Western Europe within 18 months of *The Big Issue*'s launch. Some copied the formula by observation, others through visits and phone calls to *The Big Issue*. The first were launched in Belgium and France in the summer of 1993 and within two years there were up to 60 papers in towns and cities throughout Europe.

The situation for homeless people in European towns and cities then was similar to the UK, and it was ripe for this new movement. Britain, France and Germany topped the league tables for the numbers of homeless but, on any one night in the countries of the European Union (population 340 million), around 1.1 million people were without homes, up to 5 million permanently homeless and up to 15 million living in 'severe housing stress,' in substandard conditions. This has now risen to just over 1.8 million.[1]

The nature of social exclusion differed from country to country and, in particular, from North to South. In Southern Europe, where the family structure still plays a central social role, statistics indicated that the problem of homelessness was not as acute as in Northern Europe. However, the wars in the Balkans and the persecution of the Kurds brought refugees onto the streets of European cities during the 1990s and they were joined by migrants and refugees from countries in North and West Africa.

This situation was reflected in the nature of the vendors. Many papers are sold by the unemployed as well as homeless people, and some are sold by refugees. *Das Megaphon*, the street paper in Graz, Austria, has been sold by Nigerian and Liberian refugees, rather than Austrians. Similarly with *Terre di mezzo* in Milan, Italy, which is sold mostly by Senegalese and other refugees, although not exclusively. *CAIS*, sold in Lisbon and other Portuguese towns, is distributed to different organizations working with marginalized people, whether homeless, ex-drug addicts, ex-prisoners, long-term unemployed or the disabled. Support services are therefore tailored towards the needs of these particular groups.

Diversity is the hallmark of Europe's street papers, marked by differences in editorial content, circulation figures, size and status. Circulations range upwards from 3000 per month. Some are financially supported by charities or the church, others are extensions of existing homeless projects or operate as non-profit businesses, with finance from grants or corporate sponsorship. The definition of 'business' is quite broad, but most strive towards a businesslike approach. The German street papers, for example, have a particular structure and are 'democratic' businesses, where decisions are made collectively by a board.

The papers developed in response to the different natures of social exclusion in their countries; European papers tended to focus on cities rather than on national editions, mirroring national media patterns and local politics. In Germany, for example, a street paper was launched in each major city, starting with *Hinz & Kunzt*[2] in Hamburg and *BISS* in Munich in 1993. There is no national street paper and by the mid 1990s there were around 35 German street papers, with Berlin at one time having three or four.

The situation is similar in the Netherlands, with eight or nine. In Italy, a string of street papers was launched across the cities of Northern Italy from 1993 with *Piazza Grande* first in 1993 in Bologna, followed by *Terre di mezzo* in Milan and others in Florence and Trieste. *Das Megaphon*, in Austria, was followed by around four others in the late 1990s. Despite the limitations of selling in only one city, which hinders growth, they have generally prospered.

In 1992, a team from French TV came to London to make a documentary about *The Big Issue*. One of the group, Anne Kunvari, was so taken with the idea that, with assistance in the form of expertise from *The Big Issue*, she launched *La Rue* in the autumn of 1993. It subsequently became *The Big Issue*'s partner paper in France, running along similar lines.

As with many new initiatives, there are negative aspects. French street papers encapsulated the flip side of the street paper movement. With no national paper, by the mid 1990s at least six papers were competing on the streets of Paris, and a further six outside the capital. The situation in Paris created huge problems for vendors[3] as there were no regulated pitch systems, intense competition and different prices for the papers. *La Rue* was more expensive to buy, and vendors tended to move from paper to paper. This could not last because most of the papers were losing money and by the end of the 1990s only two papers remained (*La Rue* went bankrupt in 1998).

La Rue was worried about the ethics of two of the papers, *Réverbère* and *Macadam*. *Macadam*, the first paper to launch in Europe in the summer of 1993, had huge sales throughout Belgium and France. It was a privately owned and successful business, providing an income for hundreds of homeless people. However, the profits were not going back into helping the vendors move on, but to the individual owners and the vendors were being provided with limited support. As for *Réverbère*, within a couple of years of its launch in 1993 allegations were being made by other streets papers of its racism and extreme right-wing connections. Its anti-semitic editorial caught the attention of the mainstream press and the law. No one knew what happened to the profits of the paper as there were no support services to speak of. However, the owner kept a low profile, avoiding any discussion or confrontation, and there was little that could be done to push this paper off the streets.

These two instances highlighted the dangers of lack of control and financial transparency, something which formed part of the Street Paper Charter.[4] This was formulated as membership criteria for the International Network of Street Papers (INSP) in 1995. This stressed that all post-investment profits were to finance social support for the vendors to avoid any member of the network being run solely for the benefit of its owner.

INTERNATIONAL NETWORK OF STREET PAPERS (INSP)

The development of an international department at *The Big Issue* took a step forward at the first meeting of European street papers which took place in Brussels in February 1994. Organized by FEANTSA (the European Federation of National Organizations Working with the Homeless),[5] the gathering consisted of 12 existing papers and other representatives of organizations working with homeless or socially excluded people.

Many of the European street papers were formed by people using *The Big Issue* as a model. But what was called for was some kind of body which would provide direction. The idea was put forward to establish a network of European papers that would coordinate joint projects. It would provide an advisory service to those wishing to set up papers, as well as those working on established titles. This would help raise the profile of the street paper movement in the mainstream media. But the problem, as always, was money. Although there was no money set aside for international work at the time, *The Big Issue* agreed to finance the International Network of Street Papers (INSP) and an international department from July 1994. This would be run by myself and Maria Clancy, until such time as independent funding could be found.

A donation from The Body Shop Foundation also helped in the initial stages. FEANTSA then introduced *The Big Issue* to DGV[6] at the European Commission (EC). A hurried visit to Brussels (covered by a report on BBC TV's *Newsroom South East*), followed by a manic week filling in application forms to beat the deadline, resulted in a grant of £53,000 to finance the staffing and activities of INSP for one year from December 1994.

The Big Issue's philosophy of helping homeless people to help themselves has always had an international dimension. When the opportunity arrived for the company to participate in establishing an international presence through a network, it jumped at it. However, some staff have not been behind the international work as they believe that money should be used to support vendors in the UK or invested into the magazine rather than diverted to pay for international work. Whilst the department was funded by external sources, there was little problem but there was pressure from some quarters to drop the international work if it was not paying for itself.

By the time of the first INSP conference in London in 1995, there were 16 members of the network.[7] The Street Paper Charter was adopted here as the criterion upon which papers joined the Network. The other *Big Issues* were founder members and have been involved in the international work in varying degrees. People from St Petersburg, Budapest and Johannesburg attended and this annual exchange of experience became crucial for the membership. The advantages of a network soon became apparent. Street papers had little or no spare cash and finance from the EC enabled member papers to attend not only INSP conferences, but other conferences on homelessness within Europe.

INSP went from strength to strength. In January 1996 Pat Cole, who had sold *The Big Issue* for four years and wanted to move into full-time employment, joined the department for one year as international assistant. She helped organize the staff exchange bureau in 1996 when 21 members of staff, from vendor support, distribution and editorial departments from street papers across Europe, visited their counterparts to exchange ideas and work practices. Maria Laura Bono, former editor of *Das Megaphon*, said of her visit to *Asphalt* in Hannover that 'It was very important for me to visit a street paper of a similar size and type'.

A small grant from the Gulbenkian Foundation continued this programme when Jane McRobbie from *Big Issue in the North* went to *CAIS*'s offices in Lisbon. This was then reciprocated by a visit from *CAIS*.

Pat, with Robyn Heaton, manager of JET, took a group of vendors to a conference in Copenhagen in 1996, called 'Culture from the other side'. They were joined by vendors from *BISS* in Munich and *Straatnieuws* in Utrecht. This was an unusual conference, since it brought together not simply practitioners and policy makers but homeless people themselves from all over Europe who participated in a programme of music, poetry readings and cultural events.

Street papers from four continents – Europe, North America, Africa and Australia – met for the first time at two further INSP conferences in London, in 1996 and 1997. By the third conference, the Network had 25 international members. The Reuters Foundation held a course in London in the week leading up to this conference for ten international street paper journalists which was a resounding success.

One new paper to the conference came from The Gambia. Run by Adama Bah, who works to develop sustainable tourism in his country, *Concern* is sold by young unemployed men on the beaches in an attempt to stop them harassing tourists. Adama's plan is to use the publishing link to help the unemployed to develop skills. It has been a long struggle and at one point the magazine was unable to publish for some months after the printing press broke down.

Following the 1997 conference, a social review of the charter principles was carried out, with the help of Peter Raynard, of the New Economics Foundation.[8] Social auditing is an effective way to assess the social impact and ethical behaviour of an organization in relation to its aims and those of its stakeholders. The social review revealed how the members measured up to the charter principles and provided a validation process of the members who had joined. The analysis of how the street papers assessed the charter principles provided a valuable insight into how the members would like to see the Network develop.

Having helped establish, run and part finance INSP, *The Big Issue* reliquished its role. Some members of INSP thought that *The Big Issue* was too controlling, some even seeing it as a puppet of *The Big Issue*. However unfair the international department felt the criticisms were, they were eager to take a back seat. Maria Clancy observes:

> *'We felt we had achieved what we had set out to do in terms of bringing together and energizing the international street paper movement. In effect, the desire of the Network members to actively participate was a measure of our success.'*

Subsequently, the INSP secretariat moved to *The Big Issue Scotland* where it has been run by Layla Mewburn until funding can be found for an independent secretariat. This was convenient for all concerned. Having established *The Big Issue* in Scotland Mel Young felt he wanted a new challenge and had increasingly become involved in international work. He took over the work in St Petersburg and has provided a dedication to the subsequent work in central and Eastern Europe.

The street paper movement in Western Europe is now consolidating. Like other businesses, street papers will need to develop and diversify if they are going to remain sustainable in the future.

Terre di mezzo, for example, has been producing alternative tourism guides and other books and also a second paper, *Altreconomia*, which is targeted to a more specialized audience, in the second fortnight of the month. *Terre di mezzo* is also developing an interest in fair trade and encourages fair trade shops to sponsor a vendor outside them. In turn, advertising for the shops is run or products from the shops are sold through the paper.

BISS, based in Munich, has been the first paper to employ vendors to sell the paper. Around ten employees pay social insurance contributions and the initiative has worked well, taking the vendors onto the next level. The German street papers, now numbering 40, have launched a new national network. A similar network was launched by the Dutch street papers, the Straatmedia Groep Nederland, in January 1996 in realization that working together can be more productive.

INSP's fourth conference was held in St Petersburg in 1998, sponsored by the Know How Fund and Expo 2000, and whose theme was the issue of human rights.[9] The fifth took place in Budapest, hosted by *Flaszter* in January 2000 and the sixth in Cape Town, hosted by *Big Issue Cape Town*, in March 2001. INSP's membership currently stands at over 40 members. South America is becoming a growth area for street papers, Brazil and Argentina in particular. *Hecho in Bs As* launched in Buenos Aires in June 2000, joining *Diagonal*. Initiated by Patricia Merkin, and edited by Briton Chris Moss, *Hecho* is based on *The Big Issue* and is currently sold by around 60 vendors in the city.

BIG ISSUE INTERNATIONAL

The Big Issue international department's work was extensive. As well as running INSP and providing editorial for the international page of the magazine, it ran the staff exchange bureau, met with foreign journalists, wrote articles, ran the annual conference, dealt with new members and supported new papers. It also promoted the social business idea abroad.

Many people asked to use *The Big Issue*'s name for their street papers but, except on three occasions, this was not encouraged because of the potential lack of control that the London office would have over papers so far away. Three *Big Issues* have been launched outside of the UK, all three by founders known to the UK company – *The Big Issue Australia* in Melbourne in June[10] and

The Big Issue Cape Town in December 1996. The third international
Big Issue launched in Los Angeles in 1998.

The Big Issue Australia

This was initiated by Graeme Wise, head of The Body Shop in
Australia and a friend of Gordon Roddick. Graeme pulled
together a group of organizations in Melbourne to run the
magazine and raised money through various sources, including
The Body Shop itself.

Unlike in the UK, *The Big Issue Australia* is sold by the long-
term unemployed as well as homeless and ex-homeless people.
Of Australia's 18 million people, the Salvation Army estimated
that, in 1997, 1.9 million were living in poverty. The organization
provides beds for more than 2200 homeless a night and estimates
that more than 21,000 young people and 40,000 single adults and
families are homeless, living in short-term or temporary accommodation.[11] High private rentals and long public housing waiting
lists have emerged as the main cause of poverty in Australian
cities. Therefore, many end up on the streets.

The Big Issue Australia is similar in style and content to the
UK's, being a general interest magazine. Its vendor profiles are
one of its most popular features, according to market research.
Current editor Simon Castles followed founding editor Misha
Ketchell and Thornton McCamish, to produce a wide range of
investigative and celebrity articles. Campaigning on such issues
as refugees and Aboriginal rights combines with a certain amount
of irreverant humour. There is a Missing People's page (every
year 30,000 Australians go missing) and some articles are run
from *Big Issues* in the UK.

The magazine is sold on the streets of Melbourne, Sydney and
Brisbane by over 100 vendors, some of whom have problems of
drug and alcohol addiction, or mental illness. It is sold for $3.00,
of which the vendors keep half. Around 80 per cent of the vendors
are male and over 30 years of age. The challenge for the magazine
has been to try to keep increasing circulation, which dipped soon
after the launch, but is now a healthy 21,000 per fortnight spread
between the three cities: 12,000 in Melbourne, 5000 in Sydney and
3000 in Brisbane. It is read mostly by young, professional women
and has a readership of around 60,000 every fortnight.

Sales are not high enough to be self-sustaining, so the income from sales and advertising is augmented by corporate and foundation sponsorship. Distribution points are now being set up in other areas, like Albury-Wodonga, which will raise the circulation. Editor Simon Castles says:

> 'Getting advertisers has always been difficult for us. I think a lot of potential advertisers see The Big Issue as a bit too risky, a bit too "leftie", a bit too unknown. This is obviously something we will need to rectify in order to become fully self-supporting.'

Since there are, as yet, no profits, there is no support team and vendors are referred to outside agencies for assistance. However, there are literacy and numeracy classes in Melbourne, with the help of a college of further education, as well as creative writing, sales and budgeting classes. The magazine is seen as having a complementary role to the benefit system. It receives assistance from other companies, for instance all legal work is provided *pro bono* from Corrs Chambers Westgarth and rent-free office space is provided for the headquarters at the Wesley Mission in Melbourne. A television advertisement, run in March 2000, free of charge, by ad agency Whybin TBWA, featuring vendors singing their favourite songs, brought in a great deal of positive publicity for the magazine.

The Body Shop is still involved, although its contribution is being reduced every year. Simon Castles says:

> 'The Big Issue Australia *plans to be self-supporting by the end of July 2001. It has a bright future. The profile of the magazine is growing in Australia and sales are improving all the time. The content of the magazine, whilst always able to be improved on, seems to meet with the approval of most readers.'*

Editorially, they have tried to push the magazine as 'the current affairs magazine with a sense of humour'.

THE BIG ISSUE CAPE TOWN

The experiences of *The Big Issue* in Cape Town could not have been more different from those in the UK or Australia. Here was a city in which decades of oppression had resulted in enormous poverty and street homelessness.

In South Africa, a homeless adult is defined not as someone living in a shack, of which there are millions, but as one who is 'a person of the streets'. One of the characteristics of street people is that they have lost all or most connection to their family and are likely to suffer from very poor or no self-esteem. In a country where 6 per cent of the population earns 40 per cent of the income, 66 per cent of black South Africans are poor as opposed to just 2 per cent of whites. In 1996, a survey carried out by street workers showed that around 300 homeless adult males and 96 adult females were on the streets within the central business district of Cape Town.[12]

The Body Shop Foundation again was involved, by donating £10,000 for a feasibility study and initial funding. Maria Clancy visited Cape Town, Johannesburg and Durban in 1995 to identify a team. There had already been interest in Cape Town from Shane Halpin, who was working for the Silesian Institute, and Debi Diamond, who was working with homeless people. Then, Alan Bartram, who came from Johannesburg, put money forward to publish the first issue of *The Big Issue Cape Town*. Alan, who sits on the board, had raised 40,000 Rand for his own publication. He had seen *Homeless Talk* in Johannesburg (see page 170) and was keen to help establish a publication in Cape Town. Shane and Debi then worked with Maria Clancy, mainly by phone and fax, as the paper launched and developed.

The major challenge, initially, was that street sleepers did not respond to the idea of selling the magazine. As Debi Diamond says:

> 'When we first approached homeless people they were very sceptical about the idea. But when you scratched below the surface and asked why they were so dubious they said it was the first project where they'd actually been approached and asked to be a part of it. The submissiveness of people who have been used to handouts stays with them for a very long time...'[13]

Public antagonism still exists towards the homeless who often suffer from abuse. This also would reflect on the company's finances, if they could not get enough people to sell the magazine. The staff then started to work with the long-term unemployed, who come into the city from the townships and shanty towns.

At first, the magazine was bi-monthly, going monthly in March 1998. The monthly circulation is currently around 15,000, and research indicates that the magazine is bought by the 20–50 age group. In April 1998, the total number of registered vendors was 632 of whom 528 were male, but only 131 were actively selling. In terms of ethnicity, 35 (27 per cent) were white; 48 (37 per cent) were coloured and 48 (37 per cent) were black. Sixty-six were staying in townships and vulnerable accommodation and 65 were in night shelters and sleeping rough on the streets. By October 1999, a core group of around 200 vendors were selling and another 400 were semi-active. An average vendor can make between 1000 and 2000 Rand per month (£100–£200).[14]

Now Shane Halpin believes that there are an increasing number of black, unemployed people selling the magazine. Between 40–45 per cent of the vendors are now black, 35 per cent coloured, and the remainder white. There are different responses to the vendors from the public. He says:

> 'White vendors, I think, do better. This is because the perception is that they are "one of ours". The people with the money in this country, and certainly in Cape Town, are still the white population by and large.'

Debi Diamond heads the move-on Big Step Programme. On offer to the vendors are an alcohol and substance support group, run along the lines of Alcoholics Anonymous, computer and art classes, crisis counselling, a women's support group, training and further education services, assistance with finding accommodation and a job programme (see Appendix VII). By October 1999, around 63 vendors had obtained jobs.

The Big Issue Cape Town is now recognized by the local Department of Social Services as a major supplier of services to the unemployed. 'We are being piloted for the first time this year [2000]', explains Shane. 'They are giving the money to us to see how we provide the services. It's not a grant so much as a programme of funding. It is not a huge amount of money, but in terms of the country, *The Big Issue* is part of the equation.'

The magazine was first edited by Ray Joseph, who came from the mainstream press, followed by Glenda Nevill. As in the UK, the magazine highlights the major social issues of the day, and runs celebrity features and vendors' writing. Support from the mainstream media has been impressive. However, it is not yet sustainable, relying on grants and sponsorship to underpin its work. *The Big Issue* in London has supported the magazine with substantial funds and obtained a UK National Lottery grant of £93,000. This enabled *The Big Issue Cape Town* to open a second distribution office in the suburb of Wynberg. A third depot has since opened, which will increase the sales and opportunities for new vendors.

The magazine went from bi-monthly to monthly to increase sales. An important move was the expansion into Johannesburg in March 2001. Finance has been acquired for this expansion from companies such as The Body Shop and Clicks, and the aim is to make the magazine self-sustaining through increased sales. *The Big Issue Cape Town* will be working with the Johannesburg street paper, *Homeless Talk*. Launched in 1994 by a Methodist organization, *Homeless Talk* is written by homeless and unemployed writers, mainly from the townships.

Shane comments:

> 'The people I have worked with and who have committed themselves from the beginning have been the strengths. And the vendors. People often say to us, it must be very depressing working with homelessness. And I say no, not when you're working with a project like **The Big Issue**. You see changes and positive things happening, which for me is what makes it worthwhile. There are some people you don't get anywhere with, but there are those who are so happy and so delighted just to have a job.'

RUSSIA AND EASTERN EUROPE

In the second half of the 1990s the Eastern European street paper movement has developed in response to the growth of poverty and homelessness in the post-communist era. Previously, in many Eastern European countries homeless people had been treated as criminals or imprisoned. Today, the causes of homelessness throughout Eastern Europe are similar in many respects to those in Western Europe. But it is more difficult for homeless people to find a way out of their predicament because the opportunities for access to appropriate assistance are so limited.[15] There is a massive housing crisis, with unaffordable accommodation and low quality housing stock.

St Petersburg in Russia probably held the worst record for homelessness in Eastern Europe in the early 1990s with at least 50,000 people homeless.[16] Many still on the streets have drink problems and have reached the depths of social isolation. Alcohol poisoning and malnutrition, combined with the long and brutal winters, cause over 3000 deaths on the streets each year.

Russia's first street paper, *The Depths*, was launched in St Petersburg in 1994, inspired by a copy of *The Big Issue*. It arrived, having come via Germany, at the night shelter and soup kitchen called Nochlezhka. Valeriy Sokolov, founder of the shelter and of *The Depths*, has been a tireless campaigner on behalf of the homeless in St Petersburg. He has helped bring the issue to the forefront of government and public consciousness in a country where homelessness was formerly illegal. A copy of *The Depths* was then brought to *The Big Issue* in 1995 by an English painter, Elizabeth Hinton, who had lived in St Petersburg for eight years and worked with Valeriy.

People in Russia do not exist if they are not registered with the authorities or have internal documents or passports. Valeriy set up the means by which homeless people in St Petersburg can be registered. Now, Russia is one of the few places in the world where homeless people can vote. The next five years was spent setting up soup kitchens and providing medical and legal advice. Layla Mewburn, who works with Mel Young, says:

> '*But none of that would have been available or possible if they had not done the registration of homeless people. In the first year they registered about 10,000 people who could suddenly get food, clothes, medical help, which they hadn't been able to do before.*'

Mel Young has developed and expanded the street paper movement with partners in Hungary, Russia and other countries. He obtained funding from the Know How Fund financed by the British Government's Department for International Development (DFID)[17] to help *The Depths* to become self-financing. Initially, because homeless people have nothing, *The Depths*' vendors could not afford to buy their copies. They would get them on credit, promising to return with the cash. But only a few did, creating cash flow problems for the paper. Now it is different, and around 100 regular vendors sell 20,000 papers a fortnight, at 500 roubles (six pence) each. There are now three other *Depths* newspapers selling in Moscow, Novosibirsk (Siberia) and Odessa (Ukraine). Whilst they are separate and run themselves, they are linked with inserts of local news.

There is virtually no social welfare system in Russia with the homeless having to rely on charity. However, charity is a new concept in Russia, where formerly the state provided both homes and jobs. As there are no official homelessness statistics in Russia, the current number of street people in St Petersburg is unknown; there is no housing to refer vendors on to, since there is no notion of council housing and fewer than 1000 hostel places.

The Big Issue Scotland and *The Big Issue* in London have each given part of the cover price of one edition to *The Depths* – £1500 from London and £10,000 from a Christmas edition of *The Big Issue Scotland*. Pat Cole from the international department went to St Petersburg to the first ever exhibition on homelessness in Russia in 1996, armed with £95 collected for the Russian vendors by *Big Issue* vendors. Valeriy organized the event which included street papers and items sent by the members of INSP. The exhibition contributed to breaking down the stigma of homelessness amongst the Russian public.

In Eastern Europe, there is a flourishing network of papers: Budapest (*No Borders*); Warsaw (*Bez-Granic*); Prague (*Patron-No Borders*); Slovakia and Romania (*Spune*). Attila Kenderessy launched *Flaszter*, the first paper in Budapest, in January 1997, responding to a situation where at least 20,000 were homeless. He then set up a resource centre to provide technical assistance for the existing street papers and to help start new ones. This led to the launch of *No Borders* magazine at the end of 1999. Written and designed by journalists from the UK and Hungary and produced in Budapest, it is translated into the national languages of Poland, the Czech Republic, Slovakia and Romania and is distributed to partner organizations that already work with the homeless and socially marginalized.

Flaszter is part of the *No Borders* network. *Patron*, in the Czech Republic, has been selling 20,000 a fortnight since its launch in December 1999 and has consequently been able to sell advertising on the back of its good circulation figures. DFID will continue to fund the No Borders company at least until the end of 2001. *Flaszter* is currently taking on an international research project to find out how successful street papers are across Europe, and how they help people into jobs and homes, and improve their access to health services.

The economic situation in Romania poses interesting questions for the street paper movement. Now, there are two papers in Romania: *Spune* published in Iasi, in the North West, and a *No Borders* magazine in the South East. But they are proceeding slowly. Layla Mewburn wonders if it is appropriate to have a street paper in Romania if it has to be funded from outside. She comments:

> *'People just don't have the disposable incomes there. They don't have the money to buy the paper. Pouring money into something that is going to help a few vendors, but is going to take money off people who are equally as poor as the homeless people, is there a rationale behind that?*

Then there is the question of whether street papers are appropriate for all countries. Sometimes the conditions are not right to support the production and distribution of a monthly paper. Asks Layla:

> *'Should you force street papers into other countries? If someone approaches you, then yes, you have to consider whether it is going to be a viable business. If it constantly requires outside funding, then you have to think twice about it.'*

NORTH AMERICA

The street paper movement spread westwards across the States and up into Canada, following *Street News*'s launch in New York in 1989. Today there are around 50 North American street papers.[18]

There has been much interest in American and Canadian cities in how the street paper experience has been developed in the UK. In May 1993, John Bird visited the US and Canada to meet with people in San Francisco, Vancouver, New York and Washington.

Interest centred on ways of converting existing street papers to more mass sales publications. In November 1993, Lucie Russell and John were asked to visit *L'itinéraire* in Montreal. At the time, the French-Canadian paper was interested in learning ways of tapping into *The Big Issue*'s success.

Around this time, John was contacted by a group in Chicago who wanted to start a paper. John says:

> *'They were interested in developing a popular publication based on* The Big Issue. *We talked them through our approach and sent them our blueprint. They were interested in such things as the code of conduct and our editorial mix. A representative from the group visited me in London and soon they were up and running.'*

Out of this group, *StreetWise* developed and it is America's most successful street paper. In the spring of 2000 it went weekly.

The North American Street Newspapers Association (NASNA), was launched at the first conference of North American street papers in Chicago in August 1996, hosted by *StreetWise*. A member from INSP discussed with the delegates the benefits of running a network and the advantages of shared experience.

NASNA and INSP, though, run along different philosophical lines. INSP operates a charter upon which the membership criterion is based; NASNA is 'all inclusive', allowing all North American street papers to join. American street papers are more advocate-led and shy away from the commerciality of European papers. Their preference is for papers to be run with homeless people involved at all levels, from being on the board, to writing and managing, as well as selling. Certainly, they differ from *The Big Issue*. *The Big Issue* concentrates on mass sales, leading to large numbers of homeless people earning an income. North American street papers are less mass market and see the papers as an opportunity to get homeless people making their own publications.

So far, there are two North American members of INSP who also belong to NASNA. One of the membership criteria of INSP now is that street papers have to be a social business, and that they have to be striving to make money. Layla says:

'The American street papers have a real problem with this and so we said "fine, but this is what we all believe. We believe in making money". Some wanted to take the word "business" out of the charter principles and we kept saying this is a key word. This is what we are. StreetWise were up for that totally. The members of INSP are very clear about where they want to be, and that they are businesses.'

Street News in New York still publishes sporadically but is not the mass sales paper that it was ten years ago. There had been discussions with John Bird about relaunching *Street News* as a mass circulation paper in New York which came to nothing due to the conflicting philosophies. In June 2000, the Grand Central Partnership launched *Big News*, a monthly A5 colour magazine. The first issue was given away free and now around 4500 are sold each month on the streets for a dollar, with vendors buying it for 40 cents. Financed by fundraising, government grants and its own business, it describes itself as a literary magazine.

In 1995 and 1996, John had met Ted Hayes of the Dome Village Project in downtown Los Angeles, and talked about the problems of homelessness in the US. Ted is a black activist who has worked across the racial divide on behalf of homeless people. The Dome Village, in one of LA's poorest areas, is a thriving community in which homeless people can build a life for themselves. Ted asked John to consider starting *The Big Issue* in LA. In summer 1997 John took up Ted's offer of visiting LA. He met with homeless people, social activists, city officials and the then Chief of Police. He says:

'It was impressive. Here I was with people who loved the work programme idea. The trip was a great success and it encouraged me to listen to Ted's pleading.'

At the time, there was no street paper in LA or LA County. *Hard Times* had been sold in Santa Monica, 13 miles west of the city of LA but had closed in early 1997. Founder Len Doucette also asked John to start *The Big Issue* in LA although he wanted Santa Monica included. John says:

'I listened to Len, but was more interested in working in downtown LA than Santa Monica. I wanted to work in Ted's constituency rather than what seemed like a prosperous white

zone on the edge of the ocean. Also, because of Ted's influence, I
was drawn more towards African-Americans, especially those
who would not beg and were looking for work.'

However, John agreed with Len that if *The Big Issue* started it
would be available throughout greater LA, which included Santa
Monica.

John had also developed a good working relationship with
Jeff Grunberg of the Grand Central Partnership in Manhattan. Jeff
wanted to do *The Big Issue* in New York. In 1996, Jeff had visited
the printer and publisher of New York's *Street News*. They
discussed Jeff taking over *Street News* and the publisher/owner
believed this would be simple. Jeff and John only wanted to work
with *Street News* if the existing team wanted this, but Indio, the
editor, objected. The owner therefore backed out.

John and Ted Hayes decided to launch an LA *Big Issue*.
Meanwhile, Jennafer Wagonner, a former helper on *Hard Times*,
decided to relaunch *Making Change* in Santa Monica. This was
where the complications set in. John explains:

'Because of duplications in Paris, I had suggested only having
one INSP member in each city. Paris had about six papers at
any one time and it was a problem. I therefore wanted to avoid
treading on anyone's toes in LA. But as everyone said, our brief
was to work largely with the poor African-Americans of LA.'

Santa Monica may have only been 13 miles distant but it was a
world away. Santa Monica's homeless were mainly white; many
of them were ex-surfers and musicians drawn to LA in the 1960s;
they were articulate and predominantly panhandled (begged for
money in the streets). Where Ted was, however, were the indige-
nous poor of America. Not those fallen on hard times, but those
who had lived in poverty for generations. *The Big Issue LA* would
be an LA, as opposed to a Santa Monica, initiative.

John had signed up numerous helpers, including Len
Doucette. In February, John arrived with writer Matt Owen for
what they believed was three months. Immediately, *The Big Issue*
LA (BILA) ran into problems, It was accused of imperialism with
Jennafer Wagonner as the victim. A barrage of criticism by largely
West Coast members of NASNA followed.

The launch took place in The Dome Village in April 1998. A large marquee was set up by the Village and hundreds of people attended, including leading policemen and the Assistant District Attorney. Anita Roddick and John Bird spoke. The TV, radio and newspaper coverage was positive. To John, it felt like a rerun of the original launch but it was not to be like that.

John's daughter, Diana, who worked as business manager for 18 months, remembers:

> 'The idea was that we would create a social business on the model of The Big Issue UK. There isn't so much of a street-buying history there, but having come from London, and remembering that it started the same way in Australia and South Africa, we decided to do it the same way.'

The first difficulty was recruiting vendors to sell the new monthly magazine. Whilst Los Angeles is a city where everyone goes everywhere by car or bus, there are some heavily pedestrianized areas. The vendors received 20 free copies and a pitch, and could sell them in an hour or two. Diana remembers:

> 'We'd fire them up, give them a little talk, get them to sign the code of conduct. But they didn't come back. Or they would come back a week later and buy ten papers. In the meantime, they would panhandle and they were also eligible to collect welfare and food stamps.'

The paper linked with the large number of homeless organizations in LA including an enormous number of shelters and places for homeless people to eat. Some organizers were enthusiastic, others were sceptical. Many said that homeless people have to feel that they are on some kind of programme. Shelter and employment programmes have very strict rules, like in the UK, of not being able to go out at night, drink or take drugs.

The staff talked to homeless people but they were not interested because they could make good money panhandling. The magazine then established five different distribution points, with a van stopping at various places around the city. They made it as easy as possible for people to access the papers. They asked the vendors what the problem was. Diana says:

'They were coming to us and saying, "we love what you are doing, but I don't want to sell a paper. I don't want to be out on the streets, selling a paper that is going to be recognized as a homeless newspaper".'

But isn't panhandling the same thing? Diana explains:

'There's a difference. Panhandling in America is very direct. Selling a paper, unlike panhandling which can be done with stealth, is like having a big neon sign: "Look, I'm a failure".'

What they really wanted was a job. Diana adds: 'They were saying to us, "I want a 9 to 5. I want to know how much money I'm making. I want to be part of the company".' This is a reflection of the way American culture is so success orientated. She explains:

'It's quite ruthless there. It's very easy to fall between the gaps, much easier than in the UK. There isn't the support system that they UK has, and when you fall down, it's much tougher to get up. They will take two jobs, move back to their parents' house, because going on welfare is seen as the ultimate recognition that you are not a successful person. It's because of this mentality that homeless people are kept so down and you have a lot of generational homelessness and poverty.'

After three issues, and little take-up by vendors, John Bird decided to make it free. There is a strong culture of free magazines in LA, the most popular being the listings magazine, *LA Weekly*. Four homeless people were employed to distribute BILA around the city to shops, cafes, gyms, hair salons and restaurants. Paid $8.00 an hour (the minimum wage is $5.75 an hour), they worked a full week and had all the benefits of holiday and sick pay. BILA also employed Patricia, who had been homeless and had originally sold the magazine, as the receptionist. She now has her own flat. Her life has been transformed, she says:

'I've been with The Big Issue *going on three years. It's so great to be part of something so positive and uplifting. Having been homeless myself, you learn to really appreciate a second chance at life itself.'*

One distributor was Caesar, originally from Guatemala, who has lived in a homeless shelter for over 20 years. Another was Robert, 26, who has been in and out of prison and had never held a job for more than three months. He has been with BILA for two years and has blossomed.

Cara Solomon was the editor of BILA. She had been an intern at *Spare Change*, Boston's street paper, and had spent some time at *The Big Issue* in London. Diana states:

> 'BILA was Cara's vision. She made the magazine more community orientated and socially active than the UK edition. It covered more about how to get involved in your own community. BILA made ideas and social issues very accessible and interesting. We were very much into celebrating LA.'

However, problems with some of the other American street papers continued. At the NASNA conference in August 1999 in Montreal, BILA's membership was considered. Jennafer Wagonner spoke against it; she had already resigned from NASNA in protest at what she believed would be BILA's acceptance. Many people spoke in support of John. John says:

> 'I told the conference that Making Change *could conceivably be squeezed out by a bigger paper, and I understood Jennafer's worries. I therefore withdrew our application because I did not want the movement split over* The Big Issue. *I said that if some people doubted our sincerity, it was better than we left it for a year until we had proven ourselves.'*

Though BILA was a great success with the public, who continuously phoned the offices, financially it was always precarious and the staff lived on a knife edge. It was very difficult to get advertising as the magazine was so new and the circulation was unknown, so the business was depending on little bits of investment and advertising. Diana says: 'There was six months of research done there, we were invited in. All the signs said this will work.' But a year in, the magazine was replaced by *Off the Wall*, a monthly poster of local events, financed by advertising and distributed in a similar fashion.

BILA was a very difficult experiment. It took John away from *The Big Issue* in London for two years, which created problems.

Staff in London were not happy about the situation. Nigel Kershaw, previously managing director in London, has subsequently moved to LA to develop BILA. He is working with corporations and organizations to help train homeless people.

John is adamant about the US experience.

> 'I learnt so much about moving people away from a casual existence. I saw the future in LA. It was all about new businesses and sheltered employment.'

However, the challenges produced a new attitude. John explains:

> 'Being attacked as expansionist was one problem. But most of the attacks came from people who believed in homelessness as an alternative lifestyle. I don't buy into that. If people want their own homeless paper for homeless people to read, then they are not going to create income for the homeless. The Big Issue is about creating work and mobility out of destitution.'

John continues:

> 'There were class and race issues too. Interestingly, the people who really supported us were African-Americans, who wanted opportunity. They saw no dignity in poverty. That 'dignity in poverty issue' is a white middle-class liberal thing that most poor people cannot accept.
>
> 'In the years to come, I want homeless people to have options. Not just to sell The Big Issue. We need businesses that give job opportunities.'

8

GROWTH AND CHANGE

PROBLEMS OF GROWTH

IT TOOK OVER four years after the launch to consolidate *The Big Issue*. A strategic plan was formulated and people were recruited into management to streamline the company. Until that point, the haphazard and unconventional way that the company had been thrown together affected its performance. As the company grew and the Foundation was established, a more precise and organized strategy was needed. The contradiction that this threw up meant that *The Big Issue*'s quirkiness was threatened. The excitement and dedication of the founding staff was bound to be reined as the company professionalized. John Bird's role as the visionary needed supplementing with good organizational skills, by people who could manage and develop the company on a daily basis.

Lyndall Stein had arrived in 1995 as head of fundraising for the new Foundation. She brought experience from both a political and charitable background, having worked for the African National Congress and the Terrence Higgins Trust. Lyndall tackled the lack of financial planning and for the two years she was with *The Big Issue*, her ability to challenge the status quo put the Foundation, and to a certain extent the business, on a sounder footing. She was assisted by the new managing director Andrew Jaspan, and Jonathan King, the new finance director. Lyndall discovered that for four years there had been no proper financial planning for the business. This was, she stresses, purely a result of disorganization, not impropriety. Once the Foundation was set up, budgets and an annual plan were a necessity.

Helped by the Foundation's new assistant, Rachel Stewart, she obtained money to employ external consultants, Compass, for the first time. Compass worked on the budget and annual plan for both the company and the Foundation and concluded that more money needed to be invested in extra staff in certain areas, and new equipment.

For the first time an outsider had come in to identify the company's needs. Lyndall remembers:

'John found it very difficult, the process of having Compass here. But credit to him, that he did allow it to happen, people coming and interfering with him and taking control away.'

One of the issues faced by the directorial team was that of the difficulties of being pulled in many different directions in a demand for resources for each department. They had to fight this out as a team and it was not easy. Some were inexperienced in dealing with departments and staff. Compass's work enabled the directors to pull together again, providing them with the expertise and ability to focus on the future.

Two new staff were recruited into the finance department from big City accountancy firms in 1996, joining Connie McBride and the team. Jonathan King, from James Capel, professionalized and streamlined a department that had been overstretched. Helen Montagu came from Price Waterhouse with responsibility for the Foundation's accounts.

Jonathan found the financial structures very rudimentary and the accounts team badly underresourced. He introduced formal controls and procedures. He says:

'When it becomes a £3m turnover company it has to have controls because something can go badly wrong very quickly. It became more professional because it needed to give a more professional service to its vendors, and a more professional outlook to the outside world because people start demanding more and more.'

In terms of a management structure, the company started with a 'flattened hierarchy' with everyone doing everything. Now, the structure developed into a more traditional model. As owner of the company, John has the final say within the group of directors, each of whom manages their managers who then oversee their staff. Mostly, though, John went with the consensus.

The need for for more organization led to Andrew Jaspan, formerly editor of *The Observer* newspaper, joining the company as managing director in 1996. Jo Mallabar remembers: 'Lots of people for a while had been saying that John didn't act as an MD. That he was too involved in too many things, too unreliable, always being distracted, not reading things he should read.' Andrew's brief was to take charge of the business side. He had extensive experience of the media. His task was to improve the editorial of the magazine and to raise the profile of *The Big Issue*; to make sure that the media was kept informed, and to develop the sales and distribution side of the magazine. Andrew states:

> *'John, for example, did not have a background of someone who had professionally run companies in the past, so in a sense what I was brought in to do was to augment aspects of John where he was weaker and to help him run* The Big Issue *in a better way. The spirit and the spark still came from John and the overall position of* The Big Issue *still came out of how he thought it should go. He asked me to turn that aspiration into a reality.'*

How did he do that? 'With some difficulty. I didn't really want to stamp out everything that was good about the organization by saying everything has got to be changed by bringing in new procedures and new ways of working throughout the organization.' But professionalize it he did, in many aspects of editorial, press and communication.

In June 1995, a personnel department was created to invest in training and development of staff. Personnel director Sue Hollowell and her team spent years formulating the necessary company policies to fit around *The Big Issue*'s specific work practices. It was important to Sue that she followed the best practice within the field: most of the policies in this area came from The Body Shop, which had a good reputation. ACAS (the Advisory, Conciliation and Arbitration Service) give best practice guidelines and Sue made sure that the policies met these fully. She also looked at the practices of other organizations, such as

Tower Records and *The Guardian*, which have a good reputation here too.

The Big Issue's grievance policy, for example, which has been praised by representatives from ACAS, is far broader than the standard one; it is encouraged to be seen as a positive policy, rather than a negative one. Sue explains:

> *'If you tell your manager about an idea you've got and it doesn't go any further, then you have the right to use the formal system to get that idea recognized.'*

She also took a policy from The Body Shop: if the procedure has been exhausted by going through all the proper channels, staff have the right to do a 'red letter' in order to obtain a result. She says:

> *'We did that quite early on, because we found that lots of staff were having ideas, but as the structure grew, the information coming up to John was getting more and more filtered. This is because the higher you are in an organization, the less you hear what is going on.'*

Sue has talked to many groups and organizations. For example, staff at Scotland Yard thought that the way procedures are run at *The Big Issue* are 'progressive, modern and forward thinking'. Sue comments:

> *'We have the freedom to do that here. We can bring new ideas and different ways of working. But, again, it is the resources. If we had money, we would do a creche. Lack of resources hold us back on many things.'*

Mentoring and training for staff from other organizations have both been crucial to the development of the company. Companies used to offer their services for free because they wanted to contribute to *The Big Issue*. Sue comments:

> *'We never had any resources for training here so I used to go out with a begging bowl. And we ended up getting a lot – around £56,000 worth – of staff training.'*

She talked her way onto expensive seminars for free and comments that, 'Whenever I said I was from *The Big Issue*, everyone wanted to talk to me about it and people wanted to help.'

This is an interesting aspect of social business. Companies looked at *The Big Issue* in a 'charitable' fashion. They wanted to assist, not by giving money, but by donating services free – services such as management training, legal services, PR and air time for advertisements. For example, the legal firm Nabarro Nathanson has been very supportive. Maria Clancy comments:

> 'This creates a dichotomy for the company. If we were paying Nabarro's it would cost us a lot of money. They take us on as a charitable client, part of their commitment to social responsibility.'

She adds:

> 'These kind of things should be costed up, because we would have to see, as a pure traditional business, could we deliver with all the costs incurred? And also if we had to pay market rate, what would that mean, say, to the vendors?'

Consequently, *The Big Issue* is not operating according to market forces in some areas.

The Big Issue's libel lawyers, Doughty Chambers, also carried out *pro bono* work for the first seven years. Now, they give the company a very generous deal. Nigel Kershaw has another view on it:

> 'We look at it as pro bono, but what we maybe should look at it as is that it is those people's return investment. They are investing their time and expertise. They don't look at it as "charity". They want to work with us and feel part of the way we are doing things. And they want to invest their time and experience in the business, as opposed to pro bono.'

In the summer of 1992 there were 12 people working at *The Big Issue* and at the end of 2000 there is a total of about 115 in London and the South East offices, both in the company and the Foundation. Some 20 ex-vendors have been employed over eight years, mainly worked in the distribution and outreach area. The personnel department, now comprising director Elizabeth Divver, Natasha Santos-Castellino and Maria Blaney, is still as busy as ever.

Andrew Davies, former deputy editor, links the 1990s social and political activism to the type of staff that are attracted to work at *The Big Issue*, particularly in the editorial department. Coming from a campaigning background himself, he came to *The Big Issue* partly as a way of continuing his political and social commitment. He believes:

> 'The Big Issue *was seen as an outlet for people who have perhaps been involved with groups and who wanted to change things, but realized the drawbacks of just producing left-wing newspapers such as* Militant *or* Socialist Worker. The Big Issue *has a much broader theme and has been a magnet for those who would have been politically active in left-wing movements in the eighties.'*

There are high levels of commitment by staff throughout the company. The downside is the high level of burn-out. Is that *The Big Issue*'s mismanagement or the type of person who is attracted to work at the company? He says:

> '*I think there is an element of the fact that* The Big Issue *is a terrible sponge. I could give 24 hours and* The Big Issue *would take it. You could almost die and do that. I have felt that I have given a huge part of my life, as have lots of other people. And that's not in a bitter way. Some of it has been fantastic and obviously I enjoyed doing that.'*

Despite this, Matthew Collin, editor from 1998, believes that, for journalists, *The Big Issue* is one of the best places to work in the country:

> '*Because you're part of a collective mission. You're not making money for someone to retire to a villa in Tuscany, and you have a measure of individual freedom, not a great deal but a lot more than you get in other places. It just doesn't get any better than that. You are getting paid to do things you believe in.'*

DIVERSIFICATION

Over the years, *The Big Issue* has tried to establish 'secondary income streams' or micro-enterprises. This is in addition to the publishing areas which employ and train vendors who want to move on from selling the paper. But this has created financial difficulties for the business. The most adventurous attempt was Making It, which was established in 1994 to train and encourage vendors to work in a small business environment, making products for shops. A print shop was set up in *The Big Issue* to print in-house stationery and to employ and train vendors. *The Big Issue* Film Unit was established so that *The Big Issue* could potentially become a multimedia company.

MAKING IT

Making It was the first experiment involving vendors: its mission was 'to provide employment within a secure structure to enable ex-*Big Issue* vendors to realize their true potential through training, shared involvement and social stability'. The first product was a cork board. A staff of six ex-vendors was initially employed including ex-vendor Charlie Chamberlain who still works for *The Big Issue*. The corks came from Portuguese wine producers, the glue was non-toxic and the wood for the frames came from sustainable sources. They were sold through *The Big Issue* and there were negotiations with shops such as Habitat but the production costs were too high and the boards did not sell enough to make a viable financial return.

A second attempt was made by diversifying into candle-making, a very popular consumer product in the mid 1990s. The candles were hand-rolled, from organic beeswax harvested from hives in the Miomba Forest in north-west Zambia. The beeswax was purchased on a fair trade basis and certified as organic by the Soil Association of the UK. Brazil nut shells were imported from South America and filled with the wax. It was a unique venture which united the poor of three continents: Africa, South America and Europe. Making It was committed to 'producing handmade, quality products in a commercial environment with a commitment of responsibility to suppliers, customers, its own workers and the environment.'

Chris (see Chapter 2) was one ex-vendor who played a major part in the venture. Kate de Pulford, then the manager of Making

It, introduced him to candle-making and Chris worked with Kate and 12 ex-vendors (10 men and 2 women). They were employed on a basic weekly wage, originally on a six-week contract which then stretched to twelve.

The whole enterprise posed difficulties from the very beginning. Some of the employed people's behaviour began to disrupt other workers. There were instances of racial abuse, which got so bad that one of the ex-vendors had to be escorted from the building. In the end, the vendors were paid off and the pods finished by the staff. Thousands of the hand-rolled and brazil nut pod candles were sold to organizations such as Oxfam, Shelter and The Body Shop. Most of the team went back to vending, apart from Chris. Aside from the internal problems, the pods sold to the shops did not sell and there were insufficient repeat orders. Making It ended at the beginning of 1997.

This project raised the crucial issue of how to get people who have been severely damaged by life back into work. It was realized that it takes more than just giving people a job, and that regaining lost self-respect is very difficult.

In May 1995, the whole of *The Big Issue* was sent into shock when Kate de Pulford, 23, was knocked off her bicycle on her way to work by a skip lorry; she died a few hours later. Her face beamed from the cover of the following week's *Big Issue* and the covering feature was on the dangers of cycling in London. Kate had also helped run the writing group and many poems were written in her memory and published on the Capital Lights page. Here is one by George Kirby:

Farewell Sweet Katie

Oh how we take things for granted
As we plan each forthcoming date
Entirely and so blissfully
   oblivious
To that most awesome finger
   of Fate

That fearsomely fickle finger
Which touches us all in some way
Heaps love, life and laughter
   upon us
Then snatches it all away

Oh cruel, cruel Fate, how could
  you?
To beckon sweet Katie away
How deeply we're all going to
  miss her
We so dearly wished her to stay.

George was a long-standing Big Issue vendor. He was a prolific writer, attending the writing group regularly. Sadly, he died in November 2000.

THE FILM UNIT

In 1994, John's son Paddy and Nigel Bulloch, started *The Big Issue* Film Unit in a small office in *The Big Issue* building. They had been with *The Big Issue* since the launch and wanted to move away from their work in production and design. Paddy says:

> The Big Issue *was growing and growing and there was a nice, sexy feel to have the magazine go into another form of media. We could start up a self-promotional film and TV unit, so you could expand* The Big Issue *into other avenues, apart from print.'*

They were joined by Rob Gomez and when Nigel left the company, Rob and Paddy headed up the unit. With the money from their first job, videoing *The Big Issue*/London Electricity Awards ceremony,[1] they bought a camera and equipment. With support from finance company Bloomberg, the unit started to make a presence. Whilst they picked up a few pieces of equipment along the way, they had to 'blag' editing time from editing companies, such as M2. 'If it wasn't for M2, I don't think the Film Unit would have gone very far. They were a tremendous help,' says Paddy.

They produced a training video for the vendors on the dos and don'ts of selling, in conjunction with the Vendor Services Team, a video for *The Big Issue Scotland* and one for *The Big Issue International*, which was sponsored by BT and the EC. The latter video explained how *The Big Issue* worked and was sent out to other street papers or people who were interested in setting up a paper. The unit also made a video for the advertising team to use when they were pitching to clients.

The Film Unit was officially launched at a party at Bloomberg's on 10 December 1996. Paddy remembers:

'We had a spot of luck. We didn't have our own post-production, or editing facilities. After we had nagged The Big Issue hierarchy for a while, they decided to put one of their sponsorship deals with us, which was Bloomberg. We got a very nice editing system.'

The new Avid editing suite enabled them to offer a complete range of production facilities, as well as open up new market opportunities. Paddy concentrated on the editing, with Rob as cameraman. When Andrew Jaspan arrived as managing director in 1996, the Film Unit was able to realize its dream of television production. Paddy says:

'He was very impressed with the Film Unit. He saw a lot of potential and he was the first person who gave it a lot of time. He was our new boss and set up the Media Advisory Board with representatives from C4, BBC, Granada, ITN and independent producers.'

For the first time, the Film Unit was under proper management. Sue Swinburne and Rachel Hanks joined and the unit split into a facilities house (the crewing and editing services) and a production house (to develop film ideas).

Paddy remembers:

'We had written a load of proposals for TV programmes which had been refused because we weren't an established production company. So Andrew had the idea of doing a co-production between The Big Issue and Ideal World, run by Zad Rogers.'

This became Beg to Differ which was shown on Channel 4, from an idea by Rachel Hanks. Paddy says:

'It was to get a group of six vendors to front their own small pieces on whatever subject they liked. It would be a homeless person's view on life, both funny and cutting edge at the same *time.* Beg to Differ *was the only title we could think of to do with homelessness. It caused a bit of a problem because it insinuated that* Big Issue *vendors beg, which of course they don't.'*

Ideal World employed a couple of comedy writers, a producer and a director. The pilot was successful and Channel 4 agreed to do a series.

The second TV success was *Urbanrites* for LWT. Paddy, Rob and Rachel were assisted by comedy writer Matt Owen and *Big Issue* news reporter Max Daly. They all wrote the material for *Urbanrites*. For the pilot in 1998, there was a mix of ideas taken from original *Big Issue* stories. *Urbanrites* consisted of three short films for each programme – one light-hearted, one middle-weight social film and one investigative piece. One example was an undercover visit to the Millenium Dome site to extract some allegedly contaminated earth.

A series of six was commissioned by LWT to run late on a Friday night. It was done in-house, with an external executive producer, and overseen by Sally Stainton to check on the content. This time, there were no vendors fronting the programmes, although a few appeared in some of the stories. It was a success and a second series was commissioned, with Sally Stainton and *Big Issue* editor Matthew Collin as associate producers. *The Big London Issue* was shown in summer 2000. *Time Out*[2] commented that 'it was a nice surprise. It's a rare showcase for the diversity and even bizarreness of this big, smelly city.'

GATHERING FORCE

Gathering Force,[3] a book promoting 'radical action for those tired of waiting', was published by *The Big Issue* in the autumn of 1997. Described by *The Guardian*'s environment editor John Vidal as 'essential reading for the millennium. Real change starts here...', the book documented the evolution of the 1990s' alternative cultures and direct action movement and covered all aspects of DIY culture – roads and transport, raves and festivals, land and housing, animal export protests, rights, civil rights, and community-based economics.

The Egypt trip

In spring 1997, a curious group of 21 people travelled to the desert in southern Sinai. Six vendors, *Big Issue* staff, charity staff and managers from NatWest Markets were sponsored on the trip by the McCabe Educational Trust.[4] Journalist Sarah Woodley[5] wrote it up in the magazine. Any essentials that vendors needed, like boots, were funded through The Big Issue Foundation.

Whilst the trip turned out not to be too physically arduous, it was the communication and breaking down of boundaries which was the challenge. They all slept out in the open, and went on a 50 mile, three-day trek on camelback, led and fed by the Muzeina Bedouin tribe. At one stage of the trip they climbed 7500 feet up Mount Sinai.

In a report in *The Bin*,[6] one (anonymous) vendor wrote 'The Bedouin: wicked! Ace geezers! Much nicer than I was expecting.' As for the stockbrokers:

> *'very different to the Bedouin. Very different to us. Quite nice. One of them fell off his camel, a very difficult thing to do, but in a move that indicates a good future in high finance, he managed to fall on the only bit of soft sand for miles. They all reckoned that they were going to buy* The Big Issue *in future, after having met us and realized that we were human. How nice... I realize that I've taken the piss about everything, but that does not mean that I didn't enjoy myself. I got a lot out of this trip. Thanks for sending me.'*

Vendor support worker Pete Webster tells the story:

> *'On the first couple of nights the homeless people were just taking the mickey out of the bankers because the bankers did not have a clue about homeless people or how they become homeless. When everyone started singing songs and dancing around the fire, it got on its way. I reckon if a vendor made one friend with a banker, they'd done pretty well! It was really good. The Bedouin tribe brought the camels down, they took us all round the desert, they cooked our food for us, built fires, did their own dances.'*

As to what it achieved, Webster believes it gave the bankers more of an insight into the world of the homeless. Peter, a 40 year old City banker, was quoted in an article:

> 'Some of the most cherished moments have been the one-to-ones – when no one's around to check you're confronting the issues. Discussing with people about their lives, interests, people a week ago I would have walked past. You realise that behind the suit, or the mohican haircut is an engaging personality with a lot in common – a lot to share.'[7]

Pete Webster adds:

> 'They went out of their way to be nice but they soon realized that they were in a total different world and they couldn't speak about their world. I saw three of them months after and I think it has opened their eyes. They actually said "There is a Big Issue vendor outside my station and I buy one off him every week." I think, that's nice of you, but what else can you do for them? They got a big shock out of it and they realized more about homelessness than they did before. The vendors had a brilliant holiday. They thoroughly enjoyed it.'

THE 1997 GENERAL ELECTION

The year 1997 marked a turning point both for the country and *The Big Issue*. Just before the general election, *The Big Issue* became the best-selling current affairs weekly magazine in the UK, with a national ABC figure of 294,000. The NRS figure showed that 1,121,000 people were reading the paper every week, an increase of 29 per cent.

Labour's victory in the election led to a feeling of expectation. What had been lacking in the previous government would be put right by New Labour. The May election coincided with the arrival of a new editor at *The Big Issue*, Becky Gardiner. Deputy editor Steve Chamberlain had been acting editor since Jo Mallabar resigned in March that year.

In the weeks before the election, *The Big Issue* carried interviews with Labour leader Tony Blair, Liberal Democrat leader Paddy Ashdown, and Deputy Prime Minister Michael Heseltine. Despite the fact that housing and homeless issues make up an estimated 65 per cent of MP's postbags, these issues featured little in the campaign.

From the politicians point of view, *The Big Issue* was an excellent medium in which to expound their policies. Many of the over one million readers were young, and first time voters. Prime Minister John Major, however, did not take advantage of this and refused an interview, sending along his deputy instead.

All three interviews were conducted by features editor Simon Rogers who had wanted the Blair interview to go in the biggest-selling issue of the year, at Christmas 1996, but Blair's office missed the deadline. The interview went into the New Year issue instead. This proved a godsend, since there was little other news and it consequently appeared for the whole week on the front pages of the nationals. 'There was this giant spin,' remembers Simon. 'All week it was the issue of the week.'

Tony Blair's face appeared on the 6 January 1997 cover, with the strapline, Oi Tony! What about the homeless? But it was Blair's support for 'zero tolerance' that caught the headlines. Zero tolerance was practised in New York and being experimented with in London's King's Cross, as well as in Glasgow and Edinburgh. This involved clearing beggars and homeless people off the streets, and not tolerating the smallest of crimes.This echoed Jack Straw's remarks made in September 1995.

Blair said we must 'tackle the reasons why those people are sleeping on the streets, why they're homeless or they're begging'. Beggars and street dwellers make people feel unsafe and he continued:

> *'It is right to be intolerant of people homeless on the streets. But the way to deal with that is you make sure that when those people come off the streets that you're doing the other part of the equation. You're providing them with somewhere to go.'*

He said giving to beggars was not the solution. The interview made it look as if the Labour Party were announcing a zero-tolerance policy. 'Really he was only talking off the top of his head,' alleges Simon. Blair said that his new government would release local authorities' capital receipts. There was £5 billion worth from the sale of 1.5 million council houses, which the Tory government had kept tied up. On the question of votes for homeless people he was not so forthcoming. He was not prepared to say that the new government would change the law so that homeless people would be guaranteed voting rights.

Blair countered the media response to his interview in *The Big Issue* by writing in *The Guardian*.[8] 'The usual screaming headlines greeted my interview with *The Big Issue*. From reading some reports... you would have thought I had called for beggars and homeless people to be callously driven off the streets or locked up in prison,' he wrote.

He continued: 'My argument was that we should tackle the problem of crime by not tolerating any petty offences – people are entitled to protection from crime, no matter how petty – and we should tackle the distinct problem of homelessness by providing the homeless with somewhere to go.' He went on to discuss zero tolerance and crime on the streets.

Vendor Mary remembers the Blair issue as a good seller. She says:

> 'People wanted to know what he was going to do for the homeless. They wanted to see what headway they were going to make in clearing this matter up. If it had been John Major on the cover I don't think anyone would have taken any notice. You've got to have politicians that stand up to their convictions and do something.'

A month later Liberal Democrat Paddy Ashdown was asked how a vote for him would affect homeless people. Ashdown was more forthcoming than Blair about votes for homeless people. He said he would guarantee their rights to register to vote. Provided there were safeguards against abuse, he saw no problem in people using, for instance, day centres as an address. He supported zero tolerance but as a part of a crime policy, not a crime policy in itself. He believed that if a person was begging and behaving anti-socially, they should be dealt with by the law. He said:

> 'But I don't believe in this concept, much put about by Labour, of hosing beggars off the streets or using the police. One of the things that worries me about the increasingly authoritarian trend in British politics affecting both the Left and the Right is they concentrate on the sinner not on the sin.'

Both politicians said they bought *The Big Issue*, Ashdown on a more regular basis than Blair. The third politician, Michael Heseltine[9] also said he regularly bought copies.

The huge importance of having a mass circulation magazine that is read by young people cannot be underestimated, Lyndall Stein pointed out. 'No one else is doing that. *The Big Issue* is bought by young people, not just by the traditional lefty. This means a new political audience when it comes to campaigning.'

In the Heseltine interview, Simon Rogers was keen to find out if the Conservative government took credit for the conditions that created *The Big Issue*. When they came to power in 1979 there would not have been a *Big Issue* because there were not enough people on the streets. Talking about pressure on the economy that creates unemployment, Heseltine went on to say:

> 'We must discuss what you mean by homelessness. If you're talking about rough sleepers, then I'm happy to go through with you the policies that we've created to cope with that very difficult social issue.'

He defined homelessness as 'a classification of people living in homes from which they wish to move'. Simon pointed out that Shelter would say being homeless means being insecurely accommodated, in a B&B or a hostel. Heseltine responded:

> 'Yes, but they're not without homes. They're living in homes. They wish to move for reasons which are perfectly understandable... Homelessness means no home, whereas the people we're talking about are people who want to change their homes.'

As for homeless people and the right to vote, Heseltine said that it was not up to politicians to determine whether the law was carried out, it was for the appropriate officials. To the follow-up question, 'how would you advise a rough sleeper to vote?' Heseltine's bizarre response was:

> 'I hope they vote Conservative because no government has taken more trouble to try and cope with the problems of rough sleeping... I was responsible for the policy that became the Rough Sleepers Initiative.'

Interviews with politicians were followed up in the election issue. The cover of the 5 May issue stated: 'You can't get rid of all homelessness Mr Blair... but you can have a damn good try...and we can help.' Centrepoint, CHAR, Crisis, Shelter, Empty Homes Agency, National Children's Homes, St Mungo's, Homeless Network and the Child Poverty Action Group, drew up, with *The Big Issue*, a ten-point battle plan to end the crisis of homelessness. John Bird, David Warner, from Homeless Network, Ollie Grenden from Shelter and Victor Adebowale from Centrepoint delivered the plan to No 10 Downing Street for the attention of the new Prime Minister.[10] Tony Blair subsequently wrote an article on social exclusion for the magazine.[11]

New Labour appeared to be more open and inclusive in its attempts to tackle social issues. Whilst members of the Tory government had been very supportive of *The Big Issue*, the new government appeared more proactive. Hilary Armstrong, the new Minister for Housing, visited *The Big Issue* soon after the election. An in-depth interview was conducted with Frank Field, then Social Security Minister. His views on the proposed radicalization of the welfare system appeared in the sixth birthday issue in September 1997. John Bird and Andrew Jaspan were invited to meet with Geoff Mulgan, then head of social policy at No 10, to talk about ways of working together. *The Big Issue* proposed a number of points where joint work would be conducive to social change.

Peter Mandelson, then Minister without Portfolio, accepted an invitation to speak at the Foundation's first AGM in February 1998. He noted what he saw as the many parallels between *The Big Issue* and New Labour, saying, 'The philosophy of *The Big Issue* is the same as the philosophy of the new government, lifting dependency and offering the opportunity to those previously denied it.'

Peter Mandelson had been one of the architects of the new Social Exclusion Unit (SEU),[12] set up in the autumn of 1997, by the Cabinet Office and with direct responsibility to the Prime Minister. At the AGM, Mandelson talked about tackling social division and inequality through the Social Exclusion Unit which:

> *'will help government work in a more coherent way across boundaries, across all agencies – local authorities, the voluntary sector, police, business. Rough sleepers is one issue. This is not about compassion, it is about sense. Preventative measures means a dividend for everyone.'*

One of the remits of the new Social Exclusion Unit was to tackle rough sleeping, reduing the number on the streets by two thirds by 2002. The SEU produced a report in July 1998 on how to reduce the numbers of people sleeping rough. An initial target was established of reducing the numbers in England to a third of the current level by 2002.[13]

The report recognized that rough sleepers' problems and needs crossed the responsibilities of several central government departments, so a new ministerial committee to ensure effective coordination of government policy on rough sleepers was established. The Department of the Environment, Transport and the Regions (DETR; now the DTLR) became responsible for coordinating the overall strategy on rough sleeping in England, which includes housing, health, access to employment and training and benefits.

The task of tackling the rough sleepers issue was allocated to the Rough Sleepers Unit (RSU) in April 1999 with funding of around £145m over three years. The RSU is headed by Louise Casey, formerly of Shelter and known as the 'homeless czar'.[14]

The SEU report and the setting up of the RSU were an admission that the RSIs had not entirely worked. Despite the number of rough sleepers in the capital falling from between 2–3000 in 1990 to around 400 today, there is still a constant stream of people coming onto the streets.

When the government's Social Exclusion Unit decided to target rough sleepers, *The Big Issue* was asked directly for its views, and a civil servant from the Unit visited the offices. *The Big Issue* was invited by the Prime Minister to attend a summit to launch the work of the Unit on 8 December 1997. This was the first time that *The Big Issue* was to have direct input into government policy. Sinead Hanks, then social policy adviser, sent in reports from the *Big Issues* around the country about their experiences of rough sleeping. *Big Issue* staff pointed out that rough sleeping was only one manifestation of homelessness and a more holistic approach to the problem would be preferable.

A NEW EDITOR – BECKY GARDINER

Becky Gardiner joined from the *Independent on Sunday*'s Real Life section. Under Becky the paper became more news-led and she managed the redesign of the paper in the autumn of 1997. Andrew Davies comments:

'She had that mainstream sensibility that definitely moved the magazine more towards that and it helped the magazine gain circulation. It was one of our really big growth periods then.'

Despite moving towards the mainstream arena, *The Big Issue* was still getting access to stories that the other media was not. As Simon Rogers points out:

'We have journalists like Diane [Taylor] who are great at finding things. We'll run with stories that other people know about but don't want to run with. People sometimes phone us up with stories. They trust The Big Issue.*'*

An article on paupers' graves[15] by Jane Cassidy, for example, highlighted the practice of hospitals burying penniless patients in unmarked mass graves. Information was passed on to Health Minister Alan Milburn, leading to new guidelines being issued on the subject.

Guest editing, initiated by Becky, brought in writer Irvine Welsh[16] and Suzanne Moore[17] of *The Independent*. The Irving Welsh issue was picked up by Radio 4's *Saturday Review*,[18] a discussion programme about the week's cultural events. In artist Damien Hurst's[19] issue, Jarvis Cocker interviewed David Bowie, Stephen Fry wrote on Peter Mandelson and Mariella Frostrup interviewed Dennis Hopper.

Embarrassment was caused, though, by a short piece about Dodi Fayed. Entitled 'Dead Ringer for Dodi', by Paul Sussman, who believed he resembled Dodi, it appeared in the magazine on the Monday following the death of Dodi and Princess Diana. Staff spent two days sticking an apology into every issue.

Becky decided that the international coverage was too worthy and did not fit with the new direction of the magazine, so discontinued the page. She preferred hard-hitting investigative international news. Like Jo, Becky had misgivings about Street Lights. She says:

'I really wanted to get homeless voices in the magazine. I felt that was part of our uniqueness and yet the only place we were doing that was in Street Lights which was very ghettoized at the back. It was completely unedited which meant pieces were in there which wouldn't be published for any other reason.'

Becky wanted to develop ways of homeless people being involved in the magazine. But there had to be some professional expectations about what they would produce. However, it proved difficult and the only achievement in that direction was the Street Diary, a day in a life of a homeless person.[20]

Current editor, Matthew Collin, believes Becky's great achievement (and thinks that Andrew Jaspan must take some of the credit for it too) was to professionalize the editorial department. He says:

> 'The redesign was the major turn around in the content and presentation of The Big Issue. It turned it from what was from good content which was sometimes chaotic, to something that was well organized, interesting, well presented, attractively designed, making the best of all The Big Issue had to offer.'

Becky also cut down on the working of long hours, a tradition at *The Big Issue*.

The editorial team were still collecting awards. In April 1998, *The Big Issue* won the Commission for Racial Equality's Race in the Media Award. *The Big Issue* topped the consumer magazine section for what judges described as 'an excellent body of work representing a diversity of well-written feature material and news pieces, supported by background research'. This was followed by the Mind Journalist of the Year Award. Collected by Jane Cassidy, Max Daly, Diane Taylor, Emma Cook and Sam Hart, the award was for their in-depth coverage of mental health issues.

On its seventh birthday in September 1998, *Media Week* gave resounding approval to the success of *The Big Issue*. 'Whatever is thrown at it... *The Big Issue* should accept that controversy is part and parcel of creating one of the best-value weekly titles in the country,' wrote Gavin Stamp:

> 'At £1, it has few peers for the relevance of its news coverage, its succinct reviewing style, from which many nationals could learn, and the iconoclasm of its features.'

CAMPAIGNING AND EDITORIAL

Becky left in April 1998 to edit the women's page of *The Guardian*, taking *Big Issue* staff writer Raekha Prasad as her deputy.

Matthew Collin had come to *The Big Issue* in August 1997 as deputy editor and subsequently became editor when Becky left. Previously, Matthew had worked at *Time Out*. He says:

> 'The journalism I have always done has been partly cultural analysis, journalism about popular culture and partly journalism about social issues. The Big Issue *is where those two are combined. That was why I wanted to come and work here. Editorially it is unique. It's very difficult for publications that cover popular culture to also cover current affairs or issues of social justice and vice versa.*
>
> 'I don't think there have been any major changes to what The Big Issue *is about since it started. Its core is about campaigning for social justice and providing a general interest analysis of arts and current affairs. I don't think that has changed. The way in which it has been done has changed according to the people who are there at the time.'*

His team includes Gibby Zobel who came from the direct action weekly *SchNews*, Diane Taylor, Sam Hart, Nadene Ghouri, Max Daly and current deputy editor Adam Macqueen who came from *Private Eye*.

Editorial continued to be taken by the mainstream press. For example the interview with Deputy Prime Minister John Prescott was picked up by the *Daily Mirror*.[21] Matthew criticizes the national press for 'being too obsessed with lifestyle and repeatedly falling back on news stories broken by *The Big Issue* as a result.'[22] He claims that every week at least one *Big Issue* story is picked up and published without a credit.

One example in particular was the story on Home Secretary Jack Straw's comments on travellers on 16 August 1999. *The Big Issue* sent copies to the nationals and its story appeared the following Thursday in *The Guardian*, the *Daily Express*, *The Times* and on the BBC's *Newsnight*. Matthew suggests the news team at *The Big Issue* had been first to break the story because its contacts were not mainstream and the magazine has strong links with the travelling community. *The Big Issue* also accused *The Sun*, the *Evening Standard* and *The Guardian* of stealing its story on the estate agency that opened its business to squatters.

The stories taken were not the problem, rather, it was the lack of reference to where the story originated. At times, *The Big*

Issue editorial department feels it is not unlike the unofficial research department of dailies, TV programmes and other magazines.

Press releasing articles to ensure the press picked them up has always been the role of the press office. However, it is a fine line because they steal them anyway. Andrew Davies says:

> *'I think we have always undersold ourselves... The downside is that a lot of other people have taken the credit for which* The Big Issue's *journalists actually broke. But because we didn't make a fuss about it somebody actually picked it up quietly, made a much bigger splash with it elsewhere. It's a particular skill to drumbeat for your own cause and we are usually too busy getting on doing the thing itself. It's a classic case of people involved in whatever area of social change – it's very busy and stressed.'*

As arts editor Tina Jackson remarks:

> *'Obviously we see a lot of stories ending up later in the national press. The national press evidently now sees us as a real contender. When Harry Potter author JK Rowling does four interviews, three of them are with the nationals, and one of them is with* The Big Issue. *And that is a scenario that you see over and over again. We are up there as a serious heavyweight contendor.'*

Tina sums up by saying:

> *'The Big Issue is mainstream. That's always been one of its main strengths. It doesn't seek just to appeal to people who are marginalized, although it speaks on their behalf. It campaigns for them, it gives them a voice, but it doesn't patronize them by leaving them in the margins. It brings marginal causes into the mainstream, while at the same time addressing mainstream causes and issues through its own voice.*
>
> *'Our independence means that we can tackle issues in our way. You will see that the news team, for instance, and the editorial team as a whole often run campaigning features for social issues. It means we can be very outspoken about issues which are important to us. For instance the treatment of refugees. The Big Issue has continually been unabashadly outspoken about social injustice.'*

Expectations from other organizations and the public towards *The Big Issue*'s compaigning stance have always been high. Andrew Davies explains:

> *'People expected us to do a lot more campaigns. We've campaigned for homeless people, we've given them a voice, and given the whole issue much more of a human face. Now we do it indirectly – we highlight issues, whether it's travellers' groups, refugees and people being badly done by.'*

Another important issue highlighted during 1998–99 was Stephen Lawrence's murder and the ongoing campaign for justice from the Metropolitan police.[23]

The refugee campaign was run in response to the government's proposal to provide a voucher scheme instead of cash for asylum seekers in 1999. Readers were encouraged to send in a coupon and John Bird and others then took the 4000 responses to No 10 Downing Street. On 9 June 1999, celebrities, such as Tony Blair's father-in-law, Tony Booth, actor Colin Firth, comedian Mark Thomas and actor Kathy Burke, went shopping in Sainsbury's supermarket with asylum seekers' vouchers. It was part of the ongoing campaign, spearheaded by *The Big Issue*, to outlaw vouchers, worth around £30 a week and only exchangable at named outlets, and restore benefits. The campaign also wanted to persuade MPs to vote against the third reading of the Immigration and Asylum Bill.[24] The campaign continues with some success.

Reporter Max Daly worked on the Cambridge Two campaign. Two workers from the Wintercomfort homeless drop-in centre in Cambridge, Ruth Wyner and John Brock, were imprisoned for 208 days in 2000 for 'knowingly allowing drug dealing on the premises'. Nearly 1000 *Big Issue* readers joined a campaign to demand changes to the Misuse of Drugs Act which puts charity workers at risk of jail. Both were released in July. In December, following a year-long campaign led by *The Big Issue*, the Court of Appeal told the two that they would not return to jail, but did not quash their convictions. Tina says:

> *'Max was instrumental in initially publishing that injustice, which was directly to do with the way homeless people's lives are affected by issues which many don't find palatable, like drug taking.'*

Matthew Collin concludes:

> 'The thing I am proud of is the campaigning, especially around
> the asylum issue. Before, we didn't really have a policy on
> campaigns. The problem with campaigns is that you can start a
> campaign and it fizzles out.'

With the asylum issue, it was mostly Diane Taylor's hard work.
Matthew adds:

> 'I don't necessarily think that the coupons made any sort of
> difference apart from helping kick start that debate around
> asylum. I think this is going to remain one of the crucial issues
> of this decade and is exactly the sort of thing The Big Issue
> should be campaigning about as it promotes the basic issues of
> justice. Also, it will have a knock-on effect for our vendors.'

The Big Issue ran a seven-week campaign from May 2000
highlighting the problems faced by mobile home residents, such
as illegal evictions. Since the campaign, the government has
responded with some measures to protect mobile home owners.
Matthew comments:

> 'I was also very pleased with the mobile homes campaign
> because it was one of the most unfashionable, obscure issues to
> come up with. Again it was poor, vulnerable, socially excluded
> people, pensioners being bullied by site owners. It was an aware-
> ness raising exercise and we do feel we had an impact on
> government thinking.'

There are other highlights for The Big Issue team. For example, how
chef Anton Mosimon came in to The Big Issue to cook a three-course
meal for the vendors, costing no more than one pound.[25] John Bird
and Mo Mowlem MP joining UN Secretary General Kofi Annan in
New York, to sign the Anne Frank International Declaration on
Human Rights.[26] A supplement to the magazine of photographs
by David Bailey on King's Cross, with words by Harry Ritchie.[27]
The Big Issue was included in the World Fair, EXPO 2000, held in
Hannover and was chosen as one of the 600 best international
projects submitted. Four years previously, The Big Issue had been

celebrated in Istanbul when it was chosen as one of the 100 best practices by the UN Habitat II conference. A special edition of *The Big Issue*[28] was guest-edited, with photographs, by Wolfgang Tillmans. Tillmans went on to win the prestigious Turner Prize for the year 2000.

READERSHIP AND ADVERTISING

Who reads *The Big Issue* now? Unlike most other magazines that target a specific readership, it has always been very difficult to pinpoint *The Big Issue*'s readers. According to the NRS,[29] the profile of *Big Issue* readers shows that two thirds are under 44, with the majority between the ages of 15–34.[30] Every week, *The Big Issue* reaches an average of 563,000 readers in the UK who are aged 15–34. This is more than *The Guardian, Time Out, The Independent, New Musical Express* and the *Evening Standard*. Two thirds of readers are in the ABC1 category,[31] with a 42 per cent male readership and 58 per cent female.

It appears that *The Big Issue*'s readership is quite mainstream. Andrew Davies comments:

> *'They are middle class with sensible jobs. They haven't been eco-warriors, they haven't been out on the edge doing strange things in strange clubs, so they might want to read about it. You've got to sell it to them in a kind of 'this is the strange world out there'. It's almost like a voyeuristic view about it all. Whereas before we almost accepted that they knew about it all.'*

However, there are a lot more older people outside of the 18–40 age range who read the paper. Andrew adds:

> *'But the way that youth culture dominates and where the advertising is, means that the older readership tends to be ignored. This also has to do with the fact that the editorial staff have always been in their twenties and thirties. Also, with a magazine of only 56 pages, it is impossible to be all-encompassing. It is not possible to compete with papers which have so many different sections appealing to all and sundry, or magazines which target specific age, gender or cultural groups.'*

Simon Rogers comments:

> 'I think that what has been much more important than us being strident, is us being subversive. You have the Telegraph or Mail reader who gets on the tube and they also read The Big Issue. One week they will read about Posh Spice and then about a century of homelessness. Or they'd read about this council estate in Wallasey that no one has access to, Gulf War stuff or zero tolerance stuff. All these things that they would never read anywhere else.'

Middle England, it seems, does read *The Big Issue*.

The Big Issue carries out its own readership surveys every two or three years. One was carried out in the summer of 1996 and over 2000 people responded; the overwhelming amount came from London. Another survey was carried out two years later. As with many such surveys, it was the committed core readers who responded. Whilst this is essential, in order to increase sales *The Big Issue* also needed to know why people were not buying it. This particular survey has not been carried out due to lack of finance.

In more detailed research carried out in 1999, the QRS[32] identified that 48 per cent of *Big Issue* readers read it cover to cover, higher than *The Independent*, *The Guardian* or *Time Out*. But the cross-over readership is low: only 3 per cent *The Guardian* and 5 per cent *Time Out*. Their conclusion was that *The Big Issue* does have a unique audience. According to ROAR,[33] *The Big Issue* was the third most popular magazine in the 15–24 age group.

Survey figures are the crucial factor for advertisers. The 'feel good' factor for companies advertising in the magazine has probably now gone, replaced by the need for solid circulation figures. They want to know that *The Big Issue* is getting through to young ABC1s. 'The information that we rely on to sell advertising comes from the NRS and that, if you like, is the industry currency,' comments project manager Denise McLeod. Lisa Woodman, formerly *The Big Issue*'s advertising manager and now at *The Guardian*, explains that just over a quarter of *Big Issue* revenue comes from the advertising department, with a yearly target of upwards of £1.2m.

Denise says:

'We have really worked hard to remove the 'feel good' factor in advertising. We've removed the mention of that type of thing from the media pack in terms of The Big Issue *helping homeless people. The emphasis from the advertising perspective is that this magazine is a good magazine, quality editorial, high target audience, and is very cost-effective.'*

Matthew Collin discusses the contradiction between advertising and editorial:

'We wouldn't take advertising that attacks homeless people – that's our policy – or that offended the punters. Chatlines look tacky. We have more important things to do than worry about chatlines. I don't like unattractive advertising anyway because it brings down the tone of the publication. Or dogs with their heads cut off. It looks bad. I don't think it is possible to have a fully ethical advertising policy anyway. You'd end up with no income. You'd go out of business.'

In the summer of 1999, the advertising team had worked very hard to get a series of advertisements from Nestlé, which would bring in good revenue. The subsequent battle over it highlighted the need for, if not an ethical advertising policy, then at least guidelines. The editorial department did not support the decision of the advertising department to run these ads. Many times the magazine ran features on the international Nestlé boycott. Whilst understanding the need to attract high-profile advertisers, the editorial department stated in a memo:

'Our readers believe in our independent brand values whilst enjoying our editorial coverage. Our target readership has grown up with the Nestlé boycott, and Nescafé ads would lose our core readership: an aware, young readership sick of media manipulation.'

John Bird had to broker an agreement between the two departments, and a compromise was reached. The first series of Nestlé ads would run, and then they would be cut. John stated:

'I cannot leave The Big Issue*'s financial well-being in question. We have to take the ad for the first series. We have no financial*

choice and if we don't, vendors' needs will be in jeopardy, staff jobs in jeopardy and even the future of The Big Issue.'

There is no doubt that *The Big Issue* has a very strong brand image. It goes beyond homelessness into a world of culture and the 'feel good' factor. Naomi Klein[34] summed up today's bizarre and ephemeral world of branding:

'It's a way of life. It's not advertising. It's about building a spiritual mythology around corporations. A brand is not a thing you buy in a shop. It's much more intangible than that. A brand is an idea that all sorts of companies and corporations want you to think of when you think of them. Brands have not only penetrated the culture, they are the culture.'

In a bizarre sort of way *The Big Issue* does fit exactly the criteria for 'branding', like other media, except that the connections are not so much via advertisers. The spiritual mythology built around *The Big Issue* 'corporation' is that of an individual buying into helping someone less well off than themselves.

PRINCE CHARLES VISITS AND *THE BIG ISSUE* MOVES AGAIN

The press had a field day in November 1997 when Prince Charles paid a short visit to *The Big Issue* office. One of the vendors whom he met, Clive Harold, had been to prep school with him in Knightsbridge, and the story appeared in most newspapers the next day. Another was Matt, an ex-soldier of the Royal Green Jackets, who remembered Prince Charles from routine troop inspections. He explained to the Prince that he had fallen on hard times after the break-up of his marriage. The Prince told John Bird that he found the numbers of empty properties languishing in Britain frustrating.[35]

The Prince had another chance to visit *The Big Issue* a year later when he opened the new premises in King's Cross in November 1998. He met members of the writers' group who recited their poems. He subsequently wrote an article on solutions to social exclusion for *The Big Issue*. John Bird then attended the Prince's 50th birthday party at Buckingham Palace.

By the late 1990s, Clerkenwell had developed into a trendy and upmarket area and John Bird had decided to sell the building because the value had increased substantially. It was also thought that a move near a major station would improve public transport access for the vendors. An old bank on the Pentonville Road was bought and refurbished in time to move into during *The Big Issue*'s seventh birthday week in September 1998. The bank came up with a mortgage, this time with no discussion.

Once the building in Clerkenwell had been sold, *The Big Issue* was billed for capital gains tax. If the building had been in the Foundation's name, then there would have been no tax liability. John wrote to the Chancellor of the Exchequer with a challenge. He said that the capital gains tax that *The Big Issue* owed emanated from the 1960s capital gains tax rule which was, in fact, an anti-speculative tax, and:

> '*As a social business, we are not in the business of speculation. Why can't the law be changed so that social businesses can invest this money into the Foundation to the benefit of the homeless?*'

John wrote to the Chancellor again on the same subject in January 2001 after the King's Cross building had been sold. He is still awaiting a meeting with a civil servant.

MACE were the project managers for the new building who sourced the architects, builders and structural engineers, and gave their services either for free or at partial cost. Chairman Nigel Kershaw oversaw the whole operation, with Mille Hyde as project coordinator. Many ex-vendors worked on the building, particularly those who had skills such as carpentry or decorating. Former facilities manager Natasha Santos-Castellino recalls:

> '*Rather than hire contractors who would cost a lot of money, we felt it would be better for vendors to have an opportunity to gain work experience. Sam Emsley, the facilities manager, managed them. The majority of them turned up for work. There were a couple who weren't reliable, but the majority did a good job.*'

Several vendors subsequently obtained work through MACE and with other contractors working on the site.

There is some recycling within *The Big Issue* offices, as much as possible given the lack of space. White paper is taken away for free by Paper Round[36] to a paper factory in Kent, where it is recycled and is bought back at a reduced rate.

The move, though, was not a success. Staff did not like the building. Vendors found King's Cross, at times, theatening. It was decided therefore to move again in 2001, to Vauxhall.

Chris Haslum, managing director from 1998 to the end of 2000, came from *The Daily Telegraph*. He opened up new areas of sales, particularly in towns within the M25 orbital, organized by John McFadzean, a vendor support worker. In the summer of 2000, the paper was redesigned once more, onto glossy paper with heatset colour. This has encouraged more advertising. Denise observes:

> '*One of the major problems we used to have was that advertis-ers didn't want to be seen in the mag because they didn't like the quality. That was one of the main objections. That it looked like a street paper, that it was scruffy. We have now changed all that and if you look at some of the advertisers that we have got in the relaunch issue, it's brilliant, because they couldn't use that as an excuse any more.*'

In April 2000, Matthew Collin again collected the Commission for Racial Equality[37] Race in the Media Award 2000, this time for the Asylum Seekers' Campaign. John Bird received the Marcus Morris Award from the Periodical Publishers Association (PPA) for his contribution to the magazine industry, in October 2000. He urged the PPA to set up a new training academy for homeless people who want to be journalists. He said, 'We would like you to say you will train journalists who have been on the streets and we will help them and support them.' Ian Locks, chief executive of the PPA, said the Association would discuss the proposition further.[38]

Groundswell, an organization which promotes and develops self-help initiatives in the UK with people who are homeless, excluded or living in poverty, organized the UK's first National Speakout Week in September 2000.[39] Groundswell believes that homeless people are not the problem, they are part of the solution, that they have a right to access information to make informed choices and that they must be involved in any practical solutions to tackling homelessness. The week was an enormous step forward in bringing together hundreds of service providers and over a thousand people in over 30 events. The Super Speakout was held in London's Conway Hall. Cabinet Minister Mo

Mowlam, the head of London's Homeless Taskforce, Glenda Jackson MP[40] and Rough Sleepers Unit head, Louise Casey, were there to discuss problems and solutions.

Around 50 vendors turned up to the Speakout at *The Big Issue* offices. Out of this came a Vendors Working Group which will encourage vendors to attend bi-monthly meetings to input their views into the company and the Foundation. The working group meetings are attended by a dozen vendors and relevent members of staff, who discuss such issues as the need to profile successful vendors in the magazine or getting more experienced vendors to help others in the induction. As vendor Jim Lawrie comments:

> '*I do think that a breakthrough has happened here. We are getting vendors in their own time to come. I think it's a very good idea to get vendors involved in the training. That'll push the sales up. Once the vendors are involved I want to see some figures and see if they start to go up. I'm also pleased in how the way the staff are thinking about the inductions.*'

Both The Big Issue Foundation and The Big Issue in the North Trust received £200,000 each from the Rough Sleepers Unit in the autumn of 2000. The Big Issue Foundation will split its money between Norwich and London to develop resource or activity centres, which will have JET at the centre of its work. 'We also work with people who aren't *Big Issue* vendors. This is why I'm so interested in some of the creative groups we will be starting,' Lucie Russell says. Plans include a *Big Issue* garden, access to email and the internet, web design training and taster workshops or short courses in photography and drama, and a film unit.

The appointment of Lousie Casey and the beefing up of the RSI into the RSU was a welcome turn and the RSU has been strenuous in its attempts to reach its target. But *The Big Issue* has had an on and off relationship with Louise Casey. There have been some misunderstandings, says John Bird.

Louise Casey was quoted in an article in *The Observer*[41] implying that *The Big Issue* may be helping to keep people on the streets. John Bird wrote that he was appalled to read that, after all the work that *The Big Issue* had done: 'it was suggested that we may actually be helping to keep people on the streets, and that front-line groups were perpetuating street homelessness. Included along with the likes of the Salvation Army was *The Big Issue*.'

In a response published in *The Big Issue*,[42] Lousie Casey said: 'Last week's *Observer* article… misrepresented my views. Firstly, the headline [Sweep the homeless off the streets] was the exact opposite of my view of how rough-sleeping should be tackled. Secondly, my view on *The Big Issue*, was taken out of context and missed the wider point I was trying to make.'

She wrote that she believed *The Big Issue* to be part of the solution and not part of the problem. She continued: 'I am paid to be radical and think of new ways to tackle rough-sleeping and the national strategy to be published next month will bring innovative proposals… Giving people the tools they need to help themselves off the street is the best approach to tackling rough-sleeping in the longer term. *The Big Issue*, the RSU and others are working together to reach that end.'

John Bird later commented:

> 'It is certainly true that any organization that gets involved in a social crisis will be a part of the problem as well as part of the solution. Nobody can be above the problem. Every homeless organization will encourage, strengthen and support certain people, but other people will become dependent on them. The big problem for me is that in 1991 there were hundreds of homeless organizations working in London, and now there are even more ten years later. Is the provision better? Maybe. But is there a real problem of homeless people, not only on our streets, but in hostels, bed and breakfasts, in squats and other halfway initiatives? There certainly is. And that problem continues.'

It is the continuation of 'hidden' homelessness that needs also to be tackled. Despite a commitment by the Labour government to more social housing through, for example, housing associations, there is still a long way to go.

Then, in the autumn of 2000, Lousie Casey initiated the Change a Life campaign which proved very controversial and generated much discussion in the press. Casey suggested that the public should not give to beggars on the streets but should instead give their money to charities working with the homeless. In an article in *The Guardian*,[43] she spelt out how the public in this country have come to accept people begging:

'The public face a real dilemma in this situation. Is the person homeless, in desperate need and begging simply to get by? Or do they have somewhere to live? Are they claiming benefits and begging for drink or drugs? No one really knows the answer and no one will ever really know.'

The government, she stated, thinks that 'if people want to be really sure that their money is helping someone, not trapping them in a dangerous situation, they should think twice about giving hand-outs on the street. We are not, as some would have you believe, dictating that people should not give to beggars. That choice must be an individual one.' The problem, she believed, is drugs and people on the street.

Cheap drugs, readily available throughout society, percolate down onto the streets making the work of homeless organizations far more difficult, states John Bird. But there are other ways of tackling the problem. *The Big Issue* believes that the government should not be instructing the public how to behave towards people who beg.

In December 2000, Louise Casey wrote the cover article for *The Big Issue*,[44] explaining her position and the RSU work to date. She also explained new government initiatives helping vulnerable young people; initiatives to prevent those leaving the armed forces from ending up on the streets and similarly for those leaving prisons.

THE FUTURE FOR SOCIAL BUSINESS

What is the future for social business? Mel Young comments that he was surprised after seven years that no one had taken on the social business model in Scotland. Much discussion is currently taking place within the new economy sector about the challenges and difficulties of raising money for the social business and social enterprise sector. Discussion centres around how to attract finance to businesses that have both economic and social aims, and how the traditional financial sector views this new approach.

The Big Issue comes under the umbrella of a new social economy sector which developed during the 1990s. Besides social businesses such as *The Big Issue*, the Furniture Resource Centre,[45] and Aspire,[46] the sector includes social enterprises (cooperatives and mutuals), social firms (businesses employing people with disabilities) and fair trade companies (which partner with producers in the developing world) (see Appendix IX). These all see business as a solution to a social problem.[47]

The Labour government has supported the sector with grants and development funding, seeing the opportunity that small businesses, in particular, can play in tackling social exclusion. As Matthew Taylor of the Institute of Public Policy and Research (IPPR) comments: 'Both to reinforce and to balance its image as business-friendly, the New Labour government has been keen to emphasise the social role of the corporate sector.' From the government's perspective, he adds, the social role of business activity combines public–private partnerships, corporate responsibility, with social enterprise.[48]

The Big Issue has been a member of Social venture Network Europe (SVNE) since 1993. SVNE is 'an association of companies, individual business leaders and entrepreneurs who believe they can – and must – make a significant contribution to solve social and environmental problems locally and globally'. Maria Clancy, who sits on the board, says: 'Networks are at the forefront of driving positive change in the business world. And *The Big Issue* is a member of SVNE because we believe in the merits of associating with like-minded businesses. We believe in the power of linking change makers together'.

The social and economic impact of social businesses such as *The Big Issue* on the economy and on society has yet to be formally defined. It has both directly and indirectly made a contribution. This could be costed to the public purse, as in the example below, by keeping people out of prison, or are social in value, in the creation of employment and moving people back into society. With a current turnover of £4m, and the equivalent amount going into the pockets of hundreds of vendors, this reduces the need for reliance on the state.

John Bird tells the story of vendor Tommy:

'From the early sixties until the early nineties, Tommy had never been out of prison for longer than nine months. Then he met up with The Big Issue. *Since then, he has kept out of prison and sells the magazine. We had a chat and worked out that at around £35,000 per year, the minimum cost of keeping someone in prison,* The Big Issue *had saved the tax payer around*

£140,000. Wouldn't it be great, we joked, to send the Home Office a bill for £140,000? For services rendered.'

The Big Issue has not yet carried out a social audit, which covers the non-financial impact of companies on society, but Jonathan King conducted a preliminary scoping exercise in 1999 (see Appendix X). This is a useful exercise for *The Big Issue* to assess how it is fulfilling its social mission towards the vendors and the wider community.

CHAPTER 9

CONCLUSION – AND THE FUTURE

JOHN BIRD COMMENTS on *The Big Issue*'s achievement:

> '*It started in chaos and it developed in crisis. Now more than anything,* The Big Issue *needs a new kind of leadership for the 21st century.*'

So what about the future? John had returned from Los Angeles and was beginning to reflect on 2001 and beyond. He says:

> '*I don't want to be doing this in ten years' time. Because I have not been a company man, the growth of* The Big Issue *has had to be put in the hands of others. That* The Big Issue *has grown and multiplied is probably a greater surprise to me than anyone. It's like I'm the guy who came up with the idea for Coca-Cola. One great idea, but then you need workers, managers, directors, marketeers, administrators to turn it into a reality.*'

John believes *The Big Issue* is now mature enough to move beyond the founders. He comments.

> '*Our original founder was Gordon Roddick. It was his idea. He put money, support and guidance into it. There is certainly no other person I have ever met who has had such an undying commitment into making something work. He believed so totally*

*in the concept that he brought us back to first principles again
and again. In the early days he made us face up to the lack of
commercialism.'*

If founders have to become irrelevant, how is that achieved? He
says:

*'It began early on. There was myself, and then Ruth Turner and
Anne McNamara in Manchester. They saw rightly that they
had to take possession of the opportunity. Tricia Hughes and
Mel Young did the same in Scotland. They made it their
own.They took the guiding principles and made it happen on a
bigger geographical scale. The same happened with Su West in
Wales. The South West has leapt ahead in leaps and bounds
under the leadership of Jeff Mitchell.'*

These are all signs of moving beyond the original founder
concept. After a while John was irrelevant to their development
and he adds:

*'I would say most times they knew better than me. They were
the ones who broke out of the constraints placed on* The Big
Issue *by the founder syndrome and made it happen.'*

Does this mean that he feels that they have been more successful
than the founding *Big Issue*?

*'Well, yes and no. I think it took someone like me taking
Gordon's idea and making it happen. I think my bullishness has
certainly helped to create the possibility of a sustainable social
business. But then you only have to read about the developments of the various* Big Issues *to see the kind of leadership
they have offered. We must keep personalities out of this. But
you cannot deny that the kind of things that have been done by
other* Big Issues *show a clarity and precision that must be a
reflection of personality.*

*'Jo Mallabar professionalized the magazine. It could never
have carried on with the early way of doing things. Our inspirational first year of putting the magazine together was burning
us all out. She turned a loveable wayward child into a serious
publication.'*

Later editors like Becky Gardiner and Matthew Collin have developed it further.

For the development of the Foundation, they were able to build on the services and the move-on programmes instituted by Lucie Russell. John says:

> 'Even in the early stages when we didn't have the money, she conned, pleaded and got vendors supported. And when Rory Gillert came in from the profession, he enabled us to get on a clear, organized footing.
>
> 'We have had to bring in committed people from the professions, like Lyndall Stein. Moving from bookkeepers to accountants has put meat on the business bone. All this points to a welding together of inspiration with possibility. That is why we have managed to keep delivering our remit.'

And, John stresses, the hundreds of staff who have made it all work. Without them, despite the ups and downs, especially in the early days, *The Big Issue* would never have got off the ground. So where is *The Big Issue* going?

> 'One of the things I learnt in LA is that you cannot rely entirely on work programmes from within the organization. There are simply not enough jobs to go round, to mop up the aspirations of homeless people. You can help a few here, and a few there.'

There are no big inroads to employment available. There are no big employers who are going to employ the hundreds of people that *The Big Issue* has got job ready.

> 'And even if they were, they would be what in LA they call "dumb jobs": shelf-filling, menial jobs that don't release the full potential of homeless people. You see, if you've been to the edge and looked over, you have developed a life profile that is different from the average person.'

Homeless people develop a life experience that cannot fit neatly into a 9 to 5 job. John adds:

> 'We have countless stories of homeless people who haven't lasted the course. They get some job but it does nothing for them. They

rejoin society only to find that they lose the community that, however inadequately, kept them together. They lose everything in order to take on a new identify. Only the new identity doesn't really fit.'

Was John speaking against *The Big Issue*'s job creation schemes?

'No. The schemes we have are wonderful. They work for some people, and it fills their requirements. But there are still a lot of people out there who couldn't hold down jobs.'

What is the answer?

'It's not simple. I believe one solution is to create working communities. Financially sound businesses that used to be called "sheltered employment". They are places of work where people receive support, training and education. You have to educate people away from poverty and the crises. Not unlike foyers, which take in young people for work with housing. A community is established.'

But *The Big Issue* has only ever had enough money to run itself. It has never had the big investments necessary to develop its work beyond the magazine. Everything now is aimed at creating the kind of income that will enable *The Big Issue* to move to the next stage. The organization cannot survive and develop without moving into other publications, other areas of business, because it is very difficult for businesses to survive with one product.
 Lucie Russell concurs:

'We need to start looking if we can take our vendors onto the next stage. There's a lot of people who have got very stuck selling The Big Issue *and it's a very casual existence. The two reasons why we are starting new business are absolutely integral to where we are going next. In terms of the Foundation, it's very solid, we have income. But I believe that the Foundation and the business are intrinsically interlinked.'*

Some people believe that the Foundation is now its own entity. Perhaps it needs to become more independent of the company? Lucie responds:

'I don't believe it should ever go that way. To me, it will become like any other homeless charity if it becomes more independent. The wonderful thing about the Foundation is its link to this social business which gives people a chance to earn an income.'

When he was asked about the future of *The Big Issue*, David Warner wondered, if the government was successful in its objective of reducing the visibility of street sleeping, would that impact on *The Big Issue*? If so, what does that mean for the magazine? His suggestions parallel those of *The Big Issue*:

'Should The Big Issue *be looking more and more at how it can facilitate self-employment and collective employment opportunities for homeless people that are entrepreneurially based? Should it become a catalyst in some way for the entrepreneurial skills in homeless people? Should it be looking at other forms of income or employment that homeless people can provide and services that the public need?'*

Thinking ahead, Lucie suggests that what happens after 2002 when the Rough Sleepers Unit is set to end, may well have an impact on *The Big Issue* and the Foundation. Whilst the government's commitment to ending rough sleeping will not finish, it may well take another form. Perhaps money will be channelled more locally and, she says:

'That raises so many issues for homeless people who have a transitory lifestyle and aren't based in one area. Projects like ours, where we work with people from all boroughs, and all over the country.'

What about financing these new businesses? John asserts:

'Well, that is always the problem. Where do you get the means? Banks are notoriously cautious, so you can't expect to get support from them.'

Buying the first building was crucial to this new direction, explains Nigel Kershaw:

> 'We bought the building. We grew. We made a shrewd invest-
> ment. The reason to buy was to have collateral, but more
> importantly it was to prop up our business and give it founda-
> tions. Having established these foundations, and made a profit
> on the building, we realized that bricks and mortar were hinder-
> ing our development.'

Now, *The Big Issue* has sold its second building in order to rent
and free up money for creating other social businesses. Nigel
adds:

> 'There were some people who said, don't sell the building. We
> must store up for the future, we need the security of bricks and
> mortar. They were following a traditional financial model. But
> then the argument is, what is our mission? If our mission is to
> create social change, then we must invest in social change.'

Businesses and government, as well as the public, are aware of
the need to invest in social change. But they need a rallying point.
The Big Issue is such a rallying point. Fired, inspired and driven
by The Body Shop, the homeless, the public and *The Big Issue*
team, it is unique. *The Big Issue* is going to create its own investment fund, called Social Brokers Ltd. The aim of the fund will be
to invest in socially challenged communities. Eligible businesses
will offer employment and training opportunities to disadvantaged people. The homeless and long-term unemployed will be
the main beneficiaries. Micro-credit and other means of financial
support will follow a successful development of the fund.

In ten years, *The Big Issue* has grown from the passion of two
people into an enormous worldwide business. It has changed the
agenda on homelessness. It has influenced government response
to social crisis. It has caused countless charities to question their
attitudes: are they part of the crisis or part of the solution?
Thousands of homeless and socially excluded people worldwide
owe their futures to the social experiment that turned into a social
business.

As *The Big Issue* approaches its tenth birthday, schoolchildren,
students, teachers, church leaders, politicians, policemen,
business people – an endless list of professionals and members of
the public – have become involved in *Big Issue*-led programmes.

The Big Issue magazine has created a new point of entry for many young journalists. Today's press and television are full of former workers who learnt their skills in *The Big Issue*.

Many millions of members of the general public have been woken up to the face of homelessness. Rather than homeless people asking for a handout, they see them working. They have engaged in the lives of homeless people.

The Big Issue has also created a whole group of social entrepreneurs worldwide. People who followed the example of *The Big Issue* and helped develop it onto the next stage. In Britain, the new entrepreneurs have themselves radicalized the way that *The Big Issue* has worked with homeless people.

Charles Leadbeater[1] has written about the need for an innovative and inclusive society in the 21st century to achieve its potential:

> 'We rely on institutions of welfare, insurance, education and mutual self-help to withstand the turbulence of the global economy. The welfare state was designed for a world of male full-employment and stable nuclear families which has gone for good. That is why we need to reinvigorate and revive organizations capable of creating social solidarity... Any society that writes off 30 per cent of its people through poor schooling, family breakdown, poverty and unemployment is throwing away precious assets: brainpower, intelligence and creativity...'

An innovative economy must be socially inclusive to realize its full potential. We believe that *The Big Issue* has made a major contribution to this necessary way forward.

THE CODE OF CONDUCT

SECTION 1

INDUCTEES AND TEMPORARY BADGES

INDUCTEES WILL BE issued with a temporary vendor's badge. This will remain in use for a period of one week. After one week this badge may be exchanged for a full vendors badge which will be valid for the area worked by the vendor.

The inductee will also be issued with a problem sheet. Any problems experienced by the vendor are to be noted. Verbal accounts of any such problems will be acceptable. Information is to be exchanged when the inductees receive their full badge. This is to help us, help you. Your help is appreciated.

The Code of Conduct is there to help you succeed as a *Big Issue* member. However, action will be taken if any of the following offences occur:

AGGRESSION AND VIOLENCE

1 Using aggressive or bad language towards the general public.
2 Using aggressive, harassing, or abusive behaviour towards *Big Issue* staff – in or out of the *Big Issue* building.
3 If you are found to be drunk or suspected of drinking or under the influence of drugs whilst selling or buying the magazine.
4 Fighting over pitches with other vendors, or those earning a living from the streets, eg buskers and beggars.

5   Violence towards the general public, *Big Issue* staff or other vendors.
6   Racist/sexist language or behaviour towards members of the general public or *Big Issue* staff/vendors.

Selling Areas

7   *The Big Issue* magazine cannot be sold on:
   a)   All public transport.
   b)   Public transport concourses without prior permission.
   c)   The way to your pitch.

Other Offences

8   Begging whilst wearing *The Big Issue* ID badge.
9   Obstructing the general public.
10 Committing a crime whilst wearing *The Big Issue* ID badge.
11 Vendors must not place any other literature of their own or on behalf of other organizations within *The Big Issue*.

Penalties

You have the right to appeal if you have been debadged. Please see the VST team about this.

Section 2

I understand that if I am claiming benefit and selling *The Big Issue*, I am responsible for informing the DSS that I am selling *The Big Issue*. I will also have to declare all earnings made from selling the paper. I understand that I am also responsible for paying my income tax and national insurance contributions.

KATH DANE'S
VENDOR SURVEY

A POSITIVE OUTCOME was the issue around employ-
ment but also raised the question for *The Big Issue* support services
about move-on. The majority did not feel that selling the magazine
was putting them off finding other forms of work, but all seemed
to feel that finding work was the most important. This meant either
moving on to other jobs, or as one quarter of the vendors said, for
them selling *The Big Issue* was their permanent job and they would
not be able to move on because of mental or physical health
problems, lack of secure accommodation or lack of qualifications.

The survey found that vending broke the cycle of crime. Many
vendors said that since vending, they had stopped all criminal
activities such as begging, theft and robbery. Some said that
vending was the only legal means that they had ever had of
making money.

In terms of skills, the survey found that half the vendors had
gained qualifications once they had left school, 15 per cent had a
degree and 13 per cent had held professional jobs such as teaching or engineering. Around one in ten of the vendors had served
in the armed forces. Many vendors had held jobs such as electri-
cian, mechanic or painter and decorator, before they had hit hard
times and started vending. In terms of previous work, only 5 per
cent had never been in paid employment, with two thirds having
been unemployed for over a year and a quarter having been
unemployed for over five years.

Dane's survey showed that only around 10 per cent of the
vendors used the Foundation's services. For example, the Vendor

Survey found that whilst some used the support services offered by *The Big Issue*, in particular housing, vendor support and job training, many homeless people did not feel the need to do so. Some used outside services. This is therefore an issue to address.

In terms of gender breakdown, 88 per cent of active vendors are male and 12 per cent are female. The youngest was 17, the oldest 72. The average age is 34, with two thirds between 26 and 45. It was difficult to ascertain why women stopped vending as they are not then available for interview. However, there are possible reasons in the following: they experience more stress when vending because they are women, or harassment and violence by male customers offering them money in exchange for sex, for instance. For women with small children selling is difficult as it is illegal to vend with school-age children on the streets. Few creches are available.

Vendors were worried about paying bills, obtaining more secure accommodation, health problems (one third of vendors reported poor health), and social issues, such as being able to gain access to their children. Half the vendors reported feeling depressed in particular because of their housing situation, loneliness and social relationships.

VENDOR SURVEY (JANUARY 1999)

THE AVERAGE VENDOR is male, white, from the UK, aged between 26 and 45, has been homeless for at least one year and now has his own tenancy or is living with friends. He has been selling *The Big Issue* for between one and three years, usually vends for six days a week, for around five hours per day, returning to the office three times a week to collect papers. He is likely not to have approached either the Foundation or other agencies for help and support, and, if he has, it was with regard to housing.

Eighty-five per cent of vendors are male and 15 per cent are female. Whilst most are in the 26–35 (35 per cent) and 36–45 (27 per cent) bracket, there are a significant number who are aged between 18 and 25 (20 per cent). Only one vendor was between 16 and 17; 12 per cent are 46–55, 4 per cent 56–64 and 1 per cent 65+.

There are definite patterns of vending associated with the different age ranges. In general, the younger age groups are more likely to vend for a shorter period of time than those vendors in older age groups. Moving up the age groups, the vending period increases. In the 46–55 age group, 80 per cent of vendors have been vending for more than one year, 30 per cent for over four years.

There is quite a wide range in terms of the length of time people have been vendors which seems to be relatively evenly distributed amongst the categories. More vendors fall into the one to two and two to three year catagories. The figures imply that there is a relatively stable population of vendors, with many vending for several years. Vendors may be most likely to stop vending at two points: after three months and after four to five years.

Whilst not all vendors are currently homeless, all have been homeless at some point, the majority of them long term. A considerable proportion of vendors are housed, with their own tenancy. Some of the tenancies are short term. The majority of vendors have some kind of makeshift arrangement, either living with friends or squatting (squatting 23 per cent; own tenancy 21 per cent; with friends 20 per cent; hostel/night shelter 16 per cent; sleeping rough 12 per cent; bed and breakfast 2 per cent). There are considerable differences in the housing situations of vendors depending on the length of time for which they have been homeless. More long-term homeless are sleeping rough than any other groups; more mid-term homeless have their own tenancy; short-term homeless tend to be squatting, in hostels or staying with friends.

Most vendors are UK nationals, but there are a large number from other countries, particularly from Ireland and other European countries (especially Portugal, Spain and Italy). Out of 510, only 28 are black and one is Asian. Most black vendors are UK nationals; 95 per cent of vendors are white.

There are certain patterns associated with different ethnic groups with regard to housing, age and length of time vending. For those from Spain, Portugal and Italy the average age range is much lower than the UK equivalent; 68 per cent of vendors from Portugal are in the 18–25 age group as are 41 per cent of Eastern European vendors. For those from Southern Europe, the average time of vending is between one and six months. This suggests a young and mobile population who are not likely to become long-term vendors and most are accommodated in squats (80 per cent). Eastern European vendors are mainly staying with friends or squatting, with the remainder in shared accommodation or with their own tenancy. Also, the greatest proportion of Western European vendors are living in squats.

Most vendors will be vending for four or more days in the week, with a large proportion claiming to vend seven days a week. The average time spent vending is between 3–5 and 5–8 hours. The most popular times for vending are between 12 and 4pm, with many vendors also working early and/or late, presumably to take advantage of commuter trade. Some vendors commented that their weekend vending depended on the number of papers they had left. The weather also affected the number of days they were actively vending.

Foundation help and advice

The vendors access a range of support services provided by The Big Issue Foundation and other agencies. Over one third had not accessed any support over the last year, but the majority are accessing the resources available to a greater or lesser degree. It cannot be assumed that all vendors with a particular problem will seek help for that problem and, of those who do, it cannot be assumed that they have reported it in the survey. A large proportion of vendors are seeking help from other sources than the Foundation (28 per cent) as opposed to Foundation only (17 per cent).

The services most in demand from the Foundation are those related to housing, both temporary and permanent, and vendors have requested considerably more support on this from other organizations. Help with temporary housing is requested more frequently than help with permanent housing. Approximately 80 per cent of those who have accessed support have done so for housing help.

Education and training support were accessed more frequently from the Foundation than elsewhere, as was financial support (VSF). Drug and Alcohol support is accessed from the Foundation but not as often as from other agencies. Similarly with emotional support and welfare and legal help.

Number of vendors accessing service from:

	Foundation	Other agencies
Housing (temp)	78	109
Housing (perm)	52	74
Education/training	39	19
Employment	17	19
Drugs/alcohol	31	59
Financial help	45	1
Emotional support	17	23
Welfare rights	7	14
Legal	9	21

All categories of vendors access the support offered by the Foundation, with 36 per cent of vendors using the Foundation and 47 per cent using other organizations, with new vendors being the most likely to seek help.

For education and training, mid-term vendors are more likely to seek education and training than new and long-term vendors. New vendors are most likely to seek help gaining employment, usually from other agencies. Long-term vendors seeking employment are more likely to come to *The Big Issue*.

SEVEN CENTRAL THEMES FROM THE JOHN MOORES RESEARCH

1   *Big Issue* vendors showed much higher levels of mental and emotional stability than non-vendors. This was attributed to the fact that the magazine provided them with a sense of structured stability, positive image and independence.

    It also introduced many of them to social networks and contacts which increased their sense of normality and self-respect. A small number of homeless people had met partners through selling *The Big Issue*.

2   Vendors were more optimistic about their futures, especially the possibility of obtaining permanent accommodation, a decent job and a 'normal life' than the non-vendors. The overwhelming aura surrounding the outlook of the non-vendors was virtually total despair, hopelessness and fatalism.

3   The health, particularly the psychological health, of *The Big Issue* vendors had improved significantly since they started selling the magazine, as it gave them a sense of purpose and motivation, self-respect, extra income.

4   The majority of *Big Issue* sellers were less dependent or totally non-dependent on alcohol and drugs than in their pre-*Big Issue* days, whilst those homeless people who were not involved in selling the magazine showed much higher levels of dependency problems.

5   The unanimous perception of all vendors was that central and local government were 'poisonously prejudiced' towards them. They all blamed the government for their homelessness.

6   Although the attitude of the public in general towards homeless people had become more sympathetic in recent years, in large part due to *The Big Issue*, vendors felt there still remained great hostility, lack of understanding and rejection.

7   The core message from the research was that *The Big Issue* vendors believed that the magazine provided them with a social anchor and financial support, as well as a self-help activity, which showed that these homeless people were the opposite from the stereotypes cast on them by the government and adopted by the public.

INSP FOUNDING CHARTER

1 VISION

THE INTERNATIONAL NETWORK of Street Papers (INSP) aims to be a network that:

- is all-inclusive, with both emerging and established street papers as members;
- is an internationally recognized organization, which is known for its independent activities and which has a high profile based on its core values;
- provides a voice for its members and campaigns on their behalf for changes in national and international policies by lobbying national and international organizations and governments;
- is made up of street papers, which are modelled on the principal of self-help and aim to combat social exclusion by working with those people marginalized from mainstream society;
- strives to be a self-financing social business, which is not entirely reliant upon grants and donations;
- makes money from socially responsible business enterprise, which is used as a resource by all of the members;
- works actively with its members in order to help them become self-sustaining street papers;
- is a forum for know-how exchange and also encourages its members to support one another through experience sharing.

2 MISSION

The International Network of Street Papers strives to provide effective support and leadership to its members and emerging street papers and to encourage and aid them in the production of quality street papers, which are based on the principal of self-help.

3 STREET PAPER CHARTER

All street papers, which are members of INSP, must adhere to the following street paper charter.

The charter of INSP sets out the principles of the international street paper movement. These are:

A) Aiming to help socially excluded people (in some countries only homeless people apply in this category) help themselves, through providing them with the means of earning an income and facilitating their re-integraton into society, through providing social support.
B) Using all post-investment profits to finance support for the vendors, the socially excluded or social business. Each paper supplies its annual accounts to an agreed independent organization for the purpose of financial transparency.
C) Aiming to provide vendors with a voice in the media and campaigning on behalf of the socially excluded.
D) Aiming towards creating quality street papers, which the vendors are proud to sell and the public are happy to buy. This breaks the cycle of dependency through empowerment.
E) Aiming towards social responsibility in business in terms of editorial, staff, vendor and environmental policies. Aiming not to spend excessively on professional staff, with money being targeted towards vendors and vendor support.
F) Supporting prospective street papers that share a common philosophy and intend to sign the street paper charter.
G) That no charter street paper shall enter the established selling area of an existing charter member.

INSP MEMBERSHIP (2000)

ARGENTINA
Diagonal, Buenos Aires
Hecho en Bs As, Buenos Aires

AUSTRALIA
The Big Issue Australia, Melbourne

AUSTRIA
Asfalter, Salzburg
Augustin, Vienna
Kupfermuckn, Linz
Megaphon, Graz

CANADA
L'Itinéraire, Quebec

CZECH REPUBLIC
Novy Prostor – No Borders, Prague

DENMARK
Hus Forbi, Copenhagen

GAMBIA
Concern, Serrekunda

GERMANY
Asphalt, Hannover
BISS, Munich
Hempels strassenmagazin, Kiel
Hinz & Kunzt, Hamburg
Tagessatz, Gottingen
Trott War, Stuttgart

GREECE
Dromologia, Athens

HUNGARY
Flaszter, Budapest
No Borders, Budapest

ITALY
Terre di Mezzo + Altreconomia, Milan

THE NETHERLANDS
Straat, Rotterdam
Straatnieuws, Utrecht
Z magazine, Amsterdam

PORTUGAL
Cais, Lisbon

ROMANIA
Spune, Iasi

RUSSIA
The Depths, St.Petersburg
The Depths Siberia, Novosibirsk

SOUTH AFRICA
Homeless Talk, Johannesburg
The Big Issue South Africa, Cape Town and Johannesburg

SPAIN
Tambien Contamos, Madrid

Sweden
Situation Stockholm, Stockholm

Switzerland
Surprise, Basel

Ukraine
The Depths Ukraine, Odessa

UK
The Big Issue, London
The Big Issue Cymru, Cardiff
The Big Issue in Scotland, Glasgow
The Big Issue in the North, Manchester

USA
BIG news, New York
StreetWise, Chicago

VENDOR QUESTIONNAIRE (*THE BIG ISSUE CAPE TOWN*, 2000)

A QUESTIONNAIRE WAS given to vendors in 2000 to evaluate The Big Step support programmes run at the depots. The following results were ascertained:

- 96 per cent use one or more of the social support programmes.
- 56 per cent make use of the counselling services.
- 34 per cent make use of the job club facilities.
- 35 per cent make use of the computer classes.
- 16 per cent make use of the women's support group.
- 36 per cent make use of the art/writing group.
- 16 per cent make use of the further education and training services.
- 36 per cent participate in the social outings.
- 16 per cent have made use of the assistance with accommodation.
- 45 per cent have regularly attended workshops.
- 32 per cent make use of the savings account facilities.
- 23 per cent make use of the drug and alcohol counselling support services.
- 2 per cent do not make use of The Big Step programmes.
- 2 per cent did not answer the question.

VENDORS NEEDS THAT ARE BEING ADDRESSED:

- 84 per cent said they had experienced financial relief since joining *The Big Issue*.
- 54 per cent said that their emotional needs had been or were being addressed.
- 28 per cent said that they had received assistance with their drug/alcohol addictions.
- 41 per cent felt that their self-image had improved since joining the project.
- 68 per cent felt that they were more positive about their futures.
- 59 per cent felt that their relationships with others had improved.
- 50 per cent felt that their health had improved.
- 94 per cent said that they enjoyed using the depots.

The questionnaires were given out in all three official languages and vendor support staff assisted vendors where necessary. The return rate was 49 per cent. There were suggestions given to improve the vendor support programmes and depots and these have been taken into consideration by the staff whilst planning for the year ahead.

CASP, together with *The Big Issue*, has finalized a proposal for low-cost accommodation, for which there is a huge need in this sector. The financial step for someone wishing to move from a night shelter to more permanent and independent living is unrealistic. It is a vision of *The Big Issue* project, to purchase or rent a suitable home which can be sublet to *Big Issue* vendors, ready to make this move.

From January 2000 to December 2000 the following 'new' vendor profile was recorded:

- Of the 63 new registrations, 41 vendors have moved off the project (due to the nature of the vendors' employment with *The Big Issue*, it is difficult to record vendors that have moved off into the 'mainstream', in other words those who have obtained permanent employment and accommodation).
- Only a small percentage of the 41 vendors that registered during 2000 have been recorded as successfully moving off the project.

- 22 remain active or semi-active.

Of the 63, the ethnic breakdown was as follows:

- 18 African males
- 14 Coloured males
- 11 White males
- 10 African females
- 9 Coloured females
- 1 White females

1997 General Election Ten-point Plan

1 Take homelessness seriously

THE FIRST POINT stressed that the government must take homelessness seriously by establishing a ministerial committee reporting to Cabinet and ensuring cooperation between the Home Office, the Treasury, the Departments of Social Security, Health, the Environment [of which Housing is a small department], Education and Employment.

2 and 3 Build more homes and Fill Britain's empty buildings

Then investing in housing. An estimated 150,000 extra homes for rent were needed every year until 2007. The Department of Environment's target of 60,000 per year only came in at half that number in 1996. The money made from selling off council housing could be used, according to the Chartered Institute of Housing, and could fund 140,000 new homes and 280,000 refurbishments. Also, bring back into use the estimated 790,000 empty homes in England.

4 and 5 Deal with the causes and guarantee the right to a permanent home

Then the important issue of dealing with the causes of homelessness, focusing on the vulnerable groups that end up on the streets.

The Care in the Community policy [subsequently abandoned by the Labour government] needs to be reassesed, seeing that around one third of people on the streets have mental health problems. Support given to the 800 familes who at that time were losing their homes through repossession. The guarantee to the right to a permanent home for homeless families should be enshrined in law, as it was in the Housing Act of 1977 but abolished by the Tories in 1996. There also needs to be provision for single homeless people who have been overlooked.

6 AND 7 MAKE HOUSING AFFORDABLE AND TAKE ACTION LOCALLY

The building of more homes needs to be linked to affordable rents, otherwise they too will stand empty. Benefits must link to realistic rents too. Changes in housing benefit for certain groups and support for rent deposit schemes would assist. Locally, centrally funded local initiatives with joint planning between all statutory agencies (social services, NHS, and landlords, police and homeless people). An extention of the RSI, launched in 1990 to provide short-term accommodation for those sleeping on the streets. [This was extended to Wales and other cities in 1998.]

8 AND 9 FUND MORE TRAINING AND TARGET YOUNG PEOPLE

Further points included extending employment and training schemes for homeless people. Also helping young people. The 1995 'Inquiry into the Prevention of Youth Homelessness' estimated that about 246,000 young people between 16 to 25 became homeless in 1995. Reorganizing certain parts of the benefit system to benefit young people whilst they look for jobs was one suggestion.

10 GIVE HOMELESS PEOPLE THE RIGHT TO VOTE

Finally, give homeless people the right to vote. Current restrictions mean that the right to vote depends on the local council.

SOCIAL ENTERPRISE

SOCIAL ENTERPRISES ARE businesses that do more than make money; they have social as well as economic aims and form the heart of what is coming to be known as the Social Economy or the Third Sector. Social enterprises are self-help organizations bringing people and communities together for economic empowerment and social gain. They:

- are democratic in principle, structure and practice;
- have explicit social and ethical aims and values including a commitment to empowerment and sustainability;
- earn income for financial independence and viability.

Social enterprises have a wide range of forms and functions. They include: worker cooperatives, common ownership and other types of employee-owned businesses, community-based businesses, consumer, user and buyers' cooperatives, credit unions and Local Exchange Trading Schemes (LETS). All of them are committed to the inclusion and empowerment of a membership open to all those dependent on the enterprise. Their social aims and priorities vary, but may include: the creation of opportunity for training, work experience and well-paid stable employment, the development of goods and services to meet the needs of a local area or social group, ethical trading, and care for the environment.

(As defined by Social Enterprise London which works on promotion, support and development of social enterprise.)

Social firms

A business that is created for the employment of people who are disabled or disadvantged in the labour market. It pursues its social mission through its market-oriented production of goods and services.

They are businesses with a social as well as a commercial mission, focusing on the emploment needs of disabled people. However, their express aim is to integrate and include people in the mainstream of life, through employment in a commercial business which does not make decisions based on the person's disability, but rather looks to support them in making the most of their abilities.

(*From 'Interim Report and Briefing Paper on Social Firms UK' by Bob Grove and Sheila Durie.*)

Fair trade

Fair trade is an alternative approach to conventional international trade. It is a trading partnership which aims at sustainable development for excluded and disadvantaged producers. It seeks to do this by providing better trading conditions, by awareness raising and by campaigning.

Fair trade terms of production, which licensed products must meet, include:

- minimum wages
- adequate housing where appropriate
- minimum health and safety standards
- environmental standards.

Fair trade terms of trading include:

- a minimum price
- credit terms
- long-term trading commitment.

The price paid includes a 'premium', to be used by the workers or producers to improve their living and working conditions.

(*As defined by the Fairtrade Foundation, which aims to alleviate poverty in the developing world by encouraging industry and consumers to support fairer trade.*)

STAKEHOLDER ANALYSIS AND SCOPING STUDY

IN ORDER TO formally pinpoint both the stakeholders and the social performance of *The Big Issue* after eight years, Jonathan King completed a Stakeholder Analysis and Scoping Study for The Big Issue Company Ltd[1] in September 1999 as a preliminary for a full-scale social audit.

Social auditing covers a variety of approaches by different organizations to 'the process of measuring and reporting, in order to understand and ultimately improve, an organization's social (and ethical)[2] performance'.[3] Social performance is how an organization's actions measure up against societal expectations.

The various approaches and models differ, sometimes significantly, in key areas such as use of profits, legal structure, employee and stakeholder involvement, decision making and ownership.

Whilst most companies focus on issues such as employment of minorities and disabled people, health and safety, freedom of association, and customer/stakeholder satisfaction, social businesses such as *The Big Issue* have to account for whether the organization is performing against its central social objective, outlined in the mission statement for 1999/2000 as 'to help the homeless to help themselves by providing work that brings income'.

It is the financial impact on the vendors that currently measures *The Big Issue*'s success in meeting the social objective (about £4m in 1999/2000). To date, no indicators which would enable *The Big Issue* to demonstrate that the provision of income actually helps the homeless have been defined. The 1997 Vendors Survey was the nearest. In the next stage of the process *The Big Issue* would enter into dialogue with the vendors about their suggestions of what is an indicator of an increased ability to 'help themselves'.

Jonathan saw the potential benefits of a social audit for *The Big Issue* to:

- clarify and communicate its ethical values and social objectives in relation to current stakeholders and future business partners;
- measure and demonstrate its performance against its primary objective;
- improve understanding of notions of rights and responsibilities within the employee stakeholder group;
- build and deepen two-way understanding, commitment and trust with stakeholders;
- better manage multi-stakeholder perspectives and demands;
- improve decision making and operational effectiveness.

The social audit's indicators of progress against its central mission should give *The Big Issue* ammunition for marketing, to respond to media attacks and to demonstrate to readers, staff and the vendors that its fundamental mechanism of social change really does work.

Jonathan noted that the **primary stakeholders** of *The Big Issue*, and their roles, defined as 'those individuals or categories of individuals, with a legitimate interest in the organization, who affect and/or are affected by an organization or its activities',[4] are:

1   The Vendors
2   The Shareholders (A and B: John Bird and The Body Shop)
3   The Employees
4   The Readers
5   The UK subsidiaries
6   The Big Issue Foundation

7   The Suppliers
8   The Advertisers
9   The Bank
10 The Suppliers to the editorial staff, including freelancers
11 National *Big Issues*
12 The local and wider community.

Secondary stakeholders: *The Big Issue Cape Town, The Big Issue Australia,* Off the Wall, International Network of Street Papers, other homeless organizations, families of staff, the media.

---

1 The workings of *The Big Issue* Foundation were not covered, other than through its relationship to the company as a key stakeholder.
2 Ethical performance relates to the values and aims, whether explicit or implicit, that are acknowledged by the organization.
3 AccountAbility – the Institute of Social and Ethical Accountability.
4 Ibid.

APPENDIX **XI**

LIST OF
PARTICIPANTS TO
SOCIAL BUSINESS
SEMINARS

The Big Issue Cymru
The Big Issue London
Bioregional Development Group
The Body Shop
Bug Bugs Ltd
Business in the Community
The Co-operative Bank
Day Chocolate Company
DFID (Socially Responsible Business Unit)
Ethical Property Company
Fairtrade Foundation
Forum for the Future
Furniture Resource Centre
ICOM
Kandu
Malcolm Lynch Solicitors
National Centre for Business and Ecology
National Lottery Charities Board
NatWest
Network for Social Change
POPTEL
Projects in Partnership

Rough Sleepers Unit
School for Social Entrepreneurs
Social Enterprise London
Social Firm Resource Centre
Social Venture Network Europe
SustainAbility
Traidcraft plc
Triodos Bank
Urban Catalyst

USEFUL WEBSITES

STREET PAPERS AND NETWORKS

ASFALTER:
www.asfalter.at

ASPHALT:
www.asphalt-magazin.de

AUGUSTIN:
www.augustin.bus.at

THE BIG ISSUE:
www.bigissue.com

THE BIG ISSUE AUSTRALIA:
www.bigissue.org.au

THE BIG ISSUE CAPE TOWN:
www.bigissue.co.za

THE BIG ISSUE CYMRU:
www.bigissue.com

THE BIG ISSUE LA:
www.laoffthewall.com

THE BIG ISSUE IN THE NORTH:
www.bigissueinthenorth.com

THE BIG ISSUE SCOTLAND:
www.bigissuescotland.com

THE BIG ISSUE SOUTH WEST:
www.bigissue.com

BIG NEWS:
www.BIGnewsmag.com

BISS:
www.biss-magazin.de

CAIS:
www.forum.pt/cais/index.shtm

THE DEPTHS:
www.nadne.ru

DROMOLOGIA:
http://dromologia.freeyellow.com

FLASZTER:
www.streetpapers.mgx.hu

HEMPELS STRASSENMAGAZIN:
www.hempels-ev.de

HINZ & KUNZT:
www.hinzundkunzt.de

HOMELESS TALK:
www.homelesstalk.org.za

HUS FORBI:
www.husforbi.dk

INTERNATIONAL NETWORK OF STREET PAPERS (INSP):
www.street-papers.com and www.street-papers.org

L'ITINÉRAIRE:
www.itineraire.educ.infinit.net

DAS MEGAPHON:
www.megaphon.at

NORTH AMERICAN STREET NEWSPAPERS ASSOCIATION (NASNA):
www.speakeasy.org/nasna

SITUATION STOCKHOLM:
www.situationstockholm.se

SPUNE:
www.p4g.org

STRAAT:
www.straatmagazine.nl

STRAATNIEUWS:
www.straatnieuws.nl

STREETWISE:
www.streetwise.org

SURPRISE:
www.surprise-ch.org

TERRE DI MEZZO + ALTRECONOMIA:
www.terre.it

TROTT WAR:
www.trott-war.de

Z MAGAZINE:
www.zmagazine.nl

HOMELESS ORGANIZATIONS

EUROPEAN ANTI-POVERTY NETWORK:
www.eapn.org

FEANTSA:
www.feantsa.org

GROUNDSWELL:
www.oneworld.org/groundswell

NATIONAL COALITION FOR THE HOMELESS (USA):
www.nationalhomeless.org

NATIONAL HOMELESS ALLIANCE:
www.homeless.org.uk

NATIONAL MISSING PERSONS HELPLINE:
www.missingpersons.org

SHELTER:
www.shelter.org.uk

GENERAL

ABC TALES:
www.abctales.com

THE BIG ART ISSUE:
www.artnet.co.uk

THE BODY SHOP:
www.bodyshop.com

CAN (COMMUNITY ACTION NETWORK):
www.can-online.org.uk

DEMOS:
www.demos.co.uk

FAIRTRADE FOUNDATION:
www.fairtrade.org.uk

GET ETHICAL:
www.getethical.com

IPPR:
www.ippr.org.uk

JOSEPH ROWNTREE FOUNDATION:
www.jrf.org.uk

NEW ACADEMY OF BUSINESS:
www.new-academy.ac.uk

NEW ECONOMICS FOUNDATION:
www.neweconomics.org

SCHOOL FOR SOCIAL ENTREPRENEURS:
www.sse.org.uk

SOCIAL ENTERPRISE LONDON:
www.sel.org.uk

SOCIAL FIRMS:
www.ermis.co.uk

SVNE:
www.svneurope.com

UK SOCIAL INVESTMENT FORUM:
www.uksif.org

NOTES AND REFERENCES

1 HOMELESSNESS

1   *No Fixed Abode: A History of Responses to the Roofless and the Rootless in Britain* by Robert Humphreys, p15, Macmillan Press, 1999

2   'Homelessness then and now' by John Greve in *Homelessness and Social Policy* edited by Roger Burrows, Nicholas Pleace and Deborah Quilgars, Routledge, 1997

3   In the ten years to 1989, for example, the real annual income of the average UK household increased from £10,561 to £13,084 at that year's prices. The average income of the richest 20 per cent increased from £20,138 to £28,124. However, at the lower end of the spectrum average real income dropped from £3442 to £3282

4   From Peter Townsend *The International Analysis of Poverty*, 1993, p195, quoted in *No Fixed Abode*, p176 (see Note 1)

5   Shelter stated that 145,790 households were accepted as homeless by councils in England in 1991. It estimated that this represented 418,400 individuals and that around 156,000 young people were homeless in Britain each year. From factsheet: *Homeless in England, The Facts*, Shelter, March 1992

6   The 1977 Housing (Homeless Persons) Act for the first time responded to homelessness as a housing problem, homeless families were given statutory rights to permanent, secure accommodation by local authorities, which was considered a big step forward at the time

7   'Homeless persons are defined as those who have no secure accommodation, are separated from the rest of their households, or are subject to violence or threats that jeopardise the security of their shelter. Priority is given to dependent children, pregnant women, and those vulnerable to old age or disability. Local authorities are obliged to house those individuals if they are in priority need and they are homeless.' Quoted in *International Critical Perspectives on Homelessness* edited by Mary Jo Huth and Talmadge Wright, Praeger, Westport Conn, London, 1997, Chapter 9, p167

8   Data from annual publication *Social Trends* (HMSO) quoted in *No Fixed Abode*, p156 (see Note 1)

9   *Homelessness in England: The Facts*, Shelter, 1992

10 Statistic from Crisis, 1996

11   FEANTSA (The European Federation of National Organizations Working with the Homeless) is an international NGO, founded in 1989 and based in Brussels. It brings together more than 60 charitable and not-for-profit organizations that provide a wide range of vital services to homeless people in EU member states and other European countries

12   *Housing Policy and Practice* by Peter Malpass and Alan Murie, 5th ed, Macmillan, 1999, p2

13   Greve 1991 quoted in *Homelessness and Social Policy*

14   Housing associations began as non-profit making voluntary organizations which became the principal providers of social housing since the Tory government practically ceased building council houses from 1979

15   *The State We're In*, by Will Hutton, Vintage, 1995, pp203–210

16   Anne Power in 'Poor Areas and Social Exclusion', in *CASEpaper* 35, p10, 'Social Exclusion and the Future of Cities', February 2000

17   Homeless Network is a charity working to improve services for single homeless people in London by collaboration with key homelessness member organizations

18   Bob Humphreys, *No Fixed Abode*, p158. The 1985 Board and Lodging Regulations; the Social Security Act 1986 and the Social Security Act 1988. See John Greve et al *Homelessness in Britain*, 1990, p16

19   A section of the Social Security Act 1988 involved the replacement of previous board and lodging allowances by income support and housing benefit. It also provided a lower rate of income support for those aged under 25 and removed entitlement for most aged under 18

20   Maclagan (1993) quoted in *Stakeholder Housing, A Third Way*, edited by Tim Brown, Pluto Press, London, 1999, p85

21   Ibid p85

22   The DePaul Trust is an independent organization working with 16–25 year old single homeless people, with a concentration on rough sleepers. It works with people who have been barred from any other night shelter

23   In an interview with the author, March 1999

24   From 1995 to 1997 Charles Hendry was a Trustee of The Big Issue Foundation

25   From *Homeless* by Gerald Daly, Routledge, 1996

26   From *International Critical Perspectives on Homelessness* edited by Mary Jo Huth and Talmadge Wright, Praeger, 1997, Chapter 9, p167

27   September 2000, attended by Mo Mowlem, Louise Casey and Glenda Jackson, held at Conway Hall, Red Lion Square, London

28   'Can you hear me?' by Sam Hart, *The Big Issue*, No 399, 14 August 2000, p22

29   'It's Good to Talk' by Sam Hart, *The Big Issue*, No 405, 25 September 2000, p22

30   See Charity Commissioners website www.charity-commission.gov.uk

31   From Ben and Jerry's *Double-Dip: How to run a values-led business and make money, too* by Ben Cohen and Jerry Greenfield, Fireside Book, Simon & Schuster, New York, 1998

32   *The Times*, 20 July 1995, Geoff Mulgan re: his book *The Other Invisible Hand: Remaking charity for the 21st century* by Geoff Mulgan and Charles Landry, Demos, 1995, £9.95

33   *Social Justice, The Report of the Commission on Social Justice*, p224, Vintage, 1994. Members of the Commission visited *The Big Issue* in April 1994 to discuss its work in this area

34   From *The Rise of the Social Entrepreneur* by Charles Leadbeater, Demos, 1997. For further discussion on the welfare state, see Charles Leadbeater's *Living on Thin Air: The New Economy*, Viking, 1999

35   See Business as Unusual by Anita Roddick, Thorsens, 2000, Chapter 1

36   Ibid, p14

2 THE BIG ISSUE IS BORN

1   See Lee Stringer's book about *Street News* and homelessness in New York, *Grand Central Winter*, published by Review, London, 2000

2   See *Body and Soul* by Anita Roddick, Ebury Press, London, 1991, for the whole story

3   Ibid, p24

4   The homeless community in the Bullring was finally dispersed in 1998 when the British Film Institute's giant IMAX cinema was built on the site

3 GETTING GOING

1   See full Code of Conduct in Appendix I

2   Interview with author in March 1999

3   'Beaten out of House and Home' by Sam Hart, *The Big Issue*, No 424, 12 February 2001. Reporting on a conference 'Locked Out – Women Without Homes', organized by The Big Issue Foundation, Groundswell and the National Homeless Alliance

4   See *Street Life: Young Women write about being Homeless* edited by Jane Cassidy, Livewire Books, from the Women's Press, 1999

5   As defined by *The Big Issue*, Projects in Partnership and the Social Venture Network. Two seminars were held in 1999 to develop the ideas around social business, producing a paper: 'Mapping the Social Business Sector'. See Appendix XI for list of participants

6   *The New Alchemists* by Charles Handy, Hutchinson, 1999

7   Charles Handy at the book launch of *New Alchemists* at Borders Bookshop, Oxford Street, London, December 1999

8   Anita Roddick *Business as Unusual*, pxi, Thorsons, 2000

9   Interview with Anita Roddick by Carl Frankel on 'Compassion and Business' in *YES! A Journal of Positive Futures*, Spring 1998

10   Charles Handy, ibid, pp21–52, 233–258

11   'The Hole in My Soul' by Dave Hill, *The Guardian*, Weekend, 7 March 1992

12   See also 'Streets Ahead' by Peter Silverton, *The Guardian*, Weekend, 10 July 1993

13   *Management Week*, 20 November 1991

4 GOING WEEKLY

1   The six-monthly ABC independently validates a magazine's weekly sales figures. The ABC is crucial for any commercial magazine that wishes to attract advertising

2   John Lloyd speaking at the annual conference of the International Network of Street Papers, 30 November 1998

3   See Gathering Force: DIY Culture – Radical action for those tired of waiting by Elaine Brass and Sophie Poklewski Kiziell published by *The Big Issue*, 1997, for discussion

4   See Matthew Collin's book *Altered State: The Story of Ecstasy Culture and Acid House* (Serpent's Tail 1997, 1998) on how that culture became mainstream

5   *Death by Spaghetti*, Fourth Estate, 1996

6   See 'People dying in police custody' by Lucy Johnston, *The Big Issue*, No 151, 9 October 1995

7   See Anita Roddick, *Business as Unusual*, Chapter 8, on full details of the campaign

8   All information from the Annual Company Plan 1996

9   *The Big Issue*, No 90, 2 August 1994

10   *The Big Issue*, No 122, 20 March 1995

11   *The Big Issue*, No 114, 23 January 1995

12   *The Big Issue*, No 149, 25 September 1995

13   As reported in *The Guardian*, 25 April 1994

14   *The Big Issue*, No 151, 9 October 1995

15 See article by Anna Moore in *The Big Issue*, No 81, 31 April 1994
16 *The Big Issue*, No 220, 17 February 1997
17 *The Big Issue*, No 7, April 1992
18 A new Representation of the People Act came into force in March
    2000. See new subsection 7B (Notional residence: Declarations of
    Local Connection). Declarations may be made by patients in
    mental hospitals (other than those detained as a consequence of
    criminal activity), remand prisoners and the homeless. The
    required address in the case of a homeless person is 'the address
    of, or which is nearest to, a place in the United Kingdom where he
    commonly spends a substantial part of his time (whether during
    the day or at night).' See representation of the People Act 2000,
    Chapter 2, published by The Stationery Office
19 John Lloyd speaking at the INSP conference
20 Annual advertising income continued to rise from £420,000
    (1993–94) to £620,000 (1994–95), £890,000 (1995–96) and £1,012,300
    (1996–97)
21 See Peter Ackroyd: *London, the biography*, Chatto & Windus, 2000
    pp467–8
22 *The Big Issue*, No 135, 19 June 1995
23 *Campaign*, 20 Sept 1996
24 *The Big Issue*, No 207, 11 November 1996

5 The Move Outside London

1 Former gangleader, artist and writer
2 Aspire is a not-for-profit enterprise launched in May 1999 in
   Bristol. It provides full-time employment for homeless and ex-
   homeless people by creating an opportunity for the public to
   contribute to their rehabilitation. The Aspire catalogue sells gifts,
   cards, jewellery and household items, fairly traded or handcrafted
   in the UK
3 See Shelter Cymru for statistics on Welsh homelessness

6 The Foundation and Support Services

1 Current chair of the trustees is Brian Levy. John Bird is president
   of the Foundation, Mo Mowlam is vice-president
2 See Appendix II
3 Section 6, p15, of Kath Dane's survey
4 See Appendix III for full details
5 From 'We that are left to grow old' by Anna Moore, *The Big Issue*,
   No 81, 31 May 1994

6   Inspector Steve Dyer, from the City of London police (speaking to the author in a personal capacity in 1999)

7   *The Big Issue*, No 233, 19 May 1997, p4

8   Notting Hill Housing Trust, established in the 1960s, is a charity which provides good-quality affordable homes, emergency night shelters, specialist housing and sheltered flats

9   *The Big Issue*, No 269, 2 February 1998

10   *The Big Issue in the North*, 20 November 2000

11   See: *Out of Pocket: How Banking Systems fail the Poorest*, The Big Issue in the North Trust, November 2000

12   From *the big issue book of home*, compiled and edited by Eddie Ephraums, Hodder & Stoughton in association with the Peabody Trust, 2000

13   Internal report on the London pitch system by Patrick Dennis, February 1999

14   London Local Authorities Act 1990, Part III Street Trading (d) 'trading as a news-vendor provided that the only articles sold or exposed or offered for sale are newspapers or periodicals and they are sold or exposed or offered for sale without a receptacle for them or, if with a receptacle for them, such receptacle does not… [explanation of length, position etc]'

15   *The Guardian*, 21 September 1994

16   *The Big Issue*, No 100, 10–16 October 1994

17   Up to 31 March 1999: Income: £758,379 – 44 per cent donations from individuals, 22 per cent corporate donations, 19 per cent charitable trusts, 11 per cent statutory grants and 4 per cent other income. Expenditure: VST: 72 per cent, JET: 15 per cent, VSF: 8 per cent, writing group and others: 5 per cent

18   From interview in *Professional Fundraising*, September 1996

19   John Bird quoted in the *Evening Standard*, 11 June 1996

20   The Big Art Issue: www.artnet.co.uk

21   See Andy Law's book about St Luke's: *Open Minds: 21st century business lessons and innovations from St Luke's*, Orion Business Books, 1998

22   The Grand Central Partnership (GCP) is a Business Improvement District (BID) in Manhattan. BIDs are a cooperative of property owners and managers who get together to assess and resolve the problems in their area. The success of GCP has been to reduce crime, improve sanitation and address the acute homeless problem in the Grand Central Terminal and the rest of the district during the 1990s. The project concentrates on giving training and employment opportunities to homeless people

23   Dr Sean Stitt, Ronnie Thomas and Sue Elliott (1996) 'Helping the Homeless to Help themselves: The Big Issue', Centre for

Consumer Education & Research, Liverpool John Moores University

24 See Appendix IV for seven central themes from the John Moores research

7 INTERNATIONAL DEVELOPMENTS

1 See *Homelessness: Exploring the new terrain*, edited by Patricia Kennett and Alex Marsh, The Policy Press, 1999, pp268–9. See also *Homelessness in the European Union* by Dr Dragana Avramov, FEANTSA, Brussels, 1995, and *Services for Homeless People: Innovation and change in the European Union* by Bill Edgar, Joe Doherty and Amy Mina-Coull, The Policy Press, 1999

2 See *Hinz & Kunzt*, Obdachlosenhilfe zwischen Sinnstiftung und Vermarktung, by Andrea Muller and Martina Orban, published by Agentur des Rauhen Hauses, Hamburg 1995

3 See discussion in *Les Sans-Abri: Les journaux de SDF* by Julien Damon, published by Fondations, No 1, January 1995 (financed by the Fondation Abbé Pierre pour le Logement des Défavorisés)

4 See Appendix V

5 Founded in 1989, FEANTSA has over 50 members in the European Union and other European countries. FEANTSA promotes the development and implementation of effective measures to tackle the causes of homelessness and to facilitate access to decent and affordable housing

6 The EC's Directorate-General for Employment and Social Affairs (formerly known as DGV)

7 See list of current membership of INSP in Appendix VI

8 New Economics Foundation works to construct a new economy centred on people and the environment. It is an independent think tank, combining research, advocacy, training and political action

9 See report on the fourth conference: 'A Street Paper Explosion'

10 *The Big Issue*, No 188, 'Big Issue hits Oz'

11 Figures quoted in article Good read, good deed by Catherine Fitzpatrick in 'big weekend' 6 June 1997

12 In a separate survey, 725 homeless adults were found in the city's shelters. Only a quarter of these people were working, doing jobs such as washing cars, being informal car parking attendants, collecting recycled material from waste areas and selling newspapers (from a report by *The Big Issue Cape Town*)

13 From *Orbit*, VSO magazine, 1997

14 Exchange rate at November 2000: 10 Rand = £1.00

15 From 'Housing Exclusion in Central and Eastern Europe', edited by Dragana Avramov, FEANTSA, 1997

16 *Petersburg in the early '90s: Crazy, cold, cruel*, published by
    Nochlezhka, St Petersburg, Russia 1994
17 The Know How Fund is Britain's programme of bilateral technical
    assistance to the countries of Central and Eastern Europe and the
    former Soviet Union. It aims to support their transition to democ-
    racy and a market economy by providing British skills in sectors
    such as finance, energy and health, and by encouraging British
    investment in the region
18 For the Directory of North American Street Newspapers, the
    National Coalition for the Homeless, information on homelessness
    and organizations working with the homeless in the USA, see
    Appendix XII

8 GROWTH AND CHANGE

1   The Awards celebrated groups and individuals, nominated by
    members of the public, who enriched London's life. The Awards
    were organized by *The Big Issue*, sponsored by London Electricity
    and supported by BBC GLR
2   *Time Out*, 16 August 2000
3   *Gathering Force* by Elaine Brass and Sophie Poklewski Koziell,
    edited by Denise Searle, published by *The Big Issue*, 1997
4   Project Sinai sends people from the city into the desert, and a
    donation of £30,000 from McCabe Travel enabled the McCabe
    Educational Trust to offer 50 places to vendors across the country
    to make four trips to Egypt
5   'Crossing the desert to bridge the gap', *The Big Issue*, No 222, 3–9
    March 1999
6   *The Bin*, No 25 'Wot We Did On Our 'Olidays', Anonymous
7   From 'Desert Banker', *Mail on Sunday*, Night & Day section, 2
    March 1997
8   'War on the Streets' by Tony Blair, *The Guardian*, 8 January 1997
9   See post-general election cover of *Private Eye*: Michael Heseltine
    buys a *Big Issue*
10 See Appendix VIII for more on Ten-point Plan
11 *The Big Issue*, No 291, 6 July 1998
12 See *The Guardian*, 15 August 1997, 'Peter Mandelson: A lifeline for
    youth', with an accompanying article by John Bird: 'Stop the rot
    before it sets in'
13 From DETR Homelessness Fact Sheet, November 1998
14 Outside London, under the Homelessness Action Programme
    £34m was provided to voluntary organizations over three years to
    work with local authorities to tackle rough sleeping
15 *The Big Issue*, No 272, 23 February 1998

16   *The Big Issue*, No 296, 10–16 August 1998
17   *The Big Issue*, No 224, 17–23 March 1997
18   Tom Sutcliffe, 15 August 1998
19   *The Big Issue*, No 262, 8 December 1997
20   From No 260 onwards
21   *The Big Issue*, No 312, 30 November 1998
22   *Press Gazette*, 25 August 1999
23   See 'Racism. Are We All Guilty?' by Matthew Sweet in *The Big Issue*, No 313, 7 December 1998
24   *The Big Issue*, Nos 332 and 339, 14 June 1999
25   *The Big Issue*, No 280, 20 April 1998
26   *The Big Issue*, No 320, 1 February 1999
27   *The Big Issue*, No 330, 12 April 1999
28   *The Big Issue*, No 401, August 2000
29   All this from NRS October 1998–September 1999; 1.16 million readers over five regional editions
30   *Big Issue* readers are 44 per cent more likely than the national average to be earning over £33,800; 72 per cent of BI readers have at least one credit/charge card, and 50 per cent have taken at least one foreign holiday in the last 12 months. There is a low duplication with similar titles in the marketplace; for example, 95 per cent of *Big Issue* readers do not read *The Independent* or *Time Out*. At least three copies each month are read by 51 per cent of *Big Issue* readers. A further third read at least one copy every month
31   The UK's socioeconomic grading is based on the social status and occupation of the chief income earner of an individual's household. A = upper middle class; higher managerial, administrative or professional. B = middle class; intermediate managerial, administrative or professional. C1 = lower middle class; supervisory or clerical and junior managerial administrative or professional
32   The Quality of Reading Survey aims to provide a greater understanding of the value of the print medium and the differences within it. It measures behavioural and attitudinal characteristics among readers of magazines and papers
33   ROAR: Right of Admission Reserved: a comprehensive and on-going study of the young market, run by seven media companies
34   Naomi Klein in a film on branding made for C4 News, shown 17 October 2000. See pp 39–45 'The Branding of Media', in her book *No Logo*, Flamingo, 2000
35   *The Big Issue*, No 311
36   Paper Round, 3.2 tonnes of paper were recycled by the company in 1998, saving the equivalent of 48 trees
37   The Commission for Racial Equality works in partnership with individuals and organizations for 'a fair and just society which

values diversity and gives everyone an equal chance to work, learn and live free from discrimination, prejudice and racism'

38   Reported by *Press Gazette*, 20 October 2000

39   See also Homeless Persons Charter for Scotland, producted by Speakout, a voice for Scotland's Homeless People, 1995, (from *The Big Issue Scotland*)

40   Glenda Jackson heads the homeless unit of the Greater London Authority which co-ordinates homeless strategy in the capital

41   'Sweeps the Homeless off the Streets', *The Observer*, 14 November 1999

42   *The Big Issue*, No 362, 22 November 1999

43   'Brother, Spare the Dime' by Louise Casey, *The Guardian*, 10 October 2000

44   'Homeless Czar Begs for Change', *The Big Issue*, No 415, 4 December 2000

45   Furniture Resource Centre, established in 1988, is a charity and social business. It exists to enable people in poverty to get the furniture they need to create homes for themselves. Furniture is sold to social landlords or to the public through a store called Revive, a wholly owned subsidiary of the FRC

46   Aspire is a social business run in Bristol which employs homeless people to sell goods from a catalogue

47   See work done by New Economics Foundation, IPPR and Social Enterprise London on the new social economy, See *Social Enterprise: Organizational Perspectives*, SEL, 2000

48   From *In Progress*, summer 2000, article by Matthew Taylor. See John Bird's article 'Let's Do Business for the Underclass', *The Guardian*, 29 November 1998, where he calls for a shake-up of charity laws to help launch 'social businesses'

9 CONCLUSION – AND THE FUTURE

1   Charles Leadbeater, *Living on Thin Air: The New Economy*, p11, Viking, 1999

BIBLIOGRAPHY

HOMELESSNESS IN THE UK

The Big Issue Book of Home edited by Eddie Ephraums, The Big Issue and Hodder & Stoughton, in association with Peabody Trust, 2000

European Observatory on Homelessness, National Report 1999, United Kingdom: Women and Homelessness in the UK by Robert Aldridge, Scottish Council for Single Homeless, FEANTSA, 2000

Homeless by Judy Bastyra, Evans Brothers, 1996

Homelessness and Social Policy edited by Roger Burrows, Nicholas Pleace and Deborah Quilgars, Routledge, 1997

Housing Policy and Practice by Peter Malpass and Alan Murie, Macmillan, 1999

No Fixed Abode: A history of Responses to the Roofless and the Rootless in Britain by Robert Humphreys, Macmillan, 1999

Out of Pocket: How Banking Systems Fail the Poorest, published by *The Big Issue in the North*, November 2000

Social Exclusion and the Future of Cities CASEpaper 35: Poor Areas and Social Exclusion by Anne Power; *The State of American Cities* by William Julius Wilson, Centre for Analysis of Social Exclusion, London School of Economics, 2000

Stakeholder Housing: A Third Way edited by Tim Brown, Pluto Press, 1999

Street Life: Young Women Write about Being Homeless edited by Jane Cassidy, Livewire Books, The Women's Press, 1999

INTERNATIONAL

Beyond Homelessness: Frames of Reference by Benedict Giamo and Jeffrey Grunberg, University of Iowa Press, 1992

A Dangerous Class: Scotland and St Petersburg: Life on the Margin, published by *The Big Issue in Scotland* and The Depths Publishing House, St Petersburg, 1999

Grand Central Winter: A Story from the Streets of New York City by Lee Stringer, Review, 1998, 1999

Hinz & Kunzt, Obdachlosenhilfe zwischen Sinnstiftung und Vermarktung by Andrea Muller and Martina Orban, Agentur des Rauhen Hauses, Hamburg, 1995

Homeless: Policies, Strategies and Lives on the Street by Gerald Daly,

Routledge, 1996

Homelessness in the European Union: Social and Legal Context of Housing Exclusion in the 1990s by Dragana Avramov, FEANTSA, 1995

Homelessness: Exploring the New Terrain edited by Patricia Kennett and Alex Marsh, The Policy Press, 1999

Housing Exclusion in Central and Eastern Europe edited by Dragana Avramov, FEANTSA, 1997

International Critical Perspecties on Homelessness edited by Mary Jo Huth and Talmadge Wright, Praeger, 1997

Les Sans-Abri: Les Journaux des SDF by Julien Damon, *Fondations*, No 1, January 1995

Making Room: The Economics of Homelessness by Brendan O'Flaherty, Harvard University Press, 1996

No Shame in My Game: The Working Poor in the Inner City by Katherine S Newman, Alfred A Knopf and the Russell Sage Foundation, New York, 1999

Petersburg in the Early 90s: Crazy, Cold, Cruel, published by the charitable foundation Nochlezhka, St Petersburg, 1994

Services for Homeless People: Innovation and Change in the European Union by Bill Edgar, Joe Doherty and Amy Mina-Coull, The Policy Press, 1999

Support and Housing in Europe: Tackling Social Exclusion in the European Union by Bill Edgar, Joe Doherty and Amy Mina-Coull, The Policy Press, 2000

Youth Homelessness in the European Union edited by Dragana Avramov, FEANTSA, 1998

BUSINESS, HISTORY, CULTURE AND POLICY

Altered State: The Story of Ecstasy, Culture and Acid House by Matthew Collin, Serpent's Tail, 1997, 1998

Ben & Jerry's Double-Dip: How to Run a Values-led Business and Make Money, Too by Ben Cohen & Jerry Greenfield, Simon & Schuster, 1997

Body and Soul by Anita Roddick, Vermilion, 1992

Business as Unusual by Anita Roddick, Thorsons, 2000

Cannibals and Forks by John Elkington, Capstone Publishing, 1998

Death by Spaghetti: Bizarre, Baffling and Bonkers Stories from The Big Issue edited by Paul Sussman, Fourth Estate, 1996

Gathering Force: DIY Culture – Radical Action for Those Tired of Waiting by Elaine Brass and Sophie Poklewski Koziell, *The Big Issue*, 1997

Living on Thin Air: The New Economy by Charles Leadbeater, Viking 1999

The New Alchemists: How Visionary People Make Something out of Nothing by Charles Handy, Hutchinson, 1999

No Logo by Naomi Klein, Flamingo, 2000

Open Minds: 21st Century Business Lessons and Innovations from St Luke's by Andy Law, Orion Business Books, 1998

The Rise of the Social Entrepreneur by Charles Leadbeater, Demos, 1997

Social Enterprise Organizational Perspectives, Social Enterprise London, 2000

Social Justice, The Report of the Commission on Social Justice, Vintage, 1994

The State We're In by Will Hutton, Vintage, 1996

Value-led, Market-driven: Social Enterprise Solutions to Public Policy Goals by Andrea Westall, IPPR, 2001

Index